CRIME AND LAW IN MEDIA CULTURE

CRIME AND LAW IN MEDIA CULTURE

SHEILA BROWN

Open University Press
Buckingham · Philadelphia

Open University Press
Celtic Court
22 Ballmoor
Buckingham
MK18 1XW

email: enquiries@openup.co.uk
world wide web: www.openup.co.uk

and
325 Chestnut Street
Philadelphia, PA 19106, USA

First Published 2003

A catalogue record of this book is available from the British Library

ISBN   0 335 20548 8 (pb)   0 335 20549 6 (hb)

Library of Congress Cataloging-in-Publication Data
Brown, Sheila, 1959–
    Crime and law in media culture/Sheila Brown.
       p. cm.
    Includes bibliographical references and index.
    ISBN 0-335-20549-6 – ISBN 0-335-20548-8 (pbk)
      1. Crime in mass media.   2. Law in mass media.   I. Title.
    P96.C74 B76 2003
    364–dc21   2002074910

Typeset by Type Study, Scarborough, North Yorkshire
Printed in Great Britain by Biddles Ltd, Guildford and King's Lynn

CONTENTS

ACKNOWLEDGEMENTS

My heartfelt thanks to all of my friends who as usual have been far too good to me. To Kath, as ever. Thanks to Louise, for sisterly support and the sharing of many mutual authorly tantrums (and other tantrums as well). Bob'n'Jen, thanks for being there when I needed you. Thanks to Denise, Andy, Amy, Pam and Maggie, virtual and real.

A big 'thank you' on a personal and professional level to Roger Brownsword, and also to Julie de Groot.

And to Justin Vaughan; and Miriam Selwyn at Open University Press, for constructive support (and tolerance).

1 ▪ MEDIATIZATION, MODERNITY AND GLOBALIZATION: CRIME AND LAW IN MEDIA CULTURE?

Approaching media, crime and culture

Almost every aspect of social life in western late modern societies is filtered through the 'media experience'. You can check the news and send a fax or email from your mobile phone, shop through your TV, videocam your most private moments 'up close and personal', and you may daily star (perhaps without your knowledge), on the CCTV screens of your nearest shopping mall. You can animate disasters on interactive news sites, watch TV news 24 hours a day and do nothing else (using your Internet facility in the TV to order dinner). As I write this, you cannot even have a road accident and be sure that a crew will not turn up from something called 'Road Crashes from Hell' (or similar) to expose your foolishness to about 75 million other people. Emotional problems? Take them to Trisha or a similar TV agony aunt. Money problems? Ring 'Who Wants to be a Millionaire?' and win your money on a game show. Health problems? Netdoctor.com will answer your questions anonymously over the Internet. Criminally-minded but don't know how to plan a burglary? There will be an Internet chat room for you. Who did not know a millisecond after the sordid details were revealed about ex-President Bill Clinton's penchant for cigars and buxom young White House interns? And who, by the time this book appears in print, will never have known all of this because they are already immersed in another set of here-today mediated possibilities and preoccupations? There is little dispute that we are media-saturated, although even that does not quite meet the case, as the potential for the expansion of electronic media into everyday life seems unlimited. What is less well-acknowledged are the far reaching implications that contemporary media culture has for crime and law.

The purpose of this chapter is to explore this theme within a framework that emphasizes theories of modernity and of globalization but also to consider the challenges of postmodern theory and beyond (Thompson 1990; Giddens 1999; McGuigan 1999). The discussion therefore begins 'upside-down', shelving the substantive areas of crime and law temporarily to address the fundamental question of how mediation has been theorized in relation to social life, and what contemporary developments in communications might imply about how we exist as 'mediated beings'. This will include an initial consideration of the inscription of the media in identities, of the media, the public and the private, and on the question of 'distinction' between representation and reality. Who are we in media culture? According to the critical theory of the Frankfurt School, we are passive recipients of junk culture; within more complex theories of modernity we are active subjects negotiating self and identity in an information society; if we adhere to certain theories of globalization, we are the eclectic subjects of McDonaldization and satellite TV; from a postmodern perspective we are avid surfers and grazers, stopping only for a second here or there to snatch a new fragment for our pastiche of self which has replaced identity. The media-subject is thus constituted very differently according to our theory of mediation; private life and public representation are ever more thoroughly embedded within technologies of communication, and it is crucial to grasp what this 'embedding' might entail.

Against this theoretical backdrop, the work of writers in the (broadly defined) domain of criminology will be considered; how has crime and law in media culture hitherto been conceptualized? What are the limits of 'criminology' implied by the contemporary mediascape? Mediation as a social practice – as, essentially, the defining characteristic of 'the social' – implies the interstices between medium and person, self and others, local and global, and the production of the taxonomies of everyday life through all of which crime and law become living processes rather than reified codifications. Has criminology begun to appreciate fully what media culture means for crime and law? In this, I am working from a questioning of analytical separation of media and culture toward an embedded conceptualization of media/culture which invokes 'mediatization' as a principal contemporary feature of social life with wide ranging consequences for the way in which 'we' (whether the academic 'we' or the more broadly public 'we' of policymakers, lawyers, moral gatekeepers, politicians, and social actors and collectivities) experience, construct, and relate to, crime and law. Ultimately, 'mediatization' will be argued as a social state of being which must be taken into account in any theorization of crimino-legal analysis and not sidelined into a narrowly defined 'media criminology'.

Thought-crime prevention? Early conceptions of the mass and the media

This section concerns the work of the earlier twentieth-century cultural theorists, important in its insistence upon the deleterious effects of media culture upon societies, and upon the analytical separation of 'media' (the cultural industries) and 'society' (the mass of the people upon whose consciousnesses it was inflicted) (During 1993; Inglis 1993).

Most such conceptions of media culture seem to frame culture as a domain for the prevention of thought-crime and the media industries as a narcotic weapon to dumb down 'the masses' into a stupified acceptance of consumerism. Both Left and Right of course, have adopted this view in different ways. Of most importance criminologically however, are the critical theories of the Left that presented the analysis of the media as a question of the cultural reproduction of material power relations in the 'knowledge realm'.

Historically this debate took place among an exiled European intelligentsia, notably those associated with the Frankfurt Institute for Social Research including Max Horkheimer, Theodore Adorno, Herbert Marcuse, Karl Mannheim, and Walter Benjamin. Accounts and critiques of the work of the Frankfurt School are many, and include for example, Jay (1973), Curran *et al.* (1977), Held (1980), Thompson (1990), Inglis (1993) and in the original, Adorno and Horkheimer (1972), and the Frankfurt Institute for Social Research (1973). The debate started from a moral and theoretical critique of capitalist modes of polity and economy centring specifically on the functioning of the 'mass media' in producing and maintaining capitalist relations of oppression (Adorno and Horkheimer 1973; Curran *et al.* 1977; During 1993). Its ethos is captured in the title of Adorno and Horkheimer's 1940s essay: 'enlightenment as mass deception':

> The people at the top are no longer so interested in concealing monopoly: as its violence becomes more open, so its power grows. Movies and radio need no longer pretend to be art. The truth that they are just business is made into an ideology to justify the rubbish they deliberately produce . . . the need which might resist central control has already been suppressed by the control of the individual consciousness. The step from the telephone to the radio has clearly distinguished the roles. The former still allowed the subscriber to play the role of subject, and was liberal. The latter is democratic: it turns all participants into listeners and authoritatively subjects them to broadcast programmes which are all exactly the same.
>
> (Adorno and Horkheimer 1993: 31)

The work of the Frankfurt School needs to be understood in its historical context as a development of Marxist theorizing under conditions of fascism, or specifically Nazism. The rise of Nazism and the centrality of anti-Semitism within Nazi ideology brought starkly to the fore the Hegelian problematic of the dialectical relationship between 'base' and 'superstructure', or the material and the cultural spheres of production. It was seen as necessary to explain *how* and *why* fascism could triumph, apparently against the logic of historical materialism, while German communism collapsed, virtually obliterated in the face of pro-Nazi populism.

For the writers of the Frankfurt School the core of this theoretical endeavour was an understanding of the profoundly destructive effect of capitalist modernity upon the popular consciousness through the manufacture of mass culture. The concept of 'the mass' and 'mass society' in capitalist societies was seen as closely linked to the deindividuation associated with Nazism, and required a psychoanalytic as well as more generally social–economic understanding. Thus, embraced by capitalism, mass consumerism was seen as co-opting the soul and deadening the brain, producing a universally a-critical object rather than a thinking, active, creative subject. This acts to stimulate market 'demand' for more and more commodities of mass production as symbols of the 'good life'. The good life itself was a perpetually false promise, one that ultimately is always left unfulfilled, thus securing the repetition of the whole process; the achievement of compliance with economic oppression and cultural repression through the commodification of desire itself (Marcuse 1968). Thus capitalism

> perpetually cheats its consumers of what it perpetually promises . . . it draws on pleasure [which] is endlessly prolonged; the promise, which is actually all the spectacle consists of, is illusory: all it actually confirms is that the real point will never be reached . . . by repeatedly exposing the objects of desire . . . it only stimulates the unsublimated forepleasure which habitual deprivation has long since reduced to a masochistic semblance . . . Works of art are ascetic and unashamed; the culture industry is pornographic and prudish. Love is downgraded to romance . . . The mass production of the sexual automatically achieves its repression.
> (Adorno and Horkheimer 1972; cited in Inglis 1993: 71–2)

The deadening of popular sensibility through the commodification of culture meant that the culture industries represented the truly diabolic face of capitalism; mass communication bringing with it totalizing discourses of desensitization, futile desire, empty voyeurism, and pointless, relentless symbolic consumption which serve only to perpetuate the ends of capitalist accumulation itself.

Somewhat in contrast stands the work of the Italian Marxist Antonio Gramsci. Gramsci's critical legacy from the victory of fascism (resulting in his imprisonment by Mussolini) was a drive to comprehend how widespread consent to the inequalities and injustices of capitalism are achieved, and although he too centralized the sphere of cultural production, his analysis was less bleak; he did not see popular culture as 'the site of the people's cultural deformation' as Bennett aptly puts it (1986: xiii). While the Frankfurt School was strongly bound up with a structuralist standpoint which assumes that power, in the form of cultural domination, is simply poured down people's throats, Gramsci's more complex formulation begins with the taken-for-grantedness of everyday life – the assumptions, values, beliefs and attitudes that we carry around as part of our common-sense universe. However, that universe is not forced into our psyches, it is not over and above us. There is not a 'superstructure' (realm of ideas, cultural production, belief system) which can be boiled down to a base (economy, capitalist accumulation) via a simple theory of ruling interests and domination, the seduction of the deindividuated mass. The history of ideas cannot be explained as no more than the generally accepted legitimation of the oppressors. For Gramsci the task is to expose the processes which achieve the *active* assent and participation of the majority of the people in a society, their allegiance to a particular set of social arrangements which, viewed from one perspective, might be seen as antithetical to their interests (Inglis 1993: 76).

The essence of hegemony is that it makes the 'over and aboveness' of society seem immediate, obvious, and everyday – but through a process of negotiated consent, not brainwashing. In turn this implies not a totalizing ideology, but a consideration of specific sites of cultural production and consumption, not a study of 'the media', but of their diversity, plurality, and interrelations. For Gramsci however, as with the Frankfurt School, the 'popular element' was not in a position to discover the processes of its own oppression; the very taken-for-grantedness achieved through hegemony prevented this. A class of 'intellectuals' was required who could interpret what was 'really' going on and 'educate' the people to question the basis of their assumed knowledge and culture, thereby enabling them to take 'charge' of their culture (Bennett 1986: 78).

The work of the critical school was a victim of its own contradictions. Who is to identify the difference between true, or 'high' culture, and the despoiled, defiled, popular culture of the mass? Is populism by definition contaminated? If 'the mass' exists it does not care much; if it does not care much, does it matter? Whose vision should prevail? Based on whose definitions? Exiled intellectuals, prophets, poets? People walking the street with placards declaiming that 'the end of the world is nigh'? According to Gramsci, intellectuals, who would reassert the process of cultural 'education', should make cultural definitions. Critical *faculty* was elided with a desired political end, ethics and morality with the 'science of society'. Neither the despair of the Frankfurt School nor the confined deliberations of a man imprisoned for his politics (Gramsci 1971) could 'help' if 'the mass' did not exist or if people did not share the vision of these men exiled, these outsiders. (Wilson [1956]1990).

Nevertheless, this critical legacy spawned works which have posed vital questions relating to the understanding of the media's place in social relations over time, and the relevance of these is very far from exhausted. Any study of the media could be framed as one of ideological work; as Darnell M. Hunt puts it in his study of the O.J. Simpson case, 'tracing the *process* by which we all (re)affirm what we "know" about "reality"' (1999: 11). From this standpoint the role of the media in the cultural reproduction of power relations necessitates questioning the relationship of media representations to 'reality' at two levels: first at the level of verisimilitude, especially where claims for 'objectivity' or 'factuality' are made; and second at the level of the relationship of media representations to everyday life, where appeals to 'common sense' and 'what we all know' are made.

From a criminological point of view the relevance is clear, most particularly in relation to the production of crime news. Relatively sophisticated 'materialist' or 'Marxist' analyses of news culture have formed a continuing strand of interesting research, focusing on the role of the media in transmitting selective definitions of the way the world is, and values about the way the world should be (for example Glasgow University Media Group 1976, 1980, 1982; Bennett 1986; Thompson 1990; Ericson *et al.* 1991; Allan 1999), and the question of hegemonic domination remained alive for decades (Reiner 1997). Some important contributions to the culture/ideology/media debate on hegemony also came from the work of the Centre for Contemporary Cultural Studies (CCCS) at the University of Birmingham, and from within 'radical' and 'critical' criminologies of the 1960s and 1970s. Again, extensive reviews are available (see for example Redhead 1995; Maguire *et al.* 1997; and the discussion on criminology later in this chapter.)

Such formulations of the nature of 'relations' between culture, ideology and history, between agency, subjectivity, and structure, though, retain a media/society dichotomy which is problematic. The perspective changes if we see media/society as mutually inherent and mutually constitutive. Had Adorno and Horkheimer abandoned high/low, true/false distinctions, they may have paid closer attention to the implications of their own assertion that 'real life is becoming indistinguishable from the movies' (Adorno and Horkheimer 1993: 34). The social practices of mediation entail the fusion of productive and consumptive moments (the activities of 'programme maker' and 'viewer', for instance) in a state of mediatization. The increasing trend towards passivity which they attributed to the proliferation of 'mass media' has proved with hindsight to be ever further away in the multi-faceted realities of late modernity. To understand this abstract formulation better, it is essential to consider more broadly the place occupied by mediation in the processes of modernity, and the challenges suggested to many traditional analyses of the media by the question of the postmodern.

Media messaging in modernity

In the second half of the twentieth century, partly as a result of the transformative effects of the so-called 'new media' of the electronic age, theoretical concern with media culture broadened to include a focus on the significance of technological form as well as of the ideological *content* of mediation. Whereas for the critical theorists 'technology' was simply a tool of domination, an ideological weapon given explanatory power by those whose interests it served, later analyses locate the technical as neither inherently determinant nor merely ideological tricksterism – rather it must be located as a fully social element of mediation. Mediation is as much a technological event as a linguistic one. For example Giddens (1990), Thompson (1990), and Castells (1996) have identified the contours of modernity as shaping and being shaped by the transformation of communications technologies.

The technosocial especially has framed the mediatization of identity in late modernity, and Giddens (1991) identifies the transition from 'news by ship', to print, telegraph and wireless communications, to the electronic age, as being fundamental to modernity, and to transformations in the relations between 'self and society'. In particular for Giddens, the crucial relation is that between 'dominant kinds of media and time-space transformations' (1991: 24). The evolution of media technologies under modernity is detailed in many accounts (see for example Mackay and O'Sullivan 1999), but Giddens (1991: 24) summarizes the crux of the matter simply as follows:

> Modernity is inseparable from its 'own' media: the printed text and subsequently, the electronic signal. The development and expansion of modern institutions were directly bound up with the tremendous increase in the mediation of experience which these communication forms brought in their train.

For Giddens, the subsequent sophisticated technological developments of the 'electronic age' replicated the same principles: the separation of time and space, the disembedding of interactions from the particularities of locales, and the intensification of globalizing tendencies. As a corollorary of these features of modernity, we also see an impact on the notion of identity and the public/private divide, 'the intrusion of distant events into everyday consciousness' (Giddens 1991: 27). To say, then, that fundamental changes accompanied technological developments in the media of communication is to understate the transformative power of modernity, yet as Giddens notes, Marshall McLuhan was one of the few writers to 'theorise the impact of media on social development in a sophisticated fashion, especially in relation to modernity' (1991: 24).

Marshall McLuhan referred to the 'carrier' of the message, or the medium, as a 'technology' – not in the merely technical sense of electronics or digital signals, but in a far broader sense of an 'extension of man [sic]' (his book *Understanding Media*, first published in 1964, was subtitled 'The extensions of man'). Under 'technological extensions of man' McLuhan included roads, telegraphs, housing, electric light bulbs, language, even money. For him, it was technology thus defined which altered the nature of human relationships, and thereby the forms of human culture. It is not 'light' (the message) which is of primary importance, but rather the fact that in extending 'man' beyond natural daylight, the light bulb changes the interactions between human beings, so 'the personal and social consequences of any medium – that is, of any extension of ourselves – result from the new scale that is introduced into our affairs' (McLuhan [1964]1997: 7). McLuhan argued that we tend to ignore the role of the technology, and concentrate on the content of the message enabled by it, as the foundation of culture. Whether we agree fully with his arguments or not, they are important in that they provoke us to think more clearly about the interrelationship between media and culture.

In particular, McLuhan stated that the western world was 'imploding', for 'we have extended our central nervous system itself in a global embrace, abolishing both space and time so far as our planet is concerned' (McLuhan [1964]1997: 3). As we enter the electronic age, then

> Rapidly, we approach the final phase of the extensions of man – the technological simulation of consciousness, when the creative process of knowing will collectively and corporately extend to the whole of human society, much as we have

already extended our senses and our nerves by the various
media.

(McLuhan [1964]1997: 4)

Fundamentally, McLuhan appears to be arguing that any medium in
itself – that is to say its form rather than its content – is what changes the
order of things. At times indeed he seems to be contesting that content is
irrelevant to the message of the medium: the medium *is* the message. The
'message' of any medium or technology (he appears to use these terms
interchangeably) 'is the change of scale or pace or pattern that it intro-
duces into human affairs' ([1964]1997: 8).

Following McLuhan, Giddens observes that 'the degree to which a
medium serves to alter time space relations does not depend primarily on
the content or the "message" it carries, but on its form and reproducibil-
ity' – that is, its technical properties (1991: 24).

Thus mediation can occur through linguistic signs, as in language,
through binary signals, as with computers, through image and visuality,
as with film, art, etc., through musical notation, and so on. The importance of this apparently banal observation is that each form/content
dyad of mediation carries with it a process of transformation of the original signal, and the nature of that transformation is dependent upon the
cultural context of the production and reception of the message *and* of
the medium. This is the media in its broadest sense; a form of communication which lends a particular shape to a message, *both* through form
and content.

In this book I have no particular intention of distancing myself either
from a so-called 'culturalist' perspective which emphasizes the importance of the cultural content and context of media messages, nor from a
McLuhanist stance which emphasizes the importance of the nature of
media technologies (see Stevenson, 1995, for a defence of the importance
of technological form). My contention is that the transformations of
modernity, most notably the restructuring of time–space relations and the
human–technology interface, are constituted mutually by form and content which cannot be treated separately. In this sense the debate regarding
whether or not an 'information society' exists is cavalierly set aside; with
due reverence to the richness of the debate itself (Webster 1999), of course
it does. And undoubtedly, an information society is thereby a mediatized
society. But how? How does it feel? Can we eat it, breathe it, see it? Is it

pictures, words, pixels? Is there any adequacy of language which might begin to describe it? And how are 'we' constituted through it?

The global soul? Globalization, identity and media culture

And so our dreams of distant places change as fast as images on MTV.

(Iyer 2001: 269)

The complex overlapping of the technological and the cultural form perhaps finds its ultimate expression in the assertion of the 'implosion' of media and reality developed most strongly in the work of Jean Baudrilard (Butler 1999; Genosko 1999). This strand of inquiry refers to the binding together of media and society through, in particular, the institutional and technological transformations of modernity and globalization, and ultimately leads to the question of whether media-culture is, in the twenty-first century, a postmodern culture (Morley and Robins 1995).

The most far-reaching (in all senses) change of the closing decades of the twentieth century has been the globalization of the information economy (McGuigan 1999). The breakdown of national barriers has been made possible through television (satellite and cable) and inevitable by computer (digital) technologies (Barker 1997). The keywords of informational globalism become 'convergence', 'integration', 'networking'. Castells (1996) goes so far as to see developments in information technology as constituting a new mode of development, integral to the shift from a world to a global economy. In parallel, cultures become mobile, and Stevenson (1999) contends that the 'intermixing and hybridization' of cultures through global media has become a leitmotif of modernity. Thus space is compressed and the whole of 'geography' as we may understand it in modernist terms, is dissolved. It is important here, as Lash and Urry (1994) pointed out, to differentiate between 'global culture' and 'globalization'. The interests of the media are global, and media technologies are no longer constrained by national boundaries; for Lash and Urry however, the inappropriate use of the term 'global culture' could suggest that the effect 'will be to produce mass consumers of the products of such companies on a world scale'. While global mediatization might mean *Who Wants to be a Millionaire?* the world over, what is being suggested is not a blanket 'global culture' in the way that Adorno and Horkheimer (1993) referred to 'mass culture'. Thus Lash and Urry (1994: 306–7) suggest that

> It may be more plausible to suggest that there is not *a* global culture, but that there are a number of processes which are producing the globalization of culture . . . the literature on postmodernism would suggest that these globalization processes are leading to the proliferation of multiple popular and local cultures which only in part correspond to or are congruent with dominant ideologies within particular nation-states . . . with postmodernity it is the global networks of communication and information that are crucial . . . the symbolic forms transmitted by the technical media of mass communication are central to contemporary cultural forms . . . most important of all they produce images . . . that are diverse, pluralistic, and which overload the viewer.

Thus globalization, localization, and identities need to be thought about together in order to make sense of what mediatization might come to mean.

As we have seen, Giddens was well aware that in theorizing the nature of the relationship between technological development and media culture, and the particular forms of social institutions and communications implied by this, it is also crucial to consider the transformation of identity. I refer here not only to the debates around identity which focus on the dialectic between the global and the local (Giddens 1991; Morley and Robins 1995) and on 'long' transformations of time and space (the social transformations to which notions such as diaspora refer), but also to the way in which the media infuse interpersonal social relations and concepts of self in general (Stevenson 1995). Identity is *achieved*, not given; it is a negotiated product drawing on cultural resources. As Friedman argues, it implies consumption in the most fundamental sense, and 'the old saying "you are what you eat" . . . is strikingly accurate when it is understood as a thoroughly social act' (1990: 314). Two particular features of the 'identity' project under late modernity are the *multiplicity* of resources for the construction of identity, and the *ubiquity* of cultural resources, resulting in both a homogenizing tendency through cultural globalization, and a fracturing tendency, as the traditional world of the meta-narrative disintegrates under the plethora of possible, available selves which are not necessarily anchored to time or place. Thus as Barker (1999: 33) following Featherstone (1995) argues:

> Identities . . . are narratives constructed from the intersubjective resources of language and, as such, are social and cultural 'all the way down'. That is, identities are constructed in and through cultural representations (including those produced by television) with which 'we' identify. However, our very notion of culture has begun to change, so that the image . . . of culture as an integrated, bounded, and in-place 'whole way of life' is giving way to metaphors of fragmentation and plural, if overlapping, discourses which flow across established borders . . . that is, cultures are no longer bounded by specific places but, through the migration of persons and the electronic transfer of ideas and images, transgress established boundaries.

Thus, there is the question of the 'global soul' (Iyer 2001). The ubiquity of speeded-up, technology-mediated global communication has in essence dissolved the distinction between the public and the private. Life is as confusing as an airport, redolent with ontological insecurity. When something happens 'out there', it happens 'in here'. For whom does the date-become-phrase 'September 11' now have the same meaning after the destruction of the World Trade Center in 2001 as it did for those same people on 8 September 2001? This is far from the utopian futurologist proclaiming that we are all time travellers. Indeed the enormity of the mediated global, the repeated images of the toppling towers, palpably suggesting the unthinkable – that America is not invincible, sent people shrinking back into the haven of domesticity. The very same people who slow down to watch car crashes or TV docudramas on serial killers cast around for identity, for security. We see here not a 'mass', but a teeming collective process, full of disjunctions and about-turns, one minute searching out nostalgia in the imagic artefacts of the screen, the next seeking the total experience of mock ghastliness of the horror movie. The project of identity is so multi-layered (and not just for those affluent persons seeking out psychoanalysts) and the possibilities so endless that the global soul can at one and the same time be the local soul; in its very virtuality, it is at the same time real. Thus there can be no media–society dichotomy; there can be no media–self dichotomy.

Anthony Giddens related in his 1999 BBC Reith Lecture on Globalization how:

> A friend of mine studies village life in central Africa. A few years ago, she paid her visit to a remote area where she was to carry out her fieldwork. The evening she got there, she was invited to a local home for an evening's entertainment. She expected to find out about the traditional pastimes of this isolated community. Instead, the evening turned out to be a viewing of *Basic Instinct* on video. The film at that point hadn't even reached cinemas in London.
>
> (1999: 1)

As Featherstone notes, anecdotes such as these are now common, 'yet how are we to read them?' (1995: 116). Clearly it is not just a case of everyday cultures and identities being saturated by globally marketed cultural products:

> Instantaneous electronic communication isn't just a way in which news or information is conveyed more quickly. Its existence alters the very texture of our lives, rich and poor alike . . . Globalisation isn't only about what is 'out there', remote and far away from the individual. It is an 'in here' phenomenon too, influencing intimate and personal aspects of our lives . . . Globalisation is the reason for the revival of local cultural identities in different parts of the world . . . Local nationalisms spring up as a response to globalizing tendencies.
>
> (Giddens 1999: 3–4)

Moreover this is not just about 'movements' or quasi-organized reactions or insurgencies, but about the ever more intimate interconnectedness between everyday experiences and meta-cultures; in Arundhati Roy's novel *The God of Small Things* (1998) we see it in the peculiar eclectics of going to the cinema in Kerala, watching *The Sound of Music* and drinking 'lemondrinks', or in Pico Iyer's search for a home in a 'world gone mobile', epitomized, ironically (given the restitution of the former colony) by Hong Kong: 'everywhere, I felt, a crush of multicultural props offering one goodies that answered every need except for the ancient, ancestral ones that convenience and speed could not wash away' (Iyer 2001: 98).

Featherstone refers to the term 'glocal' (1995: 118), the fusion of the terms global and local. Metaphors of 'colonization' or 'imperialism' are inappropriate to further an understanding of globalization, and are closer to the ideas of the mass culture theorists discussed earlier in this chapter than they are true to the complexities of globalizing processes. American soaps, UK quiz shows, Hollywood movies, argues Featherstone, may 'have an apparent immediacy and intelligibility which could be misunderstood as producing a homogenous response. Yet these global resources are often indigenized and syncretized to produce particular blends and identifications which sustain the sense of the local' (1995: 117). A BBC2 television programme on junk food (*Food Junkies: How We Fell in Love With Food*, 17 April 2002) reported the massive per capita consumption of Coca Cola by Mexicans and the incorporation of Coke into quasi-shamanist religious rituals. At the same time the showing of globalized TV shows and ads on TV in the UK becomes the 'humorous' fulcrum of tele-pastiche programmes such as *Tarrant on TV*, in which Chris Tarrant invites the canned laughter of a British audience over dislocated clips of indigenous adaptations of everything from condom adverts to his own game show. As the characters played by John Travolta in Tarantino's film *Pulp Fiction* (1994) points out on the subject of McDonaldization, 'And you know what they call a Quarter-Pounder with Cheese in Paris? . . . They call it a Royale with Cheese' (Tarantino 1996) – instrumentally, because of the metric system, but more, 'Royale' is loaded with everything the character sees as quintessentially Parisian: sophistication, refinement, mystery. The global burger is not the same everywhere.

Insofar as globalization means that no one can escape the (mediatized) transformations which attend modernity, then the (global) media must be considered as transformative of the dimensions of identity (Giddens 1991, 1999), for as Featherstone argues, the locality is no longer 'the prime referent of our experiences', since we can be 'immediately united with distant others with whom we can form a 'psychological neighbourhood' (1995: 117). As Thompson writes, 'the media . . . have . . . created what we would call a 'mediated worldliness': our sense of the world which lies beyond the sphere of our personal experience, and our sense of our place within this world, are increasingly shaped by mediated symbolic forms' (Thompson 1999: 21).

In terms of cultural identity, it is true that global mediatization changes the nature of belonging and memory, senses of common experiences and shared memory. Sources of symbolism, imagery, and language are more and more universalized, eroding the historical and spatial specificity of cultures (Smith 1990), but this 'erosion' does not amount to reducibility to a common denominator.

As Hannerz (1990) points out, the world has become one network of social relationships, meanings flowing across the globe just as people and goods do, but instantaneously transmitted and constantly transforming through the prism of media technologies. However such processes of constant transformation are not uniform processes, and by definition – and increasingly with the ever-expanding capacity for interactivity and intertextuality which global communications media display – are not stable or constant, or in any sense 'pre-given'.

The emergence of the media hybrid

More than this, mediatized culture also produces an apparently seamless web between spheres of representation; it leads, for me, to what Latour (1993: 1–3) terms the 'proliferation of hybrids':

> On page four of my daily newspaper, I learn that the measurements taken above the Antarctic are not good this year: the hole in the ozone layer is growing ominously larger. Reading on, I turn from upper-atmosphere chemists to Chief Executive Officers of Atochem and Monsanto, companies that are modifying their assembly lines in order to replace the innocent chlorofluorocarbons, accused of crimes against the ecosphere. A few paragraphs later, I come across heads of states of major industrialised countries who are getting involved with chemistry, refrigerators, aerosols and inert gases . . . A single thread links together the most esoteric sciences and the most sordid politics, the most distant sky and some factory in the Lyon suburbs . . . [they] are multiplying, those hybrid articles that sketch out imbroglios of science, politics, economy, law, religion, technology, fiction . . . All of culture

and all of nature get churned up again every day. Yet no one seems to find this troubling. Headings like Economy, Politics, Science, Books, Culture, Religion, and Local Events remain in place as if there were nothing odd going on . . . Press the most innocent aerosol button and you'll be heading for the Antarctic, and from there to the University of California at Irvine, the mountain ranges of Lyon, the chemistry of inert gases, and then maybe to the United Nations.

The intertextuality and interactivity of contemporary media forms highlights this tendency. As 'news' increasingly contains items about celebrities, TV shows and newspapers, and the electronic media, the news media is more and more constituted by news *about* the media.

Hence 'news' about TV soap operas and soap stars is now endemic, just as much as references to 'current affairs' are embedded in soaps (consider for instance how many episodes of popular UK soaps such as *Coronation Street* or *Brookside*, having 'dealt' with issues such as domestic violence, rape, child abuse, drug abuse etc., are followed by the trailer 'if you have been affected by any of the issues covered in this programme please send a self-addressed envelope to . . . or telephone . . . or log on to our website . . .'). At the same time as 'news' is embedded in soaps, so is promotion. Commercial breaks are being threatened by a more sophisticated version of product placement. Rather than a specific break in the programme narrative, this approach involves companies paying to have prominence for the products and marketing narratives interwoven with the dialogue of the programme itself. Already long-established in the cinema in a basic way (a Jack Daniels bottle for example, prominently sited on a drinks cabinet, a Revlon lipstick on a dressing table) the absorption of promotional into fictional narrative may lead to the obsolescence of ads. Ads are a disjunction in the viewing process which are being commercially threatened by the videotaping of programmes and the home-editing potential of emergent technologies. Television and cinema advertising itself already incorporates soap-style narratives for an increasingly sophisticated audience, using either conventions of narrative episodes as a campaign evolves or quick-flash sound-bites which 'update' the original, long format ad. We have come to expect a good story from our ads; it is a small step for them to blend seamlessly with the 'good stories' which we expect from the soaps which form threads in everyday life.

1998 was a vintage year for the media dissolution of fact and fiction in the UK. When *Coronation Street* ran a storyline in April depicting the miscarriage of justice which left Deirdre Rachid wrongly imprisoned for credit card fraud, a sequence of events followed which epitomized the fact/fiction dilemma. 'PM supports Weatherfield One' reported the BBC News online (BBC 1998):

> Prime Minister Tony Blair has promised to intervene, newspapers have launched campaigns, and thousands of ordinary people are outraged at a gross miscarriage of justice. The campaign to free Deirdre Rachid is gathering momentum with the Home Secretary Jack Straw under orders to look into the case . . .
>
> Fans are setting up Free the Weatherfield One campaigns and have jammed the switchboards of programme makers Granada . . . even in the haughty columns of *The Times*, Deirdre has made front page news . . . Initial viewing figures estimated around 16.5m watched *Coronation Street* last Sunday when Deirdre was jailed.

Meanwhile, the *Guardian* (6 April 1998) ran a 'Letters to the Editor' entitled 'Postmodernist Deirdre' and published letters on the subject which, in an ironic twist, highlighted the self-referential and intertextual nature of the mediatized legal process, for example

> I find it quite amazing that you could give publicity to a fictitious miscarriage of justice (MP's echo free Deirdre calls, March 31) when, after the Broadcast of the BBC Rough Justice programme about a real life miscarriage of justice, there was nothing.
>
> Is society so mixed up between fact and fiction that they can no longer differentiate?
>
> Raphael Rowe (M25 Three)
HM Prison Kingston
Portsmouth, Hants

The . . . theorist Jean Baudrillard advances the argument that . . . there has been an implosion of image and reality, 'a loss of the real'; 'the real is now defined in terms of the media in which it moves'. Baudrillard now argues that the world consists of an endlessly circulating morass of 'simulacra'; self generating images with no referent in reality . . . surely the occurrence of such hyperreal phenomena as the reaction to the death of Diana and the Free Deirdre campaign prove that he is right?

Richard Harris
Sheffield

In parallel vein, 'news' increasingly adopted the tone and formats of fictional or entertainment genres and the technologies of the virtual. One example was the Clinton–Lewinsky 'scandal' (see Diary of a Scandal, *Newsweek*, Wednesday 21 January, 1998), where virtuality and global TV landed the soap opera of President Clinton's alleged sexual proclivities directly in millions of homes across the world. When the story broke in January 1998, Clinton's denial of an alleged affair with former White House intern Monica Lewinsky, and his further denial that he attempted to dissuade Lewinsky from speaking to attorneys seeking a statement from her regarding an earlier alleged sexual harassment incident involving the President and another woman, Paula Jones, led to what the *Washington Post* described as 'a furor [sic] that . . . threatens to be the gravest legal and political challenge Clinton has faced in five years as president' ('Clinton denies alleged affair', *Washington Post* Thursday, 22 January 1998). On August 17 1998 the President testified before a grand jury, and later publicly acknowledged, his 'improper' relationship with Ms Lewinsky. The testimony, courtesy of satellite broadcast, treated the world to images of the president appearing by turn as sincere, shifty, embarrassed, evasive, and ultimately 'guilty'. After the Starr report hit the Internet on 13 September 1998, providing the full sexually explicit testimonies to the president's relationship with 24-year-old Ms Lewinsky, CNN.com reported that an estimated 20 million Americans 'used the internet to gain access to Independent Counsel Ken Starr's report on President Clinton (http://www.cnn./com/TECH/computing/9809/13/ internet.starr/, accessed 2/2/02). President Clinton's advisors 'flooded the Sunday talk shows in an effort to blunt the momentum building in Congress for a formal impeachment' reported the *Washington Post* (Monday, 14 September 1998). It became difficult to tell anymore where the boundaries between the White House and Hollywood might lie; as one commentator wrote, 'the president of the United States starring on the Jerry Springer–Oprah Winfrey Show of all time?' ('Comment', the *Guardian*, 22 September 1998). The next day the *Guardian* ran an 'Inside Story' special speculating on the links between Clinton and the movie representations of political figures during his administration ('Mark Lawson reads between the lines of fact and fiction', *Guardian*, 23 September 1998).

Meanwhile, back in the world of the UK soap opera, 19 October 1998 saw an Early Day Motion tabled in the House of Commons by Dr Lynne Jones MP:

> That this House congratulates the scriptwriters, actors and producers of *Coronation Street* for their sensitive and realistic portrayal of Hayley, a transsexual woman . . . and hopes the Government will soon see fit to guarantee transsexual people full civil rights, including the right to correct birth certificates and to enter into marriage.
>
> (Early Day Motion No. 1655 of the 1997–8 Session, Portrayal of 'Hayley' in *Coronation Street*, taken from the House of Commons website)

The increasingly soap opera-like and fiction-narrative structure of news programmes, such as the media promotion of iconic grief surrounding the death of Diana Princess of Wales, suggests a difficulty in knowing what is new(s). This has led some theorists into highly controversial waters, as noted by the *Guardian* letter-writers cited above. Hence Jean Baudrillard's essay on the Gulf War. In this essay Baudrillard (1995: 31) focuses on the mediated virtuality of the Gulf War, posing the question, 'is it really taking place?' for

> 'real time' information loses itself in a completely unreal space, finally furnishing the images of pure, useless, instantaneous television where its primordial function irrupts, namely that of filling a vacuum, blocking up the screen hole through which escapes the substance of events . . . The media promote the war, the war promotes the media, and advertising competes with the war . . . it allows us to turn the world and the violence of the world into a consumable substance. So, war or promotion?

Baudrillard emphasizes the sense in which messages constantly refer to other messages, and media to other media (intertextuality) until TV for example, has no referent in 'reality', but only a relation with other kinds of messages; we have reached 'implosion' (Genosko 1999: 93–8). Thus Patton, in an introduction to Baudrillard's *The Gulf War Did Not Take Place* comments upon the TV Gulf War as a seemingly 'perfect Baudrillardian simulation', that is,

> A hyperreal scenario in which events lose their identity and signifiers fade into one another. Fascination and horror at the reality which seemed to unfold before our very eyes mingled with a pervasive sense of unreality as we recognised the elements of Hollywood script which had preceded the real . . . Occasionally, the absurdity of the media's self representation as purveyor of reality and immediacy broke through, in moments such as those when the CNN cameras crossed live to a group of reporters assembled somewhere in the Gulf, only to have them confess that they were also sitting around watching CNN in order to find out what was happening. Television news coverage appeared finally to have caught up with the logic of simulation.
>
> (Patton 1995: 2)

The possibilities of contemporary media forms go beyond, indeed, the human, since the virtual 'communities' of cyberspace offer the option of a choice of prosthetic identities, the potential for disassembling of the 'self' and the prosthetic reconstruction of virtual existence, subjectivity dissociated from the 'physical substrate' of the body (Stone 1996: 65; see also Featherstone and Burrows 1995). The Internet, with its user-interactivity, collapses distinctions between producers and consumers of 'information' or 'news', and fantasy and alleged fact freely intermingle. The potential here for the erosion of boundaries – physical, social, spatial, temporal, literal, and for our purposes, criminal and legal – are discussed further in Chapter 5; and pose the penultimate questions for crime, law, media futures.

However, at the same time, even if we seem to live in a purely mediated universe, in a mediatized culture, it remains that the (mediated) practices of that culture are real in their effects: whether the Gulf War 'did' or 'did not' take place, people still died and suffered; people are still starving, and people are still imprisoned. Mediatization should, then, be taken to mean the inability to dissect media culture from reality, to imply the sense in which our identities, our actions, our beliefs, our social practices, are constantly operating in and through the media and the sense in which language and images constitute experiential reality. This does not imply the passive stupidity of the average individual, nor a hegemonic expansion of global capitalism over thought and action (harnessing ever more sophisticated digital media forms). It may be that reality is simply not available to us unmediated until the dissolution of the body, or its dismemberment, or scarification, or starvation. Arguments around prosthetics however throw even this into question; moreover the natures of embodiment are a social practice which form a major axis of media representation, and the body is a *process* and a *site* of culture (Featherstone *et al.* 1991). Even the extent to which the body can be said to 'die' is increasingly reduced to a narrow definition, with the possibilities of digital archiving (for example we can see Marilyn Monroe convincingly appearing in television adverts) on the one hand, and the prosthetic (body-extensive) capabilities of 'life-support' systems and transplants on the other. The possibilities of genetic cloning and regeneration are an even more contentious area in this respect.

Above all, mediatization in the contemporary sense refers to a universe in which the meaning of *ontological divisions* is collapsing: divisions between fact and fiction, nature and culture, global and local, science and art, technology and humanity. In talking of mediatization as a producer and product of 'modernity and globalization', we are in danger of making the mistake identified by Featherstone (1995), that is, the mistake of seeing modernity and globalization as existing in an epoch–product relationship: modernity as a specific temporal epoch from which emerges the spatial reorderings of globalism. Mediation represents precisely the spatial relationships existent across the globe, and mediatization is a product of a particular conjunction of epochal or temporal developments and spatial transformations. Mediatization, as I argued earlier, should be seen as a *condition*, or a state of being, attendant upon these developments and transformations but at the same time, transformative of them. It is more that the media in the twenty-first century have so undermined the ability to construct an *apparent* distinction between reality and representation that the modernist episteme has begun to seem somewhat shaky. This is ultimately what denotes the impossibility of a media–society dichotomy, and it has profound consequences for crime and criminology, and for law and lawyering.

The academe and the study of media, crime and law

Those who are accustomed to thinking of 'crime' or 'law' as entities, something tangible 'out there', can view the relationship of crime and law to the media as a linkage between comfortably discrete phenomena. That is to say, identifiably separate domains may be posited: 'crime', 'the law', and 'the media'. One domain may be seen to influence the other, and vice versa. However, once the dichotomy model of media/society is challenged, the picture changes in a somewhat disturbing way.

First of all, theoretical certainties which have been taken for granted in modernist academic analyses of media and crime are brought into question. The assumptions of a specifiable notion of ideology are replaced by a fluidity whereby mediation inheres in a constant flow of communicative practices where meaning is never frozen in time or space, but is continuously re-constituted through the human–technology inter-face. Moments of production and consumption are increasingly the same. The simple ideo-logical question of 'who benefits?' and the con-comitant theoretical task of peeling back layers of interpretive construc-tions, media-codified versions of reality, and conventions of representation to reveal the under-lying dynamics of power and interest at work, lose certitude and direction. The moral taxonomies, and the regulatory and censuring responses to their implications which consti-tute definitions of crime and the basis of criminal law, are no longer self-evident. This applies as much to left-wing as to right-wing analyses of crime and the media.

Second, the empirical questions which may then be asked are affected. Without an analytical allegiance to the existence of dichotomy, many of the concepts central to traditional social science studies of crime and the media prove difficult to specify. This applies most centrally to studies which address 'bias' and 'effects'. While a left-wing approach relies on the notion of a media distortion of reality which in various complex ways obfuscates the interests of the powerful by promoting certain 'ver-sions' of crime and law as normal and desirable and suppressing others as questionable or reprehensible, the right-wing approach relies on a notion of the deleterious and pernicious potential of the media with their power to undermine these normal and desirable features of social order and encourage the reprehensible and questionable. Empirical questions become ones of identifying in more or less concrete ways how this is achieved. Evidence of the concentration of media ownership in global conglomerates is assumed to imply monolithism of interests and control; techniques of formal textual analysis may be used to demonstrate, for example, the objectification of women as sex commodities; controlled experimentation may be used to correlate viewing and attitudinal shifts as evidence of the ability of media violence to incite or desensitize human beings to pain and suffering, and so on. Debate then focuses on the adequacy or otherwise of particular methodological approaches, but rarely on their underlying assumptions.

Yet if we pause to consider the implications of the ways in which mediation has come to form an integral part of everyday life under late modernity, it has probably never been more apposite to remind ourselves that 'all that is solid melts into air'. One of the greatest difficulties in modernist empirical research has always been that inadequate formulation of concepts leads to spurious correlation. Perhaps nowhere more than in crime–media research have there been so many attempts to separate fluid, ongoing transactions and re-posit them as 'variables'. However, as Sparks suggests (1992), the most interesting approach lies in the very *embeddedness* of crime as a theme in public discourse. My particular concern is the texture of this 'embeddedness', the diverse ways in which its contours find expression.

Modern media and the criminological project: dichotomies and dilemmas

Even in the twenty-first century it is surprising how often the media – despite the clear plural – are written about in criminology as if 'they' were an 'it'. The complex intertextuality of media forms, whereby the media constantly refer to themselves and to each other, is hardly considered. Most striking is that historically criminology has concerned itself with the news media, as if this could be seen as separate, or worse, speak as though 'the media' and 'the news' are one and the same. Where other genres, such as film, drama, documentary, fiction, or 'true crime' for example, are discussed, it is typically as an addition rather than as a consideration of whether the distinction between fact and fiction in crime media might be considered problematic and thus fundamental to the discipline's theoretical endeavours (see for example, Reiner 1997; for an exception, see Nichols 1994, who clearly problematizes the fact/fiction distinction).

Behind criminology's traditional concern with the media lies the now familiar, intertwining technological and cultural account of modernism. The expansion of the 'mass' media during the nineteenth century was enabled by technical innovations in the printing process (Thompson 1995, 1999) which increased the *capacity* of the printing industry, while revolutions in the division of labour under the factory system increased the capabilities of mass production processes. 'Cultural modernization' under the conditions of urbanism meanwhile proceeded apace, as new forms of popular entertainment and communication proliferated. Both work and leisure settings produced new, more populous and 'mass' forms of interaction. Contemporary middle-class commentators generally saw this as a threat. The analogy of the sewer, as Pearson notes, loomed large: the sewer was the embodiment of modernity; it both underlay (literally) the industrial success of the nation and also posed (metaphorically) the greatest threat to the nation, for the sewer 'provided a powerful controlling imagery within which to define the fearful problem of "the dangerous classes" who, if their moral contagion was not checked, might burst from their subterranean home and swamp the social order' (Pearson 1985: 22).

'The media' lay at the centre of this confusion or controversy, for the conditions of urban life, with increased rates of literacy amongst, and the increased concentration of, the 'lower orders' produced an ever greater market for print amongst the working classes as well as the bourgeoisie. Journals, newspapers, magazines, and novels grew alongside hopes and fears for the future of the 'national way of life' (and global pre-eminence) in industrializing and imperialist countries. Thus technological, economic and social change give birth to the indivisible relationship between *media* and *culture*.

The *content* of media reflected this relationship. Popular culture became a primary focus of the burgeoning media in two ways. First – a precursor to tabloid journalism – as a producer of popular culture: 'shock horror' stories for mass consumption, including horror narratives of the gothic urban; cheap, vivid accounts of crime and sin to curdle the blood and chill the marrow of every God-fearing Victorian. Second, as a vehicle for comment, debate, propaganda, and lament in general on the state of life in the cities, most notably their criminogenic nature – *fomented by the very popular cultural forms which the media themselves produced* – and the (consequent) absence of godliness among the 'dark satanic mills'. The latter discourse was prevalent not only in the right-wing press, but also in the radical press and the religious press with their dire warnings of either revolution or eternal retribution ('the wages of sin').

Thus the media were at once the primary producers of crime news and crime narratives in the city, and the chief mourners of the supposed ill effects of popular culture on public morality. Hence the media won both ways; both selling fear, and lamenting it.

This situation was to become ever more familiar and more pervasive as the twentieth century progressed, and the media surged forward on the wave of the electronic age. Electronic wave technology ('the wireless') spawned generations of radio listeners. The wireless in particular strengthened the ability of communication media to locate the discourse of 'the other' as central to conceptions of the collective 'we', and aided in the formation of collective antipathy through its manipulation of the symbiosis between the public and the private. Here lie the foundations of 'public broadcasting' in the UK; since from its inception in the 1920s, the British Broadcasting Corporation as Thompson (1999: 31) points out,

> addressed audiences as members of a national and imperial community. It advanced a highly selective version of national culture as the symbolic cement binding citizens together in a shared structure of feeling which transcended the allegiances of locality, class, and ethnicity. During the thirty years of its monopoly the BBC invented the 'sound of Britain'.

The growth of broadcasting of course reflected political and military interests, and the centrality of news and propaganda broadcasting on the domestic front of the Second World War sealed the notion that Auntie BBC spoke for *us*. The wireless represented the British Way of Life, a standard bearer for national values. BBC English, a stilted rendition of Received Pronunciation, allied speech forms inextricably with status and power relations, with vested authority. It reminded the rest of us exactly what our place in the order of things should be and reminded us who was clearly excluded from the ranks of legitimate authority: blacks, women (except on domestic matters such as household economy) foreigners, and common people. Binding 'us' together through the Second World War (a peculiar 'us', to which so few actually belonged) we knew that we were superior to foreigners and usurpers, the immoral and the criminal.

Kidd-Hewitt and Osborne (1995: 2) typify the traditional criminological approach to the study of crime and the media as constituting four lines of questioning: first, whether the media 'through depictions of crime, violence, death and aggression' can be said to 'cause' criminal or deviant behaviour (I shall refer to this as the 'effects debate'); second, whether the media unjustly stereotype groups or individuals; third, whether the media orchestrate the creation of 'moral panics' around certain groups or issues heightening fearfulness about crime; and fourth whether 'real' crime and 'fictional' crime impact upon people in the same manner.

In relation to the first of these, Howitt (1998: 59) calls the issue of potential media effects on violent behaviour the 'golden question'. The 'effects debate' concerns the potential impact which media depictions of crime and sexuality (or sexual 'deviance') may have on viewers, especially children and young people. The 'effects' debate has a history as long as popular culture (During 1993), but in its most recent manifestation controversy has surrounded so-called 'video nasties', computer games, and the Internet. The debate gathered force through high profile cases exemplified in the UK by the murder of Liverpool toddler James Bulger (Smith 1994) by two young boys who were famously alleged to have viewed video nasties. Critical commentaries and reviews of the debates are provided in Ericson (1995), Kidd-Hewitt and Osborne (1995) and Barker and Petley (1997). Again, I shall argue that to view 'the media' as a coherent institution, or specific examples of media representation (a video, a computer game) as unitary external entities which may somehow be correlated to specific acts or behavioural tendencies, is theoretically misconceived in contemporary mediatized society. This has not however, been the traditional concern of criminologists, who have largely taken the effects debate seriously. This is curious, as much of the effects research has gone very little distance on a very large budget, and despite its continuing proliferation, there is not a great deal of interest to say on the subject, as the following discussion shows.

Most of the many 'effects' studies are laboratory-based exercises in which subjects undergo various forms of violent media exposure and some aspect of their behaviour is monitored in relation to exposure. The sheer arcanity of some of these attempts at measurement is the most entertaining aspect of the literature. The more sophisticated studies, improved by a concentration on specific issues and populations, such as the viewing propensities of convicted offenders and 'non-offenders' (Hagell and Newburn 1994) are typically cautious and typically swamped by the wave of studies driven by what Vine (1997) has called the 'dangerous psycho-logic of media effects'.

Vine, in a careful exposition of causality and its research applications, shows precisely how the empirical problems facing research based on a media–society dichotomy outlined above, surface in 'effects' research:

> Whichever Behaviourist methods are used in quantitative studies of media impact, the central problem remains. If subjects' own perceptions of programmes are not directly measured, their influence on actions must be assumed or just ignored. Yet the main thrust of the hermeneutic perspective on responsible agency is that interpretation processes themselves have profoundly complex causal determinants . . . the fundamental semiotic concept of *polysemy* refers both to multiple layers of meaning being encoded within a transmitted message, and to the multiple possibilities for its decoding by different individuals.
>
> (1997: 133)

The usual – and sensible – research response to repeated failures to find anything much out would be to suggest that the wrong question was being asked, but the effects debate refuses to go away. This despite, as Howitt (1998: 63) correctly comments, that

> It may not be too hyperbolic . . . to suggest that media violence research in its totality is beyond synthesis. Apart from arguing that the research is confusing, no conclusions can be reached without disregarding swathes of contradictory research in the process. Partisan reviews have little appeal unless their criteria are accepted.

The interested reader will find as good an overview of the standard effects debate as any in Howitt (1998) and an excellent critical approach in Barker and Petley (1997). In the latter volume the contributors examine the much more fascinating question of the insistence of political and moral interest groups, and ironically the media itself, on centralizing a question which has so palpably refused to be answered. The contention that the media are a powerful source of 'ill effects' depends for its credence on 'reservoirs of dogma' argues Murdock (1997), originating in the fears surrounding modernity which flourished, as discussed above, in the nineteenth century. Therefore one is back full circle to the original doublethink: the media supposedly creates a 'problem' requiring its censorship and regulation while at the same time making a healthy income and wielding a heavy ideological stick.

The debate around pornography is just one of the many examples of this. Germaine Greer (in her journey from author of *The Female Eunuch* in 1971, to chic millennial icon of highbrow cultural criticism and 'Country Life' columnist of the *Telegraph*, a superbly manufactured media product as reinventive of self as Madonna), wrote:

> The spread of pornography into the mainstream is not, as liberal voices argue, a victory for freedom of expression but a poison in our culture – and we develop a taste for it at our peril . . . The cool post-liberal consensus about pornography misses the point. Pornography has nothing to do with freedom of expression: it is primarily business, a ruthless impersonal industry based on the sound maxims that a) there is one born every minute; and b) you should never give a sucker an even break . . . legal or illegal hardly matters except that illegal, like all crime, pays better for less work . . . It is . . . a bigger cultural presence than all our opera, ballet, theatre, music and fine art put together.
>
> (*Observer*, 24 September 2000)

This 'liberal versus anti-liberal' type of 'think' piece forms the backbone of much journalistic writing in the broadsheets, and there are many criminological questions that have interacted with it, but usually within the terms of the effects debate. *Why?* Greer backs out of the full force of the effects debate in a clever side-move; she reverts to a peculiar kind of 'Leavisism' in the sense used by During – Leavisism which 'primarily celebrated works directed towards directing the moral sensibilities of readers . . . culture was not simply a leisure activity . . . [but] a means of forming mature individuals with a concrete and balanced sense of 'life' (During 1993: 2).

In a mediatized culture many questions arise from the proliferation of 'pornography', more precisely the need for further developments in a criminology of the mediated body, and of course arguably it is the feminist criminologies which have done most to drag the discipline kicking and screaming into the twenty-first century (for example Walklate 1995; Young 1995; Green and Adam 2000). Yet Greer, for example, is or is not offering a pop version of feminist ethics, she addresses none of the really pertinent questions surrounding pornography.

Crime news and the dramas of crime

Apart from, or sometimes related to, the effects debate, the chief preoccupation of criminology has been with a critical examination of the news media's coverage of crime stories (e.g. Cohen and Young 1973; Ditton and Duffy 1983; Ericson *et al.* 1987; Wykes 2001). These, unlike the 'effects' debate per se, are areas of research that have produced a rich seam within critical criminologies in particular, linking media reporting to structural and institutional aspects of social control and hegemonic domination as well as to broader cultural significations (e.g. Cohen and Young 1973; Chibnall 1977; Hall *et al.* 1978; Ericson *et al.* 1987; Eldridge 1995; Reiner 1997; Wykes 2001).

Within critical criminologies these studies of the media and especially of the criminalization of young people, black people, and 'militant' sections of trades union movements have been a principal focus in understanding the social production of news. Analyses of news content using methodologies of varying degrees of sophistication have been the usual methods of analysis, producing some fascinating affronts to commonsense assumptions about such notions as 'objectivity' and 'bias'. In particular such studies have highlighted the quantitative overrepresentation of certain crimes and certain sections of the population (most obviously in the overrepresentation of violent crime), and the qualitatively pejorative labelling of certain individuals and groups using lurid and sensationalist language and images to create stereotypes of persons and urban myths about crime.

A useful emphasis has also been placed on the importance of the organizational processes of news production and the professional imperatives which structure that process, leading to a disproportionate emphasis in the media on the spectacular and the violent in accordance with values of 'newsworthiness'. The Centre for Contemporary Cultural Studies was of course renowned for its work on the hermeneutics of representation of deviance and otherness which often included studies of the media (Hall and Jefferson 1976; Hall *et al.* 1978). Useful overviews of these literatures may be found in Kidd-Hewitt and Osborne (1995) and Reiner (1997), and an interesting application in Wykes (2001) which approaches news as cultural text in a broad-ranging sense, and I do not propose to re-review them here.

Wykes writes in her introduction to *News, Crime and Culture* (2001: 1):

> Crime news . . . is about good and bad, innocent and guilty, heroes and villains, victims and abusers. It is the site of our national conscience and moral codes . . . The continuum of criminality is explored as a measure, mediated through the news, which informs our view of our world, of others and of ourselves.

In this volume a very different view will be adopted (this is not to criticize Wykes, of course, for purposefully delimiting her field of study); the 'news' will be seen as only one small piece within the mosaic of crime and the law, *a* site but not in any sense *the* site. Indeed, the central argument of the text is that the whole question of the media–crime–law relationship needs to be reconceived within a discourse of 'mediatization', an endeavour which attempts to swallow media culture whole, taking account of the intertextuality implied by Wykes' framing of the 'news' in terms of the dramatic narratives of heroes and villains; but at the same time addressing the dilemma of the implosion of media forms.

It is encouraging that during the 1990s a trend began to emerge around the boundaries of criminology of either directly challenging or simply ignoring its self-imposed boundaries, and an increasing number of 'textual outlaws' (Young 1996) made themselves heard. While remaining 'within' criminology, Sparks's (1992) *Television and the Drama of Crime* adopted a relatively innovative approach to crime and the media, both in its focus on TV cop shows and in its theoretical imagination. Following Garland (1990), Sparks suggests that no 'sharp separation is possible between the study of the practical conduct of affairs in crime and punishment and the ways in which these matters are publicly represented and perceived' (1992: 4). Criminological work, argues

Sparks, 'should be attentive to the ways in which images of crime, law enforcement and punishment are caught up in the fine grain of cultural and personal experience' (1992: 5). The 'moral fictions' of television crime stories are morality plays which fuse public dilemmas and private life; they present narratives which are expressive of fears and anxieties articulated as 'crime', they offer 'solutions', albeit magical and contrived, which give 'pleasure in seeing retribution exacted [which] . . . serves to stave off a degree of cynicism about a dangerous and corrupt social world' (Sparks 1992: 160). The importance of this study (which will figure in more detail later in this volume) is highlighted in his own concluding comments:

> One should seriously consider whether the moral structure of the fable can be detected in other registers of discourse (in news, in speeches from public platforms or in the dramatic reconstructions of the 'crime scarers' for example). One must therefore entertain the possibility that the plausibility of fictions and facts are mutually constraining . . . if we have grown fond of heroism and simplicity and have become accustomed to taking pleasure in seeing retribution done is it easier for us to accept rhetorics which divide the world of crime and law enforcement into simple categories . . . is this therefore a way in which the punitive preoccupation is kept alive?
>
> (Sparks 1992: 161–2)

Trials of our times: Law, the media, and popular culture

Perhaps less well known to 'criminology', other fascinating work was taking place in the 1990s in what might loosely be termed the field of law and popular culture. Redhead's work (1995) confounds disciplinary allocation, presumably intentionally so, since he conducts his debate unequivocally on his own ground and within his own definitions. Nevertheless, despite the inevitable difficulties of comprehension for the reader arising from this choice, as a 'textual outlaw' he highlights some central dilemmas for the law once media culture is taken into account. His *Unpopular Cultures* (1995), via an archaeology of the cultural criminology of the 1970s and critical, and then postmodern, approaches to law, he tackles the centrality of the media and the implosion of law and popular culture. Substantial portions of Redhead's work chart specific interrelations between the media, popular culture, and the formulation of law, notably through the processes of the escalating criminalization of music culture and football (1997). In particular he illustrates how the popular legal imagination – in and through popular cultural forms – is transformative.

The law may obviously be seen to *influence* the media – in regulating, governing, and controlling, for example through the discourses of censorship, copyright, libel, and so on, and these are areas which have received a great deal of academic and popular attention. Debates surrounding sexuality, pornography and the portrayal of violence have been, as noted above, especially prominent (Barker and Petley 1997; Howitt 1998; and the discussion of 'effects' in this volume). Other approaches have focused on the portrayal of the law and lawyering in film, television, and fiction (e.g. Denvir 1996). The purpose of these endeavours has not hitherto, however, been particularly clear. The question of why it *matters* to concern ourselves with law in media culture has rarely been explicitly tackled. Whereas criminologists, historians, and sociologists have had a fairly focused, if limited, agenda as to why crime in the media constitutes an important area of investigation, the same can rarely be said of academic lawyers interested in media representations.

So, for example, some commentators have contended that the study of law in the media is important because it can teach us about 'the law':

> I believe we can learn a great deal about the law from watching movies . . . I discovered that serious viewing of a commercial film often challenged my views on legal questions that until then I had found routine . . . I . . . recognized that movies reflect powerful myths that influence our reactions to issues we meet in real life, including legal issues.
>
> (Denvir 1996: xi)

Careful analysis of media texts may reveal the ideologies of law exploited in, for example, novel or filmic representation, the visions, languages and images of law which are held up as defining and authoritative about what the law is, what it is 'for', and what it should be. This kind of analysis often stays largely within the novel or film-as-text, rather than relating it in a sociological sense to wider social formations and structures of politics, economics, law, and everyday life. In large part such analysis depends upon a fairly detailed mapping of the themes and images within the film and how these are achieved and a reading off of debates about the nature of law from this. Thus such analyses do offer some insights into the relationship between representation and the wider social formation, but do so from a standpoint which is closer to literary criticism than grounded theory.

Even where the emphasis is on text-as-ideology, then, much writing in the textual analysis vein inevitably remains largely at the level of the descriptive, and slips easily into simply retelling the story of the film's 'story' of the law, somewhat like an extra-detailed film guide. Some of the most cutting critiques of the relationship between the law and media culture have actually come not from within academia, but in a sideways fashion from lawyers themselves in the form of a cocktail of intertextuality and reflexivity, where lawyers may be found writing fictional 'stories' with a critique of the law and of media culture at their heart. John Grisham's novels represent an accessible example. In *The Testament* Grisham (1999) describes with lively sarcasm the influence of the media on the legal process, its power to not so much pervert the course of justice as to circumscribe it. In life-imitating-art this was seen in examples such as the O.J. Simpson case. The latter is just one instance where if it had not emerged from fact, TV should have invented the story as fiction. The case is discussed more fully in Chapter 2 below. For the moment it is enough to note that the outline chronology of events contains all the ingredients for a superb plot in the genre of the legal drama, from the discovery of the bodies of Nicole Brown Simpson (O.J. Simpson's ex-wife) and Ron Goldman (her alleged lover) in June 1994 to the 'not guilty' verdict on Simpson for their murders in October 1995. Through the alleged domestic abuse of Nicole Brown Simpson by O.J. Simpson to the accusations of racism against the police and their evidence tampering, the whole saga was a media gift. It had great action, too; about to be arrested for murder, Simpson attempted to give the police the slip resulting in a police car chase. Suspense was added by considerable twists and turns in the pre-trial events including the selection of an alternative jury, hearings over admissibility of evidence, and contestation of incoming testimony (http://www.law.umkc.edu/faculty/projects/ftrials/Simpson/Simpsonchron.htm, accessed 3.3.02). Even more than this, of course, was the issue of the celebrity suspect, and whether the mediatization of the arrest and trial elevated O.J. to superstar status from ex-football star and frontman for Hertz Rental Cars' ad campaign (again discussed in Chapter 2 of this volume). A fascinating collection edited by Greg Barak (1996) also covers a whole array of events in the mediatization of O.J. Simpson. In this collection, Chancer's (1996) interviews with newspaper journalists who had covered the case highlighted that from a press perspective, Simpson was Black, but more than this, he was a celebrity. As one journalist pointed out, 'we went back and we couldn't find an instance that we know of in which a celebrity was involved in even a single homicide' (cited in Chancer 1996: 79–80).

The most frequent issues raised in relation to such cases are whether the media role was to corrupt and/or to promote justice. I would like to push this debate further towards a notion of 'mediatization' by taking up a point made John Fiske (1996; see Hunt 1999: 44) and applied by Darnell M. Hunt in his analysis of the O.J. Simpson case. Hunt details how the media coverage of the case and the events surrounding it produced a set of popular narratives which in turn produced 'The Trial of the Century', concurring with Fiske's contention that

> The term *media event* is an indication that in a postmodern world we can no longer rely on a stable relationship or clear distinction between a 'real' event and its mediated representation. Consequently we can no longer work with the idea that the 'real' is more important, significant, or even 'true' than the representation.
>
> (Fiske 1996: 2; cited in Hunt 1999: 44)

Fiske's point found its sublime expression more recently in the trial and conviction of Jeffrey Archer, the business man cum Conservative Party Chairman cum novelist cum wide boy convicted in July 2001 for perjury and perverting the course of justice. The convictions arose from Archer's manipulation of evidence and procurement of a false alibi over alleged sex with a prostitute in a 1987 libel case in which he successfully pursued an action against the *Daily Star* newspaper. Much glee was had in the British media over the delightfully ironical vision of Archer the novelist as the writer of his own script sentenced to four years imprisonment. Was this life imitating art? they pondered; or art imitating life imitating art? Or . . . dubbed 'Archer's drama' by the *Observer* newspaper, the journalist Tim Adams wrote:

Eventually, perhaps, we all get the script we deserve. Jeffrey Archer undoubtedly had plans for a lead role in Court Eight of the Old Bailey: a revival of his Great Escape of 1987. He had spent last summer on an intensive training course, conducted by RADA tutor Edward d'Souza, in how to appear authoritative in the witness box, and he had tested that training night after night in provincial theatres in his grim play *The Accused* . . . watching him in court . . . you still had the sense of a man who was acting the part of a man on trial for perjury.

(*Observer*, 'Review', 22 July 2001)

Archer the novelist and playwright, scriptwriter of his own intrigue and downfall, was the 'real' news story. Despite being described by the judge as 'as serious an offence of perjury as I have experience of, and as serious as I have been able to find in the books' the legal issues surrounding the case, apart from the judge's pronouncements, received little attention in the news media. The interest here was the drama, the intertwining of fact and fiction, a legal soap containing all the ingredients of a meaty 12-part TV series: corrupt businessman and politician turned best-selling novelist, the enigmatic and apparently long-suffering wife (Mary Archer, who had 'stood by him' through 35 years of wheeling, dealing, and philandering); the celebrity friends and associates among the *glitterati* of politics, business, the media, and show business; Archer's ambiguous status as a 'not out of the top drawer' peer, and so on. His 'news' story appeared as no more nor less than another plot for one of his own bestsellers. Were John Grisham to fictionalize it (could it be any further fictionalized) the central figure would no doubt be a charismatic, disillusioned, avenging lawyer-with-conscience who would bring about Archer's downfall.

By depicting the processes of law and justice within the dramatic conventions of reality TV, courtroom soap opera, the voyeurism of human interest, and the aesthetics of visuality, media culture and the law sometimes appear to become indivisible domains. It is this which is the most difficult and yet one of the most important dimensions of law in media culture. It is not just our notion of what the law is and what it is for that is largely media-derived, but the collective legal imagination. By the 'collective legal imagination' I mean the cultures of what is right, what is just, and what is possible. This was seen clearly in the mediation of the release in 2001 of John Venables and Robert Thompson, the young killers of toddler James Bulger. Legally and ethically one might have said that the release of the two young men after serving less than nine years in custody was contentious, but, media-processed, it turned not just the 'killers', but the nation, loose – the latter on a rampage of proclamations about the justice system and the law. Aside from the predictable headlining ('Mum Weeps as Bulger's Murderers Go Free', etc.), extra dimensions were added by the use of telephone polling on TV (increasingly used as a way of tapping into the collective sentiments of a media-dazed culture) and the immediate generation of Bulger Internet sites – including the release of an alleged up-to-date picture of one of the 'killers'. The 'Justice for James' protest movement soon gathered force, with accompanying button badges and Internet postings. The whole episode was an unnerving revelation of what happens when populism meets potent forms of media technology. In contemporary culture it is not just a matter of the blurring of fact and fiction, nor is it just a question of the media whipping up emotions such as fear, outrage, and so on, but of the immediacy and the instant pervasiveness across media forms of any given 'eruption'. In a world without the Internet, the following would perhaps have a less ominous portent:

> James' father Ralph Bulger said 'I feel angry, frustrated, and completely let down by the system'. And Mrs Fergus [James Bulger's mother] warned the killers, now 18: 'You may be free, but you'll never sleep safely'.
>
> (*Daily Express*, 23 June 2001)

Redhead (1995: 51) summarizes the question(s) of law and media representation nicely when he comments that

> Indeed, the question of law and (media) representation is a pervasive one. It alludes both to the idea of the relationship of law – national and international legal systems – to the means of communication or the mass media in general, and also, to crucially, the jurisprudential question of 'what is the object of law?': that is, what does law represent?

In general then, this book, while recognizing the contributions of the established modes of research in criminological work and crime and the media, takes a much broader view from social theory, and in doing so turns several 'traditional' questions upside down. I do not seek to re-present already much-rehearsed criminological and sociological work on media representation of crime as 'ideological work', on analyses of rela-tionships between 'the state' and 'law and order', on the structural and institutional functioning of the media in particular political climates, or on hegemonic 'crime news'. Instead, I am more concerned with delineating the features of mediatization, and with unpicking the implications of that state.

In this, I am concerned with questions of knowledge and method, such as how can crime be 'read' through the media? What *is* the problem with the endless debates over bias, 'effects', and so on, which all rely on par-ticular ways of framing the reality–representation dyad? Should some crime/law texts, those from within the academe, be privileged over others as a source of knowledge about crime and law? Or have tra-ditional dis-tinctions and dichotomies become analytical shackles, which prevent us from appreciating the richness of our mediated, global, multiply-constituted existences as crimino-legal subjects? And with the increasing challenge to traditional notions of embodiment through the technological and interrelated cultural changes in media, what *are* the objects of crime and the law? In a globalized virtuality, *where* are the objects of crime and law? Can such questions be answered empirically, or, in the end, do we face questions that are ultimately those of instrumental and ethical choice, based on an acceptance that all crime is media crime?

2 ■ REAL CRIME/CRIME STORIES: THE COLLAPSE OF FANTASY AND FACT?

This chapter explores the elision of fact and fiction in the mediation of the 'real' world. It suggests that the assumption of a self-evident distinction between, for example, 'news' and 'drama', or 'information' and 'entertainment', is continually thrown into question in contemporary media forms, and suggests that the proliferation of the genres of 'infotainment', 'docudrama', and 'reality TV', are in essence extensions of a logic which has always been present in popular cultural representations of crime and law. The development of increasingly complex technologies entailing interactivity and immediacy make fact-media more 'fictional' and vice versa. As time–space relations are revolutionized by the electronic media, notions of the simulacra and the hyperreal become less fanciful and more concrete, even (or perhaps especially) in news genres. Genres plunder each other for techniques of representation which emphasize the crossovers between 'real life', 'celebrity', and 'soap'. Rather than seeing this as a problem of 'dumbing down' or of the loss of information ('reducing the law to a soap opera', for example), the question is rather one of expansion: the proliferation of images and their myriad reproductions which includes the expansion of popular culture into the hallowed discourses of science, law, and medicine.

In a time of increasing sophistication of audiences more and more attuned to the postmodern aspects of mediation, the determination to hold onto the belief that in the end some form of reality–representation dichotomy is possible seems flawed. Yet, if we even half accept the implosion thesis, we do not seem to know what to do with it. A loosening of our commitment to belief in the self-evident facticity of the real implied by mediatization leads, moreover, to a questioning of the hierarchy of the information-values of representations. Are appeals to 'objective' reporting, 'expert' knowledges, and 'hard evidence', really tenable claims to a truer purchase on the dilemmas of social life? The wheeling out of carriers of expert knowledge is endlessly used as no more than a conventional genre of presentation in public discourse. Currently fashionable are geneticists, forensic scientists, environmental scientists, psychologists, psychiatrists, crime profilers, and even criminologists. To the media, never has the mantle of science been sexier.

By the same token, novels, movies, and TV dramas present us with the worlds of the experts as fictions. To say that all of this is in one sense 'nothing new' is to remind ourselves that the ever-buoyant demand for the crime story has always centred around the fusion of our lived and imaginary universes, our doings and our fantasies, weaving together the themes of enigma and revelation, fear and loathing, justice and injustice, the morally culpable and the moral resolution, for our voyeuristic longing. We make these demands of our crime, whether the story is told by the exclusive documentary or the latest best-selling novelist.

As this hybridization of fact and fiction becomes increasingly pervasive, it threatens to make quicksand of the bases of certainty which make proceeding with social life possible. Consequently we pretend the confusion does not exist, preferring to rely on trust (Giddens 1999). Yet, in our constantly mediated beings, even the most immediate tragedy takes on an element of the imitation, of the vicarious, of the surreal. Thus we need to have an understanding of what the 'collapse of the real' might mean with a clear caveat that if such a collapse is happening, it does not detract from the validity of experience, nor absolve us from the burden of ethical choice.

Crime: metaphorically speaking, a practice?

Surprisingly, while cultural studies and anthropology have been so attentive to matters of language, image, and iconography, much criminology has tended to regard these aspects as inconveniences. This is perfectly comprehensible from the point of view of the 'origin stories' of criminology, which delineate the emergence of the scientific, administrative and bureaucratic norms governing its project within modernity (Garland 1994). It is more difficult to understand when one considers that 'crime' has been eloquently shown from within criminology itself to be a matter of metaphorical and mythic negotiation, of taxonomy and intersubjectivity. Most of the latter work, however, has the sticky handprints of the sociology of deviance all over it, now a somewhat unfashionable notion. It bears the stigmata of relativism, imprecision, and naïve radicalism. An obsession with a rather crude exposé of the bases of social control made it unpopular with funders and policymakers alike, particularly in the UK during the dark years of Thatcherism (1979–1991).

When Burrows (1997) poses his rhetorical question of who now reads what in social theory, there is an echo to be found in criminology. Except in those tedious criminological theory courses where hapless students are dragged, yawning, through the narratives of criminology from A to Z, who now reads Matza? Or Becker, or the early radical studies which produced cultural criminology (Hall and Jefferson 1976)? They were effectively stomped on by those reinvented Madonnas of crime, the 'new left realists' (Young 1986), and criminology now pays little more than lip-service to the richness of their texts. The early work of Stuart Hall *et al.* (1978), Stan Cohen (1973), and Geoffrey Pearson (1983) remain as extant reminders that crime is actually produced through language, wars over meaning, and generalized metaphoric constellations, but even this work remains often only as tracer in the referencing conventions of academic writing.

If Foucault (1977) had not been resuscitated by feminist criminology, perhaps even the value of discursive archaeology would have been lost (Young 1996), outside of its applications to the disciplinary techniques of the carceral in modernity (Cohen 1985). The conventional discourses of criminology have been to see the mass media as a form of 'distortion':

> To be realistic about crime is not an easy task . . . We are caught between two currents, one which would grossly exaggerate the problems of crime, another covering a wide swathe of political opinion that may seriously underestimate the extent of the problem. Crime is a staple of news in the Western mass media and police fiction a major genre of

television drama . . . the media abound with images of the dangerous stranger. On television we see folk monsters who are psychopathic killers or serial murderers yet offenders who even remotely fit these caricatures are extremely rare . . . the criminologist knows that this is far from the humdrum nature of reality . . . the nature of crime, of victimization and of policing is thus systematically distorted in the mass media.

(Young 1986; reprinted in Muncie *et al.* 1996: 446)

It was not until 1992 that a sophisticated criminological analysis of crime–media representation finally appeared in the UK, in the form of Sparks's *Television and the Drama of Crime*. Sumner notes in his introduction to Sparks's book, 'His analyses should prevent us from ever again dividing up television and its impact into a kind of base/superstructure topography' (Sumner 1992: xii). In interweaving a mind-boggling array of philosophical and social analysis from Aristotle to Ricoeur, Sparks finally blew the criminological myth that the interstices of everyday practice, emotion, feeling, public representation, and that fluid construction we assign to the category 'crime', could be magicked away. He gestures, as did Cohen (1973) and more particularly Pearson (1983) in much more partial ways, towards a gaping theoretical lacuna at the heart of the criminological project. This is a misunderstanding of (or merely inattention to) the most vibrant categories of everyday life as they inhere in, produce and are reproduced by, the discursive practices of crime mediation: the categories of unreason, of fear, anxiety, and of censure. At last the study of the language of crime and retribution in public life was taken further than the imposed second-order category of ideological construct; Sparks has indirectly rooted language in social practice, so that to take crime seriously must be to begin with taking language seriously.

To face outward again from criminology, crime is a concept we live by. Lakoff and Johnson's classic study of metaphor in everyday life (1977) will not be found in the index of many criminological texts (for an exception see Wykes 2001), even taking Sumner's broad definition of criminology as 'any kind of study concerned with crime and criminal justice'. Lacan has received better press, and indeed the importation of subjectivity into criminology has mainly been achieved through psychoanalytic categories (see for example Young 1996; Jefferson 1997). While recognizing the importance of this project, I remain for the moment concerned with everyday practice, with the collective, negotiated, externalizations of subjectivity through the expressions of shared language.

> The concepts that govern our thought are not just matters of the intellect. They also govern our everyday functioning, down to the most mundane details. Our concepts structure the way we perceive, how we get around in the world, how we relate to people. Our conceptual system thus plays a central role in defining our everyday realities. If we are right in suggesting that our conceptual system is largely metaphorical, then the way we think, what we experience, and what we do every day is very much a matter of metaphor.
>
> (Lakoff and Johnson 1977: 3)

Lakoff and Johnson contend that metaphors 'allow us to understand one domain of experience in terms of another' (1977: 117). We need not share their assertion of the 'final instance' state of human nature to recognize the power of the metaphor as the outcome of intersubjective work. As a sense-making process, the realm of the metaphoric does display the systemic properties that they attribute to it. Orientations towards experience, the values and emotions attached to it, are made concrete through metaphor. Hierarchies and other structures of relation such as similarity and difference enable feelings and emotions to be metaphorically indicated, and create frameworks of response to events. Mediated experience (and in a language-based culture, all human experience is mediated) in thus explicating the world through metaphor, thereby indicates potential courses of future action and legitimates or condemns past and present action. It is utterly crucial in understanding the role of the public representational domain in framing the emotional and attitudinal work of actors and collectivities and their correspondent practices. To acknowledge this from a 'criminological' perspective is to centralize the metaphoric dimension of crime and the public response to it. Before I even embark upon further discussion of this, I want clearly to state my position on 'reality'. Looking over my shoulder, I can see the realists in hot pursuit. *Centralizing metaphor is not prioritizing image over reality. It is not divorcing the imaginary and the real. It is not disputing pain and suffering, politics or inequality, culpability or responsibility.* To begin with metaphor however, is to refute once and for all, for all practical purposes, the existence of the unmediated real to which we have access. What an appreciation of metaphor enables is an analysis of what is being actualized through language-concepts, an analysis essential in 'taking crime seriously'.

Consider some of the most used crime metaphors, in isolation for the moment from narrative. We are 'lost in a tide of porn' (*Independent on Sunday* 16 August 1998) apparently. This is a container metaphor – albeit a rather strange one, since we might presumably be immersed in a tide or drowned by a tide or pulled by a tide etc. Still, the inaccuracy of the metaphor is important, since it shows that metaphors do not have to be exact in order to be evocative. Metaphors are economical in their communication of meaning; they 'cut to the chase'. Minimum verbiage, maximum impact; a clear appeal to the news media is evident. The writer of this article was clearly fond of natural disaster metaphors, since 'London's Soho . . . is at the epicentre of Britain's porn industry'.

The accusation of 'sensationalism' levelled against news coverage of crime, that handy fallback for students grown weary of analysing the news media, ('they do it for sensationalism') is more interesting when it is considered as a particularly visual or tactile use of metaphor: 'chilling', 'blood curdling', 'sick' and so on. A 'cold-blooded murderer' is worse than a 'hot-blooded murderer' with its connotations of the passions; thus 'the concepts that occur in metaphorical definitions are those that correspond to natural kinds of experience' (Lakoff and Johnson 1997: 118). Pornography is 'poison', crime is a 'plague', retribution should be 'tougher', the enemy should be 'crushed'. Disease and body metaphors are some of the most popular for crime; crime is never a 'snuffle' or a 'sneeze', however, but a plague or cancer, although policymakers sometimes have it that sudden apparent rises in crime are 'hiccups'. Crime usually affects the 'face' of our society, disfiguring its appearance, although, when really bad, it is buried 'deep in the body'. Attack metaphors give physicality to crime as they do to disease; we are 'in the grip' of an 'epidemic'. Action against crime is 'war'; terror strikes 'deep into the heart' of civilization. Spatial metaphors give immediacy to crime; it is 'on our doorstep', there is trouble 'round the corner'.

What gives such metaphors their resonance is not actually their 'distortion' of reality; it is their proximity to experience. Anyone whose home has been burgled knows what it is to be 'violated'. Metaphors for criminals create the appropriate sense of otherness, either through disease or perhaps animal metaphors. 'Criminals are a normatively proscribed other' hardly meets the case; 'criminals are animals' does. The past is 'rosy', the future 'bleak'; after all, 'storm clouds are gathering' and 'it never rains but it pours'. The words merge into images, fashioning the visual from the language, and slide imperceptibly into the actual visuals of representation: photographs, TV cameras, video footage, digital imaging; the image–words and image–images interlock and resonate with each other in mutual reinforcement.

Thus metaphors are not a substitute for 'reality' but an expression of categories of reality; the notion of objectivity where language or image is concerned is simply odd, because it denies the bases on which everyday life works. The meaning systems that we apply to the category 'crime' are metaphoric systems; the coherence and consistency of their application operates to sustain certain relations: relationships of similarity/otherness and inclusion/exclusion, most commonly. 'Crime' is grounded in the way in which conceptual metaphorical devices ground it in other experiences and render it of the same class. The importance of this (and why I have laboured the point) is that metaphoric media representation intertwines with the sense-making activities in which we engage every time we use language to communicate. One phenomenon is made to stand proxy for another, and hierarchy, asymmetry and equivalence metaphors both explain and provide the conditions for action. People in positions of trust are thought of 'highly' or, if they abrogate that trust, break the criminal code, or cause harm to others they are 'lowered'. They are 'no better than a common criminal'. Vocabularies of motive are replete with metaphor; 'she drove me to it', 'I was pushed into it', 'I wanted my share of the cake', 'it was too sweet to pass over'. They justify action retrospectively, but are not therefore dishonest, since they may be the product of careful reflexivity on the part of the actor. Personal life and public stories exist in a state of dependence upon each other. Metaphor, as Lakoff and Johnson show, is thus intricately connected with notions of truth, and action, and is both social and political; it connects recursively with everyday life in a constant exchange of meaning.

Action and interaction produce change, so neither is the metaphoric static; new situations create new experiences, and new metaphors arise out of the resources available, framing more action and interaction. Thus the metaphoric conceptual world of the cyber is not in equivalence to that of the embodied world; but it demonstrates constant parallels and reformulations. Much of the appeal of William Gibson's writing, so central to the subsequent theorizing of cybercultures (Burrows 1997), lies in its sensitivity to metaphor, creating a world within a world, one world being the unknown virtual world of the future, and the other being the conceptual world of everyday life. He makes his created world both familiar and unfamiliar by manipulating metaphors and creating new ones out of the elements of the old; the new metaphors make sense only within the narrative of the text because they require context. Once the fictional context is in place, it retains enough systematic metaphoric links to the 'outside' to render it meaningful, even though the fictional reality is not a reality we currently live. The fictional thereby becomes a source of action. Its practical languages are taken from the real world and loop back into the real world just as 'news' stories do. Much Gibsonian language is now cyber language, framing the meaning and actions which constitute cyber life, not to mention social theory. The metaphor that the matrix (global virtual computer net) is a 'consensual hallucination' (Gibson 1984) must be one of the most frequently recurring citations of the 1990s in writing on cybercultures. Bell and Kennedy (2000), a comprehensive collection of papers on all things cyber, is liberally peppered with the phrase.

Many pronouncements about postmodern culture are about death, ending, and the collapse of boundaries, about the disjunction of past and present and the end of memory and narrative. The notion of what things are not (or no longer are) however, depends on certain assumptions about what things were. The idea that the referent bears no necessary relation to the real, and that everything is therefore surface, making reference to other surfaces, is neither revelatory nor startling if one accepts that memory is (has always 'been') a consensual hallucination; that everything stands proxy for something else, and that reality for human beings exists only in practice, which exists only in language. At this point there is nothing to choose between fact and fiction beyond the distinctiveness of their genres and conventions that flag up that one is 'real' and the other is 'fiction'. A fictive text adopting the conventions of the non-fictive becomes 'realist' or 'almost documentary', a non-fictive text adopting the conventions of the fictive becomes 'soap opera'. Increasingly genres cross-dress, borrowing each other's conventions and formats, so that if we hold on to our notions of a separate 'real' which could possibly be faithfully represented through a transparent, metaphor-free language devoid of practice, then we have indeed reached a watershed. Having rejected the reality/referent distinction initially, these aspects of the 'postmodern' seem neither controversial nor new.

McLuhan's formulation and subsequently Baudrillard's adoption of the notion of 'implosion' however (Genosko 1999) is more than this. The technological scope of contemporary media forms enhances the complexity of, and speeds up, these processes, investing them with a sense of decisive discontinuity from other eras which may not be all that it seems, or may be more than it seems. Before returning to this, which in a sense goes beyond the fact/fiction question in its emphasis on technological form, I turn to some of the fairly recent facts and fictions of crime.

Crime dramas: the collapse of the 'real'?

> A variety of evidence ranging from reality TV to how-to publishing points to a pervasive hunger for information about the historical world surrounding us. But our hunger is less for information in the raw than for stories fashioned from it.
>
> (Nichols 1994: ix)

Crime dramas ('fiction' or 'non-fictions' or something 'in between') have in common that they address conceptual reality rather than empirical events.

Empirical event: February 1993. Robert Thompson and Jon Venables, two 10-year-old boys, abducted 2-year-old James Bulger from a Liverpool shopping mall, took him to a railway line and killed him. Although CCTV footage of the abduction was available, and some witness statements reported brief sightings along the way, there is no further direct record of events.

Empirical event: June 2001. 'Justice for James' campaign launched. A picture allegedly of the adult Robert Thompson taken from recent CCTV footage during a 'trip out' from the secure unit is posted on the Internet, circumventing a high court injunction preventing publication of pictures of the teenagers. 'Justice for James' stage protest marches, with James's mother at the front, and hold press conferences. Campaigners wear 'Justice for James' T-shirts and button badges bearing a picture of James. There are denials of vigilantism.

Documentary: 21 June 2001. BBC2 screens a documentary film, *Eyes of the Detective: The Murder of James Bulger.* Based on the same empirical event, this hour-long documentary concentrates on retrospective interviews with police officers and other 'experts' involved in the case, solicitors, teachers, and James Bulger's mother. In a series of reconstructions it depicts the police interrogation of Thompson and Venables from police tapes. Contextual footage to a melancholy musical background contrasts the grim deindustrialized landscape of Bootle and visits to the crime scene (where, it is pointed out, the 'scene of crime' markers still show us the ferocity of the attack by pinpointing the spattered blood) with home videos of the victim joyfully playing in the garden and living room of a comfortable, pleasant home; archive footage from 1993 is shown: the ubiquitous CCTV record, original press-release photographs of the cherubic-faced victim and of his murderers, ugly scenes outside the court at the time of trial, a devastated Denise Bulger. The whole is an archaeology of the emotions in the wake of the murder, giving glimpses of retributive passion, the 'cushy' secure units which are presumably 'the same' as those in which the killers were incarcerated, and the opinions of a young man who had allegedly been in the same unit as one of the boys.

Lacking direct footage from the time, we are provided with a detailed forensic reconstruction of the 'nature of the attack' (frenzied) which the careful viewer will note is principally a detailing of the post-mortem damage done to the victim's body by a train and the absence of clothing from the lower half of the body (implying a sexual perversity which was not forensically upheld in the case itself). Since the social workers, psychiatrists, and secure unit workers who were directly involved with the killers' custodial lives cannot be interviewed, there is no actual information as to the specific regimes followed by Thompson and Venables, nor their psychiatric or rehabilitative programmes, beyond the revelation that they were allowed computers in their rooms, to cook meals for their families, and to go on reorientation outings to shopping centres, a football match, and the countryside.

Neither are there any further discussions of aetiology, even of a speculative nature, echoing the journalist David Smith's astute observation of the trial that 'perhaps 20 minutes out of 17 days, was the full extent of the trial's inquiry into the boys' mental health' (Smith 1994: 211). Therefore the basis of the judicial decision to free the killers on licence remains literally inexplicable. The conclusion covers the 'Justice for James' campaign.

Empirical event: 22 June 2001. Robert Thompson and Jon Venables, convicted of killing of a 2-year-old in 1993, when they were 10 years of age, are released with new identities to undisclosed locations.

Crime news: 'They're Out . . . and we're all left to hope, and pray, that they don't do it again. And last night James's distraught mum Denise warned: "They can never be trusted where there are little children" '. (*Mirror*, 23 June 2001).

Crime news: 'No other city in Britain attracts as many myths as Liverpool. And the latest one doing the rounds – that there is a seething mob of vigilantes ready to hunt down and kill Jon Venables and Robert Thompson – is down there with the very worst of those myths.'

'The overwhelming majority of Merseysiders are more sad than angry that these two killers are walking free after so short a time, when Denise Bulger's tears have barely dried on her cheeks.'

'In a recent *Liverpool Echo* poll a staggering 35,000 people voted to keep the killers behind bars with 7,000 demanding their release.'

'To an outsider that may seem a harsh and reactionary ratio; it is a ratio I imagine would be echoed across the land if everyone had been as close to the events of eight years ago as we had.'

'Far from viewing the Bulger murder as a legal test case, or an ideological debate between left and right, for those who remember the case as though it were yesterday, the pain is still raw' (*Mirror*, 23 June 2001).

Crime news: ' "They will get the boys". The shopping centre passageway where James Bulger was led to his death fell silent yesterday afternoon. People braced themselves for the lynch mob. "It won't be here and it won't be us, probably. But they will get the boys," said a mother-of-three . . .

' "We wanted them to rot in prison," said one grandfather. "The British justice system is a joke. It would never have happened in America." Outside AR Tyms butchers, site of the closed circuit television that recorded footage of James holding hands with his killers, shop owners turned up radios to hear local newscasters. Local newspapers warned that relatives would hunt the teenagers down . . .

'The campaigner for Justice for Jamie [*sic*], Merseyside Radio City DJ Pete Price, burst into tears on air . . . "Now is when the sentence starts. This is when the fun and games start . . . If the boys had a taste for blood once, they are going to want to taste blood again, just like an animal that needs to be put down." Mr Price said he abhorred the notion of revenge attacks. But he said: "There will be a witch-hunt" ' (*Guardian*, 23 June 2001).

What lies within the events? The 'facts' are brief and bald. The 'story' is the retelling of the murder story and the revenge story. The metaphors structure the conceptual framing of the events in an interaction between people's everyday worlds and their public representation. The repeated visuals are of the past, not the present: pictures of Thompson and Venables as small boys; the angelic photograph of 'blonde James' as he was typically described; Jamie Bulger in the original news reports of 1993 has now become James Bulger, looking out on the world; the images of the distraught relatives and angry onlookers of 1993 are juxtaposed with the present, the funereal dignity of the 'Justice for James' march. The metaphors reveal the meanings; they refer to different domains of experience, and are spatial, bestial, social, and emotional (Lakoff and Johnson 1977: 59). The evil and the avengers of evil are separated clearly. Thompson and Venables should be 'behind bars'. The 'lynch mob' are 'out there'. The evil ones have 'a taste for blood', they *need* to be 'put down' like 'animals'. The pain of the surviving victims – the relatives, the inhabitants of Liverpool – is a wound, 'still raw'. There is no (legal) justice in our society, the aftermath will be 'fun and games', 'a witch hunt'.

The narratives offer a story which is partly fashioned from the metaphorical frames directly 'lifted' from the populace, expressed in 'their own words', the journalist interrupting the duree of their everyday lives to extract a decontextualized snippet of reaction. The contextual commentary resonates with these metaphors, setting it within notions of history and memory which include 'our' remembered shock and pain, the transformation of 'our' society by a tragic event. The emotional immediacy of the historical past collapses time to show how soon (i.e. after eight years) Thompson and Venables have been released, most powerfully by the reversal of the literal in 'the tears had barely dried on her cheeks'. The tiny revelation of confusion here gives the lie to this compression, but is glossed over: these are the cheeks of Denise Bulger, but she is now Denise Fergus. Her physical appearance has changed from that of a shell-shocked, respectable working-class parent to a well-groomed, professionally made-up vision of measured grieving and sad testament to the unfathomable leniency of the judicial system.

The metaphor of the drying tears stands proxy for the intensity and pervasiveness of grief, which bears only a tangential relationship to calendrical time. The immediacy of the past is reinforced by the iconic image of James as he was then, a little boy who will never grow up, and the repeated retrospective screening of *that* mondo footage of all time: the CCTV record of James being led away by his murderers, his life behind, his death ahead. The absence of the only three people who actually know what the other events of the abduction and killing contained (Thompson, Venables, and James Bulger) is turned to advantage, and full rein is given to the fictionalization of the imagined:

> We see and hear the grotesque torture they put him through, stripping off his underwear, battering him with an iron bar, kicking him in the face, and other details too stomach-churning to repeat, before laying his naked and lifeless two-year-old body on a railway line and heading home for their tea.
>
> (*Mirror*, 23 June 2001)

The question is not one of factual accuracy. If one were to insist on a fact–fiction divide, this account might be deemed 'sensationalist'. But the latter is only a loose word for the narrative's use of the visceral and the emotional domains of everyday life, and loses the sense in which the narrative is *authentic*. The imagined and the metaphoric, which go hand in hand, establish the connectivity of the account to everyday imagined and metaphoric worlds. A particular feature of the 'Bulger story' is the lack of access to the key players (something which was also used to full effect in the media coverage of the Fred and Rosemary West 'story'[1]). The absence of knowledge about what the 'treatment' and 'rehabilitation' programmes applied to Thompson and Venables consisted of is exploited to the full. Instead, the visible fragments of their incarceration are taken out of context and displayed as aberrations: days out, visits to shopping malls captured on CCTV, the computers in their rooms, a 'good' education. 'They have had twice as good an education as any of the kids around here . . . absolute anger' (interview in the *Guardian*, 23 June 2001). Artefacts of the events (police interview transcripts, forensic evidence transcripts) are creatively interpreted and refracted back into the everyday.

Then the overall construct of the crime is deployed metaphorically to stand proxy for the 'failure of society' and the 'failure of our justice system'; '[James Bulger] is the one society has let down once again. His is the memory that our legal system has disgraced' (*Mirror*, 23 June 2001). Trust in abstract or disembedded systems has been abrogated; our legal system 'is a joke'. The metaphors render feelings coherent, helping 'us' to visualize what the problem is: there is a gaping hole at the centre of our justice system. It has failed to deliver censure. The ethical implications for action become clear: it must be remedied by the people. Thus retributivism, not sated by the abstract systems, finds expression in the impulse toward vigilantism, to direct and concrete action. Whatever the empirical events were or are, how they were experienced and constituted by those directly involved in making them (the perpetrators, the victim, the police, lawyers, social workers, psychologists and so on), what matters now is the authenticity of the narrative to other everyday lives. Action is to be based on, and legitimated by, this reading off of the general from the corporeal and the specific (Nichols 1994), and coherence derives from the sense of history and memory evoked. The narrative solves the 'coherence problem'. It produces closure around interpretation, soothing 'any inclination to despair over the failure to solve it by revealing what might be called its form in "plot" and its content in the meaning with which the plot endows what would otherwise be mere event' (Nichols 1994: 3).

If this property of the news, its necessary authentic fictionalization of events through metaphor and narrative, reveals the falsity of the fact/fiction opposition, then it is not in the least surprising that 'factual' and 'fictional' television borrow constantly from each other. The metaphoric conceptual structures of crime drama on TV and their appearance as morality tales have been amply demonstrated by Sparks (1992), and I do not intend to revisit cop shows here, except to highlight some of his more general conclusions regarding the fictive world and the everyday. Sparks is concerned in part with 'the distribution and ordering of moral and other emblematic categories within narratives' (1992: 146). I want to dispense with Sparks's caveat however, that while 'matters of metaphor and resonance' are central (1992: 146) televisual images retain intrinsic meaning. The 'intrinsic' meaning is a product of the resonance of the text, not a quality of the text. The text *cannot* be abstracted from its metaphoricity and its resonance; these remain 'in' the text itself only in so far as the text is resonant. His injunction that we should consider seriously 'whether the moral structure of the fable can be detected in other registers of discourse (in news, in speeches from public platforms or in the dramatic reconstructions of the "crime scarers" for example)' (1992: 161) is a necessary one. Most importantly,

> one must therefore entertain the possibility that the plausibility of fictions and facts are mutually constraining, and that stories and entertainments contribute to the setting of parameters on what rhetorics, political postures and policies we are inclined to believe or accept.
>
> (Sparks 1992: 161)

It is the televisual which has above all reduced the apparent gap between 'news' and 'fiction' in its generic cross-dressing. The constant juxtapositioning of programming schedules, interleaving fact and fiction as we 'break for the news' no longer represents the conventional divide of the television world. This is a multifaceted phenomenon as the 'news' and 'fiction' undergo a rapidly accelerating process of hybridization. The body of the news, now clothed in the brasher, more dramatic style of entertainment formats, provides a resonance not just through its moral and metaphoric structure as such, but in its surfaces. The 'star' has been replaced by that hybrid creature, the 'celebrity', a position as open to news presenters as to actors and footballers. News is no longer 'read', it is presented. The cross-dressing permits easy genre-travel, not just through the props of the set, or the animation of the production (in the sense that the UK news programmes of the pre-1980s were static and text-based), but in the exchange of formats and styles. While the news borrows crime from drama and soap operas, soaps and drama borrow from the news and 'reality TV'.

The UK programme *The Bill* has famously been transformed by its cross-dressing activities, sporting videocams and ditching action music; policing now occurs in the drug-ridden spaces of a run-down estate. Issue-based crime soap stories (drugs, domestic violence, male-on-male violence, general criminality, incest, and the like) lend an air of authenticity and moral guardianship, particularly with their associated help lines. Miscarriages of justice were a popular theme of the 1990s, stealing the limelight directly from the news. The trials and tribulations of Deirdre Rachid in *Coronation Street* have already been noted; it took the *Daily Star* (11 October 1999) to call the wrongful conviction of East-Ender Matthew Rose for manslaughter 'the worst miscarriage of justice ever'.

Sport-related crime has become popular in the 2000s, with soap/dramas such as *Footballers' Wives* highlighting the tension between players' deviant, drug-taking, alcoholic, criminal tendencies and the imperatives of clean-image global football and the hybridization of cultures brought about by the importation of non-UK players. This interleaves with the news stories which are less and less about 'hooliganism' and more and more about the on-, and more often off-pitch behaviour of players, often crimes of racism and violence involving alcohol and English player-thugs. The iconic figure of David Beckham and his happy-families celebrity former Spice Girl wife is the essential feel-good factor against which the public censure of boozed-up thuggery is counterpoised. The foregrounding of football as entertainment for general consumption, dominating the prime time, has made it inevitable that a vamped-up crime angle would emerge around the celebrity identity and the international stage.

What is emerging from the hybridization of crime is that analyses resting on interpellation of the content or structure of a particular genre ('the news', 'the cop show' 'the soap opera') face increasing difficulties. A glance at a UK TV guide for terrestrial television alone demonstrates this; during the course of one evening there can be *Crimewatch UK*, *Crimewatch UK Update*, a profile of serial killers, *Police, Camera, Action*, one or more variants of the cop show, the mock-up court TV of Judge Judy, and probably a couple of crime movies, as well as the news. Satellite, cable, and digital TV of course enhance the prospects tenfold at least, with anything from televized trials to stories from death row. The narrative, while it is still the organizing principal for a great deal of metaphoric structuring of meaning (and thereby action), is cross-cut all of the time by the importing in of references and techniques, and the sending out of references and techniques. In this, the interplay between crime representation and everyday life, which formerly had remained at the level of metaphor-resonance, becomes more immediate and interstitial than ever before.

Reality TV, a superbly cheap alternative to fictional TV, has burgeoned with the rise of 'the voice', a miniaturized camera technology which allows cameras to be fastened easily to the body or the dashboards of cars, and of CCTV which provides ready-made footage; then there is footage of the police in action (car chases, drug and pornography seizures and similar), and ultimately the global distribution of the televized trial. One of the final bastions of the separation of the media and everyday life is crumbling: the 'professional' separation of actors and 'real' people, between those who tell the news/drama and those who are the stuff of the news/drama. In a process which has long been familiar to stars or icons (Hollywood names, members of the royal family, prominent soap stars) everyday life and media life are meshing. Soon, the term 'audience', always imprecise, already anachronistic, will disappear altogether.

This transformation has two salient facets. The first is the proliferation of crime-celebrities through the shunting of the legal process into the public domains of TV and the Internet. For example in 1998 we saw Louise Woodward, previously a mere nanny to a rich US family, winding up as a celebrity at the Edinburgh Television Festival. The celebrity circus was set in motion by the televized trial of Woodward in 1997, broadcast globally by satellite. She was accused of killing Matthew Eappen, the baby son of her employers. Her photo-image, a sullen-looking pudding-faced person with scraped back mouse-coloured hair and no make-up, set her up as a believable image of evil. Convicted and freed on appeal, a turning point was the legal history made when Judge Hiller Zobel decided to post the verdict of her appeal on the Internet. Virtual justice was paralleled by the unfolding of the legal soap in the terrestrial media. By May 1998 the *Independent* was running 'Sex, Lies, and Louise Woodward's Lawyer' (30 May 1998). In a bizarre tale eminently worthy of its soap status, Woodward's lawyer was arrested on a drink-driving charge:

> She allegedly told the investigating officer: 'I thought she was innocent, but now I know she is guilty and I can't handle it'.
> The lawyer has since denied making the statement and alleged that the officer . . . said he would let her off if she agreed to have sex with him, something he has denied.
> (*Independent*, 30 May 1998)

A freelance journalist secretly taped a telephone conversation with the defence lawyer, Elaine Whitfield-Sharp. This time the issue was an allegation that Woodward was going to sell her story to the media – something she had promised not to do. In a superbly ironic statement, Woodward said on her release in November 1997, 'I have no intention of exploiting this tragedy. It is not a subject for sensationalism or profiteering' (reported in the *Guardian*, 30 May 1998).

According to the taped conversation, Whitfield-Sharp called Woodward a 'duplicitous monster' and said, 'I don't want any more trouble with Louise Woodward than I have already got. She is a fucking pain in the ass' (*Independent*, 30 May 1998). Predictably, the *Mirror* ran the headline 'Louise is a Lying Monster' (29 May 1998).

By August 1998 Woodward was speaking at the Edinburgh Television Festival. The transformed Woodward appeared, well made-up, with the mouse hair replaced by a stylishly cut blonde bob and wearing an elegant suit and jewellery. Woodward attacked the dramatization of the televisual soap which her trial became, and said:

> People are not able to distinguish between notoriety and celebrity. I never wanted to be in this position. I don't want to be a minor celebrity – I am not famous for anything good and people ask me to sign baseball caps . . .
>
> Should we just replace 12 people as a jury with an opinion poll on [the television chat show] Richard and Judy?
>
> Television turns a courtroom into a soap opera, turns it into entertainment, but a courtroom is a serious place dealing with peoples' lives.
>
> (reported in the *Independent*, 1 September 1998)

Meanwhile, it was also revealed at the festival that ITV was planning 30 further documentary soap operas for the coming year, using fly-on-the-wall techniques to draw more 'ordinary' people into the ambit of celebrity (*Independent*, 1 September 1998).

If media events such as the Woodward trial and the antics of fly-on-the-wall documentary-makers produce celebrities out of the unknown, there is also the media production of the celebrity trial. Nowhere was this better seen, perhaps, than in the case of O.J. Simpson, as has been suggested earlier in the discussion (Barak 1996). Moreover, this was not just a celebrity trial, but a fully intertextual, globalized, no-holds-barred imploding trial. Ferrell (1996: 47) argues that

> With the Simpson case, we cross once and for all the postmodern divide, the final representational frontier, the borderlands that once separated criminal justice processes from media dynamics. From the first the case existed not just as a 'media event', as the media themselves described it, but as a

media construction, a made-for-television slasher movie
serialized day after day, week after week.

Ferrell makes the point that this was only 'fair' given that O.J. Simpson was himself 'exclusively a media construction' (1996: 47). In other
words this was the media constructing the media, making no reference
to anything other than itself. The media movie of the trial contained
movies within movies and TV programmes within TV programmes; the
pornographic movie of O.J.'s 'personal' life, (Ferrell 1996: 48) the law
movie, the 'Police, Camera, Action' of the car chase. As the 'reality TV
of reality TV' it marked the apotheosis of the genre, but perhaps where
things really crossed over was into the virtual. The web pages, chat room
exchanges, and news groups postings proliferated as the computer users
took over the trial. The Net trial gave 'trial by media' a new slant: not
governed by 'legal' procedure or the dramatics of lawyering, not produced by the 'professional' (!), organizational, conventional (genre-
bound), or commercial imperatives of the 'mass media', this was trial by
disembodied, virtual, global and glocal (Featherstone 1995) voice.
Greek's (1996) analysis of the cybertrial by news group postings suggests
that salient themes were race and gender cross-cut by procedural issues,
O.J.'s celebrity status, and desire for retribution. This was a normative
trial, a trial in part by prejudice and ethics, frequently graphically
expressed; for example,

> FREE O.J. Jail Mark 'the racist dog' Fuhrman [Fuhrman was
> the white police officer who planted evidence].

> O.J. Simpson, a black man who has already been tried and
> convicted in the eyes of the white (Jew) controlled media is
> going to fry unless black people stand up with him, and try to
> assert the common principle of presumed innocence.

> Q: Can anyone confirm presence of Nicole's brain tissue
>   exposed at the time the body was discovered/examined at
>   scene of murder?
> A: Can anyone confirm the presence of Nicole's brain tissue
>   when she continued a relationship with an abusive man?

Not got one to beat, never will have, look at any man that is in any sort of trouble and you will find somewhere a bitch is responsible for it. Take O.J. as a very good example

(From Greek 1996: 69)

Other postings found by Greek, however, went into considerable detail regarding problematic aspects of evidence and procedure, while others reflected on the media circus, and who was about to get rich from the trial. Postings came from criminal justice and other professionals as well as lay people (so far as can be ascertained), and 'scientific facts, personal opinions, and urban legends were all part of the mix of Internet coverage/discussion of the case' (Greek 1996: 76), while the debate was infused normatively with raced and gendered ways of seeing, and tactically by the Internet culture of gaming. The most important point is the immediate translation of O.J. into cyberculture; here the issues are no longer just 'about' the trial; the trial is just one way of doing cyberculture. It fits gaming culture; it fits UseNet groups' 'debate culture'; it provides a focus and materials for the kind of debates that Net geeks like to have.

Whether or not the Internet trial did as Greek claims, 'democratize' the trial is contestable. It didn't do anything *to* the trial/media event outside of the cyber, nor particularly make 'more' of the trial visible beyond some postings of detailed transcripts and photographs of evidentiary material. Given that the trial was already so highly visible across the globe through live coverage and satellite links, the cyber was probably less important to the media event than the 1997 watershed in which the terrestrial media had to find out about the Woodward verdict from the Internet; or the 1998 instance of the James Bulger retributionist movement which resulted in material that the terrestrial media were banned from making public being posted on the Internet.

There is something curious about the celebrity trial however, involving a media created icon; the icon himself occupies the virtual and metaphoric space. This is not merely trial *by* media; it is a trial of whatever it is that the celebrity icon stands for. On this, the O.J. Simpson trial offered rich pickings: a trial of the justice system; a trial of race; a trial of gender; a trial of celebrity personality; a trial of the sporting hero? Certainly, as Barak argues, 'In the *People versus Simpson,* space is open for alternative perspectives on "domestic violence", "racist police", and "legal ethics" ' (1996: 4; readers unfamiliar with the full context of the trial will find an excellent account in Barak's volume.) Yet

above all the celebrity stands for celebrity, a trial at once about everything and nothing; a trial about spectacle and entertainment, power and
manipulation; about the mobilization of 'information' which is not
really information; a trial as popular culture; a trial as consumption; a
trial waiting for Baudrillard to happen. Everyone, it seems, wanted a
piece of O.J. The two dead people were already forgotten. Their
absence was not forged into being, mythical beings placed centre stage.
Theirs was not the iconic death of Diana, nor the elevated death of
James Bulger. It was just a prop for the media circus; dead people as bit-
part players. There are no grand moral oppositions here; no innocence
of childhood abrogated by evil; even the racial oppositions and the gendered violence referred to by Barak were ultimately reduced to mere
tactics, feint and counter-feint.

As Hunt suggests, Simpson became the focal point of a media event of
a particular kind – 'a societal [global?] wide celebration *and* contestation
of dominant knowledge about reality' (1999: 249). 'Political' groupings
clustered around the available facets of the show. Hunt identifies for
example the Celebrity Defendant project, the Just-Us Project, and the
Domestic Violence project (1999: 251). Anyone who suspects this
presentation of the trial as a celebrity show to be overly cynical should
read Hunt's report of 'Camp O.J.': a million dollar 'media complex of
cable, scaffolding, and newsworkers' (1999: 87). He noted that 'two-
hundred and fifty phone lines had been installed in the court's twelfth
floor press room to accommodate the . . . communications needs of the
1,159 credentialed newsworkers who covered the case' (Hunt 1999: 87).
As for the public, there were queues for hours before dawn to enter the
lottery for the remaining seats – 'standby tickets', in other words. Outside the building, millions watched TV while

> As I scanned the scene, the telescoping transmitters of satellite
> trucks, which were poised to instantly feed video and audio
> narratives about the verdicts to any point on the globe,
> obscured my view of the skyline. Some eighty miles of cable
> had been run throughout the encampment . . . media owned
> helicopters circled directly overhead.
>
> (Hunt 1999: 87–8)

In an important sense race was not the fulcrum of the O.J. Simpson
trial. Raced narratives provided the resources of language and the

conceptual framework within which the show was played, but above all it was a show, and

> The norm-like quality of race-as-representation . . . provided the grounding for this 'relay circuit of race'. That is, it supplied the rules for the racial performance . . . ritual maneuvers that ultimately work to celebrate and (re)affirm our raced subjectivities. Rituals, at base, are about faith – about renewing our faith in a particular worldview.
>
> (Hunt 1999: 264)

Does this observation mean that the trial was devoid of content? Was it fragments of narrative tangentially related to a forgotten historical and political order, a metaphorical memory-space, playing off against each other? Did the spectacle empty the crime of content, and race of content? Were the 'raced subjectivities' mobilized in attendance upon the event, inherent to it, or merely vehicles for the spectacular, resources for adaptation by journalistic conventions and technological possibilities? Hunt retains a grounded theory of subjectivity, if not a belief in reality; the operation of the media spectacle *in relation* to authentic conceptual experience is not disputed in his text. Still, he is not so far from a position where the spectacle authenticates a non-existent reality, speaks not to a referent but to other mediatized configurations or images. Nothing could have been less important than the crime itself. Simpson's innocence or guilt 'is *not* the knowledge that mattered in the ritual I have called the Simpson media event. What was at stake, what continues to matter, is how we differentiate "fact" from "fiction" and (re)affirm what we believe about "reality" ' (Hunt 1999: 274).

The 'stakes' in the reality debate however, are suitability upped by the advent of the millennium. Not to be outdone, have we already produced 'the crime of the century'? What does the spectacle of ' global terrorism' do to our ways of reading crime and mediation?

Argument is war – war of words. We declare war: the war against crime; the war against terror*ism*; the war against terror. If you are not with us you are against us. Germs are weapons. The pyrotechnics of, and subsequently surrounding, the attack on the World Trade Center on September 11 2001 made the O.J. Simpson saga pale into insignificance. A personal interjection: I hope that I am as compassionate and humane as most people, as capable of emotion and of appreciating loss. They are worlds of feeling which I understand 'in myself' before naming them. I have lost loved ones and grieved, and felt inexplicable sadness for those whom I do not even know. I feel it necessary to establish my credentials as a non-monster before I record for public consumption my reaction to the media spectacle of September 11th. My mediatized state finally got me: half the time while watching the television or reading the newspapers or surfing the Net, seeing and hearing and reading the endless reworkings of 'the atrocity', I *forgot to remember* that this loss of life was really that; that for so many people, this grief was real and immediate, and would last for their whole lives. What was wrong with me? I hadn't been well recently, hadn't been 'myself' . . .

This was not the 'de-sensitization' thesis in action. I was not numbed into indifference by repeated exposure to media violence; except in the sense that the images and words seemed more surreal each time they were replayed and reworked in the global mediascape. This was not indifference. Thankfully, feeling came back as soon as I got out of physical proximity to the communications technology, in the open air, taking a walk along the valley near my home. But gazing at the TV, mediachosis descended again. The media spectacle was dematerializing reality before my eyes. In an inevitably raced way of seeing, perhaps I was more shocked at my reaction because this was an attack on the West; shouldn't I have felt *more*? Perhaps I would not have felt so strange and monstrous if I had been like this watching scenes of famine in the Third World? That did not hold true either, because I have watched such footage without experiencing the same bizarre dislocation.

The events had been mediated out of existence as they unfolded, almost instantaneously. The crime was just a media spectacle when it had hardly begun to launch the ensuing war-story. The 'human interest' stories didn't help: none of the people seemed real, none of the tears looked real. I logged on to *Guardian Unlimited* (http://www. guardian.co.uk) 'Special Reports', 'Manhattan Skyline – before and after'. Click! A virtual Manhattan appeared. For before, click! For after, click, and like a mouth with two front teeth missing, the 'after' image appeared. I took up the invitation to visit the interactive site. I clicked for the simulation of the actual attack and demolition. I clicked for 'Attack on America' guides. This was getting ridiculous. I clicked on 'Archive'. 'How this morning's broadsheet newspapers covered yesterday's terrorist attacks on America'. 'How this morning's tabloid newspapers covered yesterday's terror attacks on America'. And so it went on. Twenty-four hours after the event, the history of September 11th was already the history of the media.

Turning to the press, I found a blend of mutated Wild West outlaws and infotainment. 'Wanted: Dead or Alive' headlined the photograph of Osama Bin Laden. In a mix-up of genre, the *Independent* captioned it 'prime suspect' (from the quasi-feminist TV cop series of the same name). This was soon followed by 'FBI names its 22 most wanted'; the *Guardian* investigation displaying 22 Internet mugshots of suspected 'followers', 'accomplices', 'disciples' of Bin Laden, 'Publicised in the UK in a Crimewatch-style television programme'.

On 14 December 2001 the *Guardian* newspaper reported the release of the videotape starring Osama Bin Laden: 'The Bin Laden video: is this the clinching evidence?':

> Osama Bin Laden laughs and boasts in a captured videotape released by the Pentagon yesterday as he describes how he sent the September 11 hijackers to their deaths without revealing their mission until moments before they boarded the planes . . . The tape's release may turn out to be an ironic death knell for Bin Laden's terrorist career. In the aftermath of September 11 he used carefully staged videos with great effect to rally Muslim support for his cause. By contrast, most analysts agreed that this amateur video was never intended for broadcast . . . a Middle East expert at Georgetown University in Washington said the video would have an 'important impact in demystifying and dehumanising Osama Bin Laden' . . . The defence secretary, Donald Rumsfeld, said: 'It should be clear from the very matter of fact way that he refers to the attacks that killed thousands of innocent people, from several dozen different countries, why terrorists and terrorism must be defeated before they get their hands on weapons of mass destruction' . . . But many people in the Arab world claim the tape was doctored.

A cartoon underneath the still photograph of a blurred, smiling Bin Laden, taken from the video, portraying (presumably) Bin Laden and the Muslim cleric also featured in the video. The cleric says: 'In Paradise you get your own chat show'.

The embrace of 'terrorism' has predictably broadened to widen the scope when the war grows a little quiet; the spores of anthrax powder (and even talcum powder, as it transpires, and other 'harmless white substances') containing the threat of global biological warfare; debates over which forms of biological warfare are and are not amenable to terrorist use. We move from the war that is (or is not) 'taking place' to the war that might take place; gas masks and protective clothing sell out as soon as they hit the shops. There is a discussion on CNN about whether there is too much news coverage of the crisis, reported in *Guardian Unlimited*, which chides CNN with 'physician, heal thyself'.

There are further ironies yet in this portrayal of the 'real' on the run. It is all very well for the West to play the postmodern. The Arab world meanwhile has been in hot media pursuit, not just through Bin Laden's appropriation of the western media, but in its own search for the absent real, presumed to exist behind the wall of censorship, via a 'window through which we can breathe'. This is how Ahdaf Soueif, Egyptian novelist, described the satellite TV station al-Jazeera (*Guardian*, 9 October 2001). Based in 'Doha, the capital of Qatar on the Arabian peninsula', Soueif recalls the moment of discovering the station:

> [In] a hotel room in Cairo, I was channel hopping at two in the morning and suddenly, there was a channel, speaking in Arabic, but in a way I had only ever heard people speak in private – away from the censorship and the various state security services that dominate our public discourse.

Back in London, Soueif had a dish installed, and when it blew away in a gale on the night when the US and Britain commenced the bombing of Afghanistan, 'I was so bereft I found myself gazing at the black screen, trying to stare through it to what al-Jazeera might be transmitting'. Whatever the satellite window is enabling Soueif to see, it is a different Arab world from the one of terrestrial Arab TV. It has, writes Soueif, 'made censorship of news and opinion pointless'. In reverse, the western journalist Brian Whitaker reports on 'how al-Jazeera cornered the conflict' for 'this time round, CNN found itself in the wrong place and al-Jazeera has become our window on to the war, providing exclusive footage from Taliban-held areas of Afghanistan' (*Guardian*, 9 October 2001).

This is a timely reminder that postmodern culture does not a postmodern world make. The loss of context in describing the mediatized nature of the world shunts us towards proclamations of 'the death of the real', 'the death of the social' and by implication 'the death of crime' and 'the death of war'. Media absences are as important as media presence, explaining Whitaker's attraction to al-Jazeera, and there are still many people who inhabit a space not suffused with the proliferation of signs. It is hasty moves from postmodern manifestations to the assertion of a postmodern existence-for-all that have earned writers such as Baudrillard a bad reputation in some quarters, even when they themselves have not made such moves. Soueif's sudden loss of his satellite dish left him staring at a black screen, trying to imagine the world of signs; Whitaker's access to al-Jazeera is a manifestation of the western insatiability for yet more signs, trying to imagine the world through the 'black hole of the screen' (cf. Baudrillard 1995).

Will the missing context please stand up? 'Implosion' and its problems

The convolutions that some social theorists have attempted to try and dispense with the inconvenience of materiality and the distribution of materially-dependent power seem to suggest only that the failure of (male) meta-narratives to satisfactorily describe, predict, or control the world has induced a state of denial. Since satellite and digital technologies are the materiality upon which global flows depend and through which they are constituted, we can no longer give the 'old' narratives of theory a makeover and hope that they scrub up well in the face of global economics and politics. Yet the fear of relativity has long haunted western social science and wherever social theory has arrived at a point of questioning the real, the richness of this discovery has consistently led to cries of 'relativism!' It could aptly have been, as it turns out, 'Turkey Lurkey, the sky's falling!' The sky, actually, appears to be held up by the likes of satellite TV corporations such as Sky but 'Turkey Lurkey, the sky's proliferating an endless loop of images and simulacra' does not have quite the same ring. So the material and the cultural coexist but are not separable; the material has become virtualized at the global level. Materiality at the same time becomes more dispersed, more flexible, more ethereal in its manifestations while at the same time examples of good old fashioned poverty and oppressions inscribed in the body of daily existence necessarily coexist with the world of signs. As materiality becomes ever more virtual (money is information, information is money) at the global level, so the 'effects' of the postmodern work themselves out at the glocal (Featherstone 1995). This is not, as such, an analytical problem, unless one is trying to hold on for sanity's sake to the base/superstructure models tied, one-legged race style, by ideology.

Ironically, it is the grim determination to hold onto the possibility of an unmediated access to some entity called reality that seems to block much potentially rewarding discussion. Maybe this arises partly from the choice of language of postmodern theorists; an obsession with death is so gloomy and so final in its connotations that it implies looking into the future will reveal only a blank page with a full-stop in the middle; the future is dead, too. This is why postmodern writing provides so many pithy quotations either to savour with delight or bombard with epithet. It delights in the sound (byte). The kinds of 'death' with which postmodern theory seems obsessed is only metaphorical death or metaphysical death; postmodern writers are not immune from language, and therefore from metaphorics, and therefore from resonance, and therefore from practice . . . which is inscribed in the material. The 'theory' of the postmodern is like any other theory in one respect at least: it is part of what it describes. We should expect it to use the language and images of MTV in a kind of bricolage with the leftover traces of philosophy, linguistics, and social-theoretical abstraction. It is not there to be 'comprehensible' as such. It promotes only itself; 'the death of the social' is a much better brand-builder than 'the erosion of the tangible' or the 'gradual disappearance of an easily identifiable, coherent and institutionally based social order'. None of this means that money and power aren't happening or that the 'natural' process we label photosynthesis is not taking place, for example.

The genius of postmodern 'theorizing' and the 'death of theory' is that it banishes the formalistic requirements of modernist social science: to 'prove', to 'explain', to 'logically extrapolate'. It allows the kind of knowledges back in that criminology so firmly shut out in its administrative mode. More generally, the traditional academic text can no longer be privileged over other texts; imagining and intuiting and reading the world regain their vitality, no longer consigned to 'the fictive', since that category too, is dissolving. All of those claims of privileged access to reality are thankfully swept away; it is just that academics are paid to spend a lot of time reflecting on such things. While being accused of an anal obsession with its self, what postmodern theory has done is really to highlight academia's traditional pomposity while splendidly ignoring its own.

Baudrillard, in *The Gulf War Did Not Take Place* (1995) wrote a good deal of the script for the media spectacle of the present 'war against terror'. While *Simulations* (Baudrillard 1983) is probably one of the most plundered texts in discussions of 'the postmodern', *The Gulf War Did Not Take Place* has been seen as one of his more scurrilous and – well – downright daft, outpourings. As Patton notes in his introduction to the 1995 edition,

> The central thesis of Baudrillard's essays ['The Gulf War will not take place', 'The Gulf War is not taking place', and 'The Gulf War did not take place' appear together in the 1995 volume] appears to be directly contradicted by the facts. What took place during January and February 1991 was a massive aerial bombardment of Iraq's military and civil infrastructure. According to some accounts, the amount of high explosive unleashed in the first months of the conflict exceeded that of the entire Allied offensive during WW II. This was followed by a systematic air and land assault on the Iraqi forces left in Kuwait . . . official estimates of lives lost as direct casualties of these attacks are in the order of 100,000, but these do not take into account the subsequent loss of life due to hunger and disease. On the face of it, Baudrillard could not have been more wrong.
>
> (Patton, in Baudrillard 1995: 1–2)

The essays were denounced not only as 'wrong' in the sense used above, but as 'reprehensible'. One critic cited by Patton attacked them as a demonstration of 'the depth of ideological *complicity* that exists between such forms of anti-realist or irrationalist doctrine and the crisis of intellectual and political nerve' among western intellectuals (Norris 1992, in Patton 1995: 15).

My own reading of these essays, thinking of them in relation to crime and issues of law and censure, and the post-1980s criminological penchant for 'realism' as a basis for the analysis of these, took me in a completely different direction from Norris. Intellectually the essays seem possessed of considerable nerve, especially in their unashamed parading of apparent contradictions and self-refutations, which parody those of everyday life experience; but more fundamentally in their sweeping away of 'reality' as unimportant, non-existent, or irrelevant, by turn. What Baudrillard really stands accused of is *bad taste,* in the way that 'there are some things you just don't make jokes about' (it is all very well writing this sort of thing about Art, but the legitimized murder of thousands of people?) – and in 'intellectual' work of course, one should not make jokes about *anything.* The joke analogy is useful because a joke is a complex thing. The definition of a 'bad taste' joke is one that masks the reality of suffering and which is therefore assumed to adopt complicity toward the infliction of it. The joke of course, does nothing to the lived experience of suffering; indeed it does not refer directly to that 'reality' at all; it plays with the signs in which it is inscripted.

In *Simulations* a more staid Baudrillard (1983: 147) argues:

> And so: end of the real, and end of art, by total absorption of one into the other? No: hyperrealism is the limit of art, and of the real, by respective exchange, on the level of the simulacrum, of the privileges and prejudices which are their basis. The hyperreal transcends representation . . . only because it is entirely in simulation. The tourniquet of representation tightens madly, but of an implosive madness, that, far from eccentric (marginal) inclines towards the centre to its own infinite repetition . . . Hyperrealism is made an integral part of a coded reality that it perpetuates, and for which it changes nothing.

The way in which crime and war (which is crime by other means) inhere in the mediatized world is consistent with such a view. With so much to see, there is nothing to see. Hence a sense of dislocation viewing the 'war against terror'. The archive is 'the complement of the event in real time, of that instantaneity of the event and its diffusion', and the event 'vanishing in information itself' (Baudrillard 1995: 47). September 11th, except in the case of those intimately connected with it, has already vanished in information. It is already a simulation, as simulated as the *Guardian Interactive* page. If we replace many of Baudrillard's usages of 'the war' by 'crime' it makes as much sense of the contemporary mediascape as do many more structured and 'materialist' accounts. For example:

> The war's programmed escalation is relentless and its non-
> occurrence no less inevitable: the war proceeds at once towards
> the two extremes of intensification and deterrence.
>
> (Baudrillard 1995: 47)

Certainly the war against crime is promotion; the media promotes itself. The war against crime is a domain of mass production and consumption. Crime is an aesthetic product, a highly visual as well as linguistically metaphorical project; it is a media project of desirable commodities generating multiplicities of fickle brand loyalties. It must be endlessly reinvented in different formats, repackaged and rebranded. Perhaps most interestingly, it occupies a space where, being dislocated entirely from the real by the media, it has to be reinvented by the media; resting on the crucial question of otherness, in accordance with the third order of simulacra (Baudrillard 1983) it must resurrect difference and otherness, so 'it is always a question of proving the real by the imaginary, proving truth by scandal, proving the law by transgression' (Baudrillard 1983: 36). Thus,

> all hold-ups, hijacks and the like are now as it were simulation
> hold-ups, in the sense that they are inscribed in advance in the
> decoding and orchestration rituals of the media, anticipated in
> their mode of presentation and possible consequences. In brief,
> they function as a set of signs, dedicated exclusively to their
> recurrence as signs, and no longer to their 'real' goal at all.
>
> (Baudrillard 1983: 40)

It would be a mistake, however, to assume that this is a cultural shift which simply bamboozles an audience. By its nature, the audience being part producer and part consumer learns from the very techniques of simulation. Baudrillard reveals the high culture/low culture, Frankfurt School-like subtext of his nihilism however when he refers to archival cassettes, that will 'be something to see for the . . . generations of video-zombies who will never cease reconstituting this event, never having had the intuition of the non-event of this war' (1995: 47).

Sophistication is required for, and produced by, the negotiation of postmodern media forms; it is a stylistic imperative that the viewer comprehends the notion of bricolage and intertextuality, of the instantaneity of images and their immediate death, only to be recycled and reinvented in a parody of the preceding simulations. It goes with interactive TV, the logical development of channel-hopping, and the pause, rewind and fast-forward of video-taped programmes (Barker 1997) and the simulation of crime is part of the process. Similarly reflexivity in postmodern culture becomes a more complex process than in modern culture; reflecting on the multifarious and interrelated nature of mediated experience, identity operates in many directions at once. (I discuss the implications of the virtual for multiplexed identities further in Chapter 5). Barker (1997) further makes the point that reflexivity in postmodern media culture also acknowledges that everything has been said before, and is constantly said again in different ways, so that one is never inventing the new but playing with the existing. This constant unoriginality produces irony, 'because it encourages a widespread awareness of the history and techniques of cultural production' (Barker 1997: 170).

At the same time, the media constantly undermines their own claims to veracity through their self-revelatory activities. The *Independent* ran a full-page article in its 'Home News' section (20 August 1998) on media falsification. Headlined 'The Sun did it. Stalin did it. This is how simple it is to retouch history', it reported:

> Stalin did it to Trotsky. Ronald Reagan did it to Oliver North. And last week *The Sun* did it to Shelley Ann Emery and her wheelchair . . .
>
> With computer software and digitised photographs, almost anyone can make improvements on reality. And they can almost never be detected.
>
> The most infamous recent newspaper case included *The Guardian* removing an irksome child from Gordon Brown's arm on Budget Day last year and *The Mirror* creating an embrace between Dodi Fayed and the Princess of Wales on a yacht . . .
>
> A computer program called Adobe Photoshop is to blame . . . editors, picture editors or chief sub-editors can do what they like to an image . . .
>
> We were even able to make Gordon Brown smile and put a champagne bottle in the picture. Mr Brown's smile was taken from *The Independent*'s electronic picture library.

The medium is the message? 'Now with a £1,200 PC and photoshop software, anyone can play Stalin' (*Independent*, 20 August 1998). The *debate* in the article surrounded the technology, but also the ethics of deception: the 'dangerousness' of 'changing content so that the meaning is changed'. Thus the cultural (news) values of allegiance to reflecting the truth are reinforced; and while the practice of 'deception' is clearly identified as being nothing new, the sophisticated and convincing nature of the contemporary technology highlights the 'dilemma'. It assumes a consensus among the public that the camera never lies; that *as opposed to the meaning of words* the veracity of the photographic image is wrongly assumed by those who see it. Of course there is no particular justification for either assumption, but the newspaper has obligingly added to the readers' already extensive grasp of the dubious nature of media truth-claims.

Indeed, viewers and readers are constantly reminded by the media themselves of the provisional status of apparent reality. BBC Radio Four news reported on 14 October 2001 that the BBC had been contacted by Downing Street regarding certain 'editorial dilemmas', particularly surrounding BBC TV's showing of video broadcasts by Osama Bin Laden, the Afghan Taliban leader. Downing Street had briefed them against showing unedited Bin Laden broadcasts due to concern that they could contain 'coded messages' (BBC Radio 4 News, 14 October 2001). Nevertheless, despite this 'slip', which both the BBC and Downing Street agreed to 'draw a line under', it had been declared that 'the BBC was having a very good war' (BBC Radio 4 News October 2001).

The techniques of representation used in television are constantly on display; from MTV to Crimewatch UK the media wears its image-manipulation and editing technologies on the outside. As the speeding up and slowing down of sequences, visual distortions and contortions, looping, and cam-flexibility develop and proliferate in front of our eyes, so the images we see are constantly boasting of their own ability to transcend realism. When 'realism' is used, it is so self-consciously and self-evidently a technique that it too assumes an ironic dimension; used frequently in satirical and entertainment formats, there is little that is subtle or hidden about the construction of meaning. Like the Pompidou Centre, the image is turned inside-out so that its functioning becomes its aesthetic. The apparent seriousness with which 'objectivity' and 'facticity' are debated is nothing more than an advertising ploy, or a mere vestige of news and documentary culture in modernity.

What is not so clear, in relation to crime at least, is whether this sophistication and sense of the ironic operates equally in relation to different signification practices. Since the contours of postmodern 'viewing' culture arise from the intertextuality, the interactivity, the bricolage, and the dynamics of simulation; and since increasingly the 'news is soap' and 'soap is the news', 'law is soap' and 'soap is law', etc., it is tempting to take a homogenizing approach to thinking about how mediatized identit(ies) interact with the various modalities of crime representation. This is not a presumption that should be made, however, since scepticism and irony will by no means necessarily apply to the same degree across the board. There is nothing particularly to suggest that the search for narrative resolution, authenticity, and therefore resonance, has been abandoned. *Claims* to authenticity remain strong grounds of contestation, suggesting that authenticity is a desired attribute. Crime programmes 'based on a *true* story', films 'based on a *real* case' or 'our correspondent reports *now from the scene*' compete for an illusion of veracity which is by implication denied to other 'stories', whereas at other times veracity is implied by denial ('the characters in this film are entirely fictional and are not based on any living persons' – clearly a protective caveat which encourages rather than discourages the viewer to invest the story with authenticity). The use of metaphoric resonance together with such stratagems as these are aimed at undermining the wily sophistication of the inhabitants of imploding cultures.

We live in contradictory (crime) times. Is it necessary to cling to oppositional postures (modernity versus postmodernity) and final statements (the death of the metanarrative, the death of history, the death of the law, and so on; for all is irony) when clearly all is flux, or to a directional imperative (we are moving towards implosion, for example) when unidirectionality seems to be the least self-evident impulse of mediatization? Nichols writes, in his multiply layered analysis of 'the trials and tribulations of Rodney King' (1994: 19):

> What the insulated world of television could not contain was Rodney King's metonymic linkage to a far greater community. What was done to him had been done to others like him . . . Reminding ourselves that images of a man being beaten are only signifiers, floating in the ether of an autonomous signifying practice, may be formally correct but also strangely alienated. Critics like Jean Baudrillard, who refutes the 'reference principle' . . . opts to celebrate how alienated we

have all become. He wants us to enjoy a decathected free-fall
through the shadow play of simulacra . . . But along comes a
moment such as the beating of Rodney King and the historical
referent once again cuts through the inoculating power of
signifying systems to turn our response to that excess beyond
the frame.

Nichols is pointing out that the reality TV, the live footage of the beating of Rodney King,[2] makes clear reference to the event and to all other
Rodney King-like events, and that the image is transparent rather than
obfuscating. Yet clearly the impact of reality TV can *also* be obfuscating
and alienating, can further distance us from a sense of reality. It can do
both these things at once, depending upon the constituency of those
viewing it. Nichols indicates the nature of his own normative and moral
engagement with the reality text; yet this does not necessarily mean that
postmodern perspectives can be easily dismissed as 'voodoo semiotics'
(Nichols 1994: 19).

As Callon (1986) once pointed out, nature has no preference, a line
also taken by Callinocos (1989), who argues that scientific rationality is
a successful outcome, not of its uncovering of the inherent properties of
an unchanging natural reality, but of the will to power. Western modernist culture as it is inscribed in practice, including the practice of language,
selectively imputes properties onto nature and claims an unmediated
access to 'reality'. These interpretations are multiple, and find numerous
expressions. To accept Nichols's point is not thereby to reject Baudrillard's; it is Nichols himself who is doing this.

A frequent response to Baudrillard's writing is based on revulsion
against its supposed implications (i.e. that there are no implications for
ethical response) rather than on an effective rejection of his insights – or
on annoyance that his work is not a corpus; it is not 'a theory' or 'a
body'; it is not coherent. As Redhead (1990) points out, this is simply not
in the nature of Baudrillard's eclectic writings, and could not be, since he
anyway rejects coherence. Hebdige finds Baudrillard's work difficult to
accept on both counts; on the first, 'although in one sense I realise the
pertinence of what he is saying . . . I also have my suspicions that
the kind of will motivating his work seems to be poisonous', and on the
second, 'the language he uses is not very fruitful, there's not much future
in it.' (Hebdige in interview with Harley, Harley 1987: 70, quoted in
Redhead 1990). Barker (1997) meanwhile, seems to seek an antidote in

finding optimism in postmodern theory. Increasingly differentiated global societies, the decline of theoretical and actual commonality of culture and the acceptance of diversity are identified by Barker as contours of 'postmodern culture'. As a result,

> the 'other' of modernity, those voices which had been suppressed by the modern drive to extinguish difference, have increasingly found ways to speak within postmodern culture(s). Hence the emergence of 'new social movements' and 'life politics' connected for example to ecological or feminist concerns. Likewise the development of multi-ethnic communities, the disengagement with mainstream politics.
>
> (Barker 1997: 169)

There are two problems here. One problem is that postmodern theory tends to be celebratory of difference in a superficial and ultimately consumerist sense, and could not be connected in any deep or structural sense to what are clearly enduring power-domination formations of gender and imperialism. It is highly questionable whether it opens up a space for the *changes* which would be necessary to unravel these formations and replace them with a more pluralistic and heteropian landscape (Sardar 1998). To see such optimism in postmodern theory is to treat it as a theory of a society rather than of an account of culture. Unless one adopts an explicitly idealist philosophy as unproblematic, this is misplaced. McGuigan (1999: 89) points out that to overstate postmodernist claims to the proliferation of difference is to deny the inherently ethnocentric nature of postmodern thought, since 'crises of identity and epistemology, the chronic choices of those freed of tradition and restraint, do not much concern the famine stricken and dying of Africa'.

Moreover, while touting the unreality of the Gulf War (or the 'war against terror') there is a danger of sublime indifference to those oppressions, which continue to arise directly out of the imperatives of western modernity, such as ethnic cleansing in Bosnia (McGuigan 1999: 89). Let us be quite clear about it: there is no postmodern *future*. This is where the alleged nihilism of postmodern theory rests. The second problem is that the third procession of simulacra (Baudrillard 1983) reconstitutes the Other as a simulacrum.

Taken together, the critical stances towards postmodernist thought, and towards Baudrillard in particular, suggest a number of questions relevant to criminological thought (if not to criminology), while post-modernist thought seems also to offer a number of interesting *possi-bilities* for 'reading crime'. First of all, there is the ever-present question of referent-reality. In one way, to assert the fracturing of this relationship can be seen as a mire of cultural relativity. However, handled with cau-tion, the notion of simulacra is powerful and helpful. There seems to me to be an error in slipping from what is essentially descriptive of the process and form of mediatization, to the assumption that therefore no reality exists. As Butler (1999: 17) points out, Baudrillard uses 'real' in two senses: one, the disappearing real referring to the internality of the system, and another real, the real–real which is an absolute limit to the system.

If we prefer to call real crime 'crime-like acts' or engage in any other form of linguistic gymnastics, we can. It is good enough for most people that they know when they have been assaulted, when their property has been forcibly taken from them, or when they have been swindled out of their pension funds or their loved ones violently deprived of life. Any denial of this would be so patently inhuman that it would imply direct collusion with such acts; it would indeed be 'voodoo semiotics' (Nichols 1994: 19). If we choose to *only* consider war (or crime by other means) as a simulacrum, then clearly we are supporting murderous regimes. This would make a Baudrillardian reading of crime poisonous. But this is not a 'required' way to approach the idea of postmodern culture. Post-modernism does not 'magic away' the sustained inequalities of power and materiality which pattern both the nature of the construction of crime, the motivations of criminals, and public censure, including dis-courses of the law.

However, postmodern thought allows us to recognize that mediatiza-tion does not distort the 'true' nature of crime and criminality, and their distribution. It is never capable of representing them in the first place. Crime and criminality do not have a fixed existence or meaning. They are taxonomic categories, culturally produced and sustained in more or less patterned ways; crucially metaphoric categories, but ones which give visual form to indescribable pains; evasive sensations of suffering, grief, loss, fear, anxiety, irresolution, regret, anger, loneliness and despair. These are as amenable to metaphoric signification through the categories of for example, love, death, or war. The truth–reality debate is *unneces-sary*, being based as McGuigan (1999) notes, in logocentrism. It is brought into being only by language, and specifically by writing. The centrality of metaphor is that it constitutes and is constituted by the symbolic articulation of experience, only inadequately gesturing toward an underlying reality. 'Crime' is not the reality; 'crime' is the metaphor.

This does not prevent us from seeking to understand the experiences of people who consider themselves victims, nor from seeking to understand the contexts in which the patterning of such experience inheres. It does not require a callous decentring of experience. Therefore, it can comfortably accommodate the normative and moral demands of a 'realist criminology', as well as some of the empirical demands of, say, 'new left' realism (Matthews and Young 1992). It is not inherently obstructive of social policy which would seek to ameliorate people's fears and experiences of victimization. To oppose a realist epistemology and postmodernism is a formal exercise which detracts from the benefits of postmodern insights.

These insights actually increase an understanding of 'crime'. Postmodernism's decentring of academic or scientific truth claims, contingent on the representation–reality fracture, allows for a much fuller way of approaching crime. Accepting crime *as* metaphoric, and accepting the blurring of fact and fiction, enables us to approach anything from the news, to film, to crime novels, to the cyber, as spheres of representation through which we can read crime (and by definition what crime is not). To 'read' crime is neither to measure nor to invent, but to explore the inventions we call crime, their metaphorical resonance, their inherence in structures of feeling and in experience, to recognize languages as practices, and to accept the multiplicity of available readings.

The determination to hold on to the notion that the media exist in a linear/measurable relationship to factual reality, rather than recursively in metaphorical resonance with experience *and* as simulacra, can only land criminology in a time warp – one that is not even inhabited by most of its contemporary young students. The latter tend to be sophisticated postmodern subjects who (at the time of writing this) entered adulthood through TV programmes like *Big Brother* (2000, 2001, 2002) and *Pop Idols* (2001, 2002)[3]; and films like *Natural Born Killers* (1994) and *The Blair Witch Project* (2000). They were weaned on sampling and rapping, garage and house (Redhead 1990), grew up on the post-punk novel (Redhead 2000). From Irvine Welsh's novel *Trainspotting* (Welsh 1993) onwards they have been born of a (cultural) chemical generation, symptomatic of an era where 'a literary underground became overground in a rapidly accelerating global culture at the end of

the millennium' (Redhead 2000: xii). They are the repetitive beat generation (Redhead 2000), interactively, intertextually (post)literate, post-
pop (*cf.* Redhead 1997a), multiply-identitied beings.

Perhaps in the end the problem lies not with postmodern theorizing,
but rather in knowing what to do with it. If we believed in the notion of
simulacra as a thoroughgoing theory of an epoch, there would be nothing to choose. If we rejected the 'postmodern nonsense' as mere voodoo
semiotics, we would have to address the galaxy of simulacra and ask
'Will the real context please stand up?' If we are prepared to accept the
implosion of media forms as an unavoidable aspect of the glocal, and the
fact/fiction collapse as part of a much broader tendency which undermines the hierarchizing of epistemologies, we are left with an ethical, not
a scientific dilemma. Perhaps one of the challenging aspects of developments in crime/media culture has been the rise and rise of 'audience
polling'. I want only to consider this briefly in the context of the mobilization of allies around certain normative dimensions of crime and law,
although clearly it does raise the broader and complex question of the
'opinion poll' phenomenon in general. For the moment I use the example
only to highlight the pertinence of ethics if 'science' can no longer be
wheeled out as a legitimation for action.

The media frequently give the rest of the general public bit parts as
judges and jurors. Audience polling (by telephone, mobile phone, texting
or email) is now an integral part of reality TV as well as the tabloid press.
Less commonly used for crime shows than for entertainment formats like
Big Brother, the *Crimewatch* formula of viewers ringing in to give information (and have a go at potential reward money) has proved highly
popular in the UK and elsewhere. Television news polls have been run on
crime stories such as the Thompson–Venables release. The *Mirror* ran an
(in)famous campaign asking readers to call a hotline supporting 'Sarah's
Law'. Sarah Payne, aged 8, was murdered by a convicted sex offender.[4]
On August 5 2000, the *Mirror* ran a headline chiding its readers for not
supporting the campaign for 'Sarah's Law' (seeking changes in the law
to establish registers of known child sex offenders) in sufficient numbers:
'Did YOU Back Her? . . . 32,000 readers did. What's keeping the rest
of you?'. The following day, the headline was 'YOU'VE DONE IT . . .
Authorities approve Sarah's Law . . . Deal after 93,000 call our hotline'
(*Mirror*, 5 August 2000). Without this sort of context, the *Daily Star*
campaign to free 'Matt' (BBC1 *East Enders*' 'victim' of miscarriage of
justice Matthew Rose, dubbed D.J. Matt, was wrongly imprisoned for

the murder of a female character in the soap) would be nothing more than a joke, but being enjoined to join the campaign for justice and 'send your message of support for DJ Matt . . . on 071–922–7386' (*Daily Star*, 11 October 1999) in hindsight, was one end of a continuum.

The popular legal imagination becomes, increasingly, subject matter in the fact/fiction interstice. At the time of writing, *The Jury*, an ITV1 television drama, which is a kind of anodyne *Twelve Angry Men* for the twenty-first century, is the latest offering. 'The jury in context' is a timely shift in the mediascape: 'it's the second day of the trial, and the jurors try to ignore the media hype surrounding the case . . . but the dead boy's brothers are determined to take the law into their own hands' (*TV Quick*, 23 February 2002).

With each of these developments, the illusion of any serious fact/fiction divide in mediated production recedes. 'Democracy' and 'the law' as soap opera and simulacrum? Undoubtedly. However, since it is so patently obvious that meaning has not disappeared, any more than experience has, the imperative is not so much to comprehend an 'it' but to address a question of purpose: the instrumental use to which the proliferating hybrids of knowledges shall be harnessed. The knowledges themselves have no logical or necessary outcome. We cannot blame a 'science of causes' for eugenics. We cannot blame postmodern cultural analysis for a mediachosis which may seem powerless to address the real experiences and sufferings attendant upon crime. We cannot blame an undifferentiated 'mass', duped into mindless compliance with media agendas. We are still left with a question of the bases of power, institutional and more broadly social, and with the crucial question, addressed eloquently by Smart (1999) of 'ambivalence, reflexivity, and morality'.

3 ■ NOVEL FORMS, DRAMATIC SCENES: CRIME AND LAW IN POPULAR CULTURE

Within the broad themes of this book, how might one begin to think about the fictive voices of crime? What would be the interest, the point, of studying crime in fiction or film? I am concerned about the process of reading crime, and yet to adopt a particular standpoint is at one and the same time to silence the relevance of others. Then again, to begin with complete methodological openness would fall merely into redescribing the themes of the text itself. The subjectivity and the social of the interaction with the text is one which students constantly raise; when I ask them to theorize about the texts with which they are engaging, what do I mean? It is a task that can be archaeological and personal, anthropological and yet biographical. In this spirit I want to begin with a consideration of some expressed agendas of authors who have written on fictive voices, while also considering what it might mean to take an anthropological orientation toward reading crime fiction or crime film. Then I shall take my own agenda and plunder fictive voices. This is not a chapter about textual analysis as such, but about the mode of interacting, of living the text. It belongs to anybody, because above all, like love, crime is anything we want it to be. That is both its beauty and its horror, its lure and its repulsion.

Reading crime fiction: crime in popular culture

When Young (1996: 79) talks about reading detective fiction, she phrases it thus:

> I wish to examine its ability to stage aspects of the crimino-
> legal process in a form that engages with our fears and
> pleasures in criminality. The chapter will deal with crime as an
> aesthetic form that combines the body as a repository of clues
> and signs with the trauma of witnessing the event of
> victimization. The genre's laws of representation will also be
> considered; its codes of naming, its location of crime in the city
> and in sexual difference, its heroic detectives and its foundation
> upon a primal moment of betrayal. My argument concerns the
> dialectic between appearance and disappearance, law and
> ethics, masculinity and femininity. And finally, in a genre that
> has often been dismissed for its inherent conservatism, I seek to
> discover a place for ethical feminism.

As Young points out, in a culture where assumptions are made constantly about the fearfulness of people, it is interesting to broach the question of the ways in which people may actively wish for texts which allow them to enjoy fearfulness. She is intrigued by the demands that a text 'makes', so that detective stories require someone 'who is uniquely able to decode the puzzle', to apply 'rationality, forensic science, re-enactment, intuition' (Young 1996: 81). These are, then, requisites of the narrative structure of the genre. Geographical location, she suggests, is also important as well as historical timelessness. Reader allegiances to certain authors are based around attractions to specifics within the same genre, the characters of the detectives and the ways in which characters and locations are portrayed. Detective stories, for Young, are 'textual exemplifications' of censure. This is an aesthetic censure, developed through the conventions of modernity. Hence she appears to be primarily concerned with laws of genre, thematic similarities that consistently appear across different texts and produce the particular experience of reading through that structuring.

'Reading the city' is an important law of detective genre for Young, its criminogenic nature, its need to be decoded through the signs (in the semiotic sense) of crime. In the work of Conan Doyle for example, the detective is a semiotician who can decode the city. He utilizes stringently positivist methods based on contemporary criminological orthodoxies where criminality must be based on observable features of body, psyche, or environment. The role of the detective is, through his expert reading, to restore the meaning lost when a crime is unsolved. This is consistent with the development of the modernist urban: the fear of the mass. The detective as a superior individual possessed of extraordinary powers of reasoning is able to defuse the fear by fathoming the unfathomable. Young then invokes the notions of surveillance and the panopticon; detective fiction 'watches the detective watching the criminal and thus institutes a panoptic relationship between reader and fictional offender' (1996: 87). Thus glancing toward the work of Michel Foucault (1977) on surveillance and disciplinary power as dominant modalities of power under modernism, she argues that detective fiction exemplifies a representation of the panoptic principle.

Next Young turns toward the writing of Patricia Cornwell in her best-selling Kay Scarpetta novels, focusing on a reading of Cornwell that emphasizes the logic of pathology as being the ultimate expression of a procedural semiotics of the body. Retrospection, linear causality and logic require, again, expert application if the signs are to be read correctly: blood, hair, skin, bones. The scientized body, the opacity and threat of the city (in this case, Richmond, VA), and the rational method represent for Young crucial aspects of modernity that are articulated by detective fiction. Detective fiction, on this reading, resolves the pains of modernity while enabling the reader to enjoy the pleasures of fear; this is also a question of visibility and invisibility, permitting voyeurism with reference to its necessity. It also requires that the detective have an interlocutor, a significant Other who may either be a different character or the inner voice of the detective herself, or even a spiritual presence. The Other creates a space, within which an interpreter, justifier, explicator, of the detective can operate, presumably (although Young does not make clear the significance of the Other for her) to make visible the self and identity of the detective as part of the modernist project of identity. In this, masculinity and femininity also figure. Detection is a masculine narrative function, although Young argues it can sometimes be occupied by a woman.

Young cites feminist detective fiction, such as the work of Sue Grafton, Sara Paretsky and Val McDermid, as offering a 'reappraisal of the laws of crime which govern the genre of detective fiction' (1996: 102). By this she seems to mean that the limitations of a masculinist genre demanding merely reason, logic, and the making visible of the invisible, are translated by feminist writing. That is to say, the detective's 'entire existence is criss-crossed with tensions, riven with ambiguities' (Young 1996: 102). Unlike the masculinist narratives, feminist narratives do not separate the personal, the ethical and the detection. Everything is a struggle, because the woman detectives as feminists and/or lesbians, occupy a site of personal and political struggle, and the world is not made, by these authors, necessarily dichotomous of emotion and reason.

Young concludes that it is clear that detective stories project the image of a given social order and 'the implied value system that helps sustain it' (1996: 107) while at the same time denying the possibility that the law itself could be unjust. They offer the reader a trajectory from fear (of the city, of the Other, of the mass) to pleasure in the narrative resolution and the re-establishment of order. At the same time however, 'detective fiction has also been the scene of a legible feminist ethics' which 'is prior to law, and for which detection (and law) can only ever constitute a surrogate' (Young 1996: 109–10).

I have dealt with Young's work at some length because it exemplifies a methodology that is now common in the social analysis of fictive cultural crime texts; a methodology that eschews literary or semiotic analysis for a more fully social treatment. It treats both the form and content of the message as fully grounded in the historical moment of modernity. 'All' that it is necessary to do is to apply modernist modes of interpretation of the culture, politics and economics of a society to the text and the meaning will be revealed.

The value of this approach is that it reads crime fiction as representative of the well-documented transformations outlined in Chapter 1, producing an intelligible and believable social contextual reading. It seeks a match between two narratives: the narrative of what happened, and the narrative of what the text says. It also opens up the text as a culturally relative project, making no judgements about 'goodness' or 'badness'. At the same time it allows of the possibility that the fictive voice may be one of revelation or dissent about crime and the law, as well as reaffirmation. Laying a more or less sophisticated template over the text, it allows us to see the story as telling the story of the culture from which it emanates, and it does so free of the complexities of either literary–critical or cultural textual analysis. It is essentially a sociology of the fictive text. In this it is a method that enables the interpreter to read off a culture from the text. In particular, for example, Young emphasizes fear and pleasure surrounding crime, and of course in doing so throws into question the commonsensical notion that crime is necessarily a bad thing. Rather, crime is a metaphor for the modern condition. It stands proxy for the modernist identity project; it is concerned with the self and the Other. Crime operates as a representational category, which allows the voicing of dissenting realities, of women and lesbians, precisely because it renders problematic the taken-for-granted conventions of social order. The crime novel can use the narrative structure to produce subversive definitions of what 'the problem' is, and subversive resolutions of that problem.

In the end, genres notwithstanding, fictive texts are reading crime. This is their importance for criminology. For example, in *Neon Noir* (1999), describing fictive texts as 'skip tracing the culture', Haut places examples of crime fiction and film in what seems on the face of it a rather bizarre analytical juxtaposition with the USA's record on the Vietnam War. Through this, however, he presents an interesting delineation of contemporary 'crime America'. He justifies his method thus:

> To examine a culture, one need only investigate its crimes. Thus the fictionalisation of crime has become a favourite pastime and a means of analysing society . . . *Neon Noir* concerns crime fiction from the mid-1960s to the 1990s . . . reading the era alongside particular authors and texts. Yet *Neon Noir* makes no attempt to be a definitive history of contemporary crime fiction . . . the writers included in this study reflect the author's personal tastes.
>
> (Haut 1999: 3)

Actually, since Haut positions this caveat in a section headed 'Locating the Evidence', one suspects him of disingenuity. Why should not *Neon Noir* be as 'authoritative' as any other history? Moreover, why should it be a 'history of fiction', when clearly it is also a history of crime? And how could the 'personal' be excluded from any such reading? I will address these issues later in this chapter; for the moment the important point is that the fiction, as Haut emphasizes, is the tool for reading the culture. He reads American history as bifurcated by the Vietnam War, and his book is described in the publisher's note on the back jacket as 'a roller coaster ride through the American nightmare'.

'Neon Noir' fiction constitutes the fiction which for Haut is both an urban genre, and also traces an electronic culture; it

> suggests an electronic culture consisting of half-lit signs adorning cheap hotels, the sound of crackling synapses induced by hallucinogenics and the war in Vietnam, the power of the media, and the flash of self promotion as crime writers hammer out stories on the frontage of the information superhighway.
>
> (Haut 1999: 4)

Haut's work is an interesting process of excavating the dialectic between history and fiction; he uses the history to read the fiction, and the fiction to read the history. Many criminologists might take note of his method. The Vietnam War raised the vexed question of state crime – which as anyone familiar with McCarthyism will know, is not a favoured way to stay healthy in that culture (witness George W. Bush's pronouncement, broadcast on television news on 1 February 2002, extending the 'war against terror' in the context of the September 11th bombings to a threat to 'any nation who is not with us'). Hence fiction tended not to tackle state crime head-on, but rather adopted an oblique approach to the war, rarely criticizing it openly. One factor, he points out, was the crime writers' status as literary workers – they were as dependent on their publishers as criminological researchers on their funders. Later, there was to be a critical resurgence among crime writers so that the war (as it became memory) was arbited by fiction, and discourses of murder, state crime, and corruption infused the fictive voice; 'as everyone's war and everyone's crime, Vietnam would become the subtext of numerous crime novels' (Haut 1999: 48).

In general, Haut points out, detective fiction has always been important as a historical text, and can therefore provide a rich source of information on state crime, while at the same time providing a particular perspective: history viewed through the methods of the private eye. American crime fiction is far richer in its range of perspectives and accounts of corporate and state crime than is 'official' criminology, which has traditionally neglected the subject for various reasons (Giddens 1985, Maguire *et al.* 1997).

Haut pursues the adventures of a wide range of fiction writers on his trail across American urban history, unravelling the twists and turns of America's shame through the eyes of Lawrence Block, Stephen Dobyns,

James Lee Burke, Gar Anthony Haywood, Walter Mosely, James Sallis, and others. The statement that it is a male genre precludes him from mentioning any female writer except for Sara Paretsky. It is interesting that when Haut gets to Paretsky, he is merely condescending, even in his faint-hearted praise for her work. 'Hard boiled' it seems is not for softy girls, who should presumably stay on their own side of the fence. He contends that ultimately Paretsky fails in the genre precisely by trying to 'be a man'. Her V.I. Warshawski has too many morals, is too human, too predictable, and is one-dimensional, her narratives are overly neat. For 'political though it may be, detective fiction requires complex characterisation and narratives that address the contradictions of everyday reality', and Paretsky 'lacks a warped edge' (Haut 1999: 97).

Haut has nothing else to say about the rise of the feminist detective novel, and as a result his excavation of American crime through the fictive voice is too predictable, and is one-dimensional! It is necessary to look elsewhere for an account of the 'spectacular rise of the American feminist detective novel' (Vanacker 1997). The gendering of the crime fictive voice, like the gendering of crime itself, provides an essential perspective from which to view the mediation of crime. Unlike Haut, Vanacker (1997) reads Paretsky, in siting her feminist detective within the hard-boiled genre, as acting to 'subvert its frequently misogynist ideology'. The traits that Haut identifies as weaknesses are strengths in Vanacker's eyes. Along with the work of Sue Grafton and Patricia Cornwell, Vanacker cites Paretsky's work as interesting precisely because it is ambivalent within the traditional male bastion of the genre; in particular she notes they 're-examine the whole business of the gathering of information and the pursuit of knowledge to show the limitations of the male epistemological ideal and to suggest a preferred feminist alternative' (1997: 64). Vanacker's approval and Haut's disdain reveal how crucial gender is to the perspective which one brings to the reading of crime. Whereas Haut sees Paretsky as failing in the genre, Vanacker sees her as a subversive. She links her discussion of feminist crime writing explicitly to epistemology, and indeed implies that the feminist detective novel is superior as a text from which to read crime, since the protagonists display an explicit and enthusiastic pleasure in gaining information and knowledge 'seldom seen in the male detective novel' (Vanacker 1997: 80).

No discussion of reading crime through the fictive voice could be complete without a consideration of the lesbian thriller. Although having been accused of being flawed in being too bound to genre (Drucker 1992), the notion of a transgressive reading of crime through the detective novel is intriguing from a 'criminological' point of view. Within debates among literary academics and writers themselves, controversy has tended to be genre-bound – that is, back to Gair's (1997) question of when is a novel not a crime novel or, since the terms of hard-boiled are already defined through a masculinist paradigm, how does the notion of a lesbian detective fit in? As Palmer (1997) points out, the 'discrepancy of values' that is brought to the lesbian thriller can be seen as a strength or a stumbling block from a literary–critical point of view. Since we are not here bound by such concerns, it is possible simply to explore what kind of difference the 'lesbian' in the thriller does bring to reading crime.

No bigger contrast could be found than between Sherlock Holmes or Philip Marlowe and the lesbian sleuth. Much of the lesbian thriller writing occurs in the US, but British examples include the work of Manda Scott and Val McDermid. McDermid's Lindsay Gordon mysteries are probably the most well known (for an example see McDermid 1996) whereas Scott's work is given an extra twist in its Scottishness and part rural, part urban settings (for example Scott 1996, 1999). Well-known US examples are Barbara Wilson (1984, 1991) Sandra Scoppettone (1993), and Mary Wings (1986) among many others.

For the purposes of reading crime, the most significant difference is the gendered power axis of the perspective adopted. This operates both at the level of the detective herself, her methods, and at the level of the crime. The lesbian sleuth exists in a world riven by contradictions and dilemmas specific to her sexual orientation as well as her gender. She is usually located firmly within a lesbian feminist social network, bringing personal relationships to the fore during the process of crime-solving in a way alien to mainstream hard-boiled texts. Her dilemmas include personal safety, loyalty to her friends and concern for their welfare as they may become embroiled in her work or put at risk by it; the impact of her work on her lover/s, and other emotionally contextualizing issues. Her sexual relationships are often somehow bound up with the plot, and many issues of trust are raised. The crime itself is usually, however indirectly, linked to her network, either through the victim or the perpetrator. The problematic attitudes of authority figures, notably the police, can be palpable (although there is frequently an ally within), and witnesses often react negatively.

The space of crime is used differently in the lesbian thriller or detective novel to explore the dynamics and problematics of transgressive sexuality. In this the 'modernist' paradigm could hardly apply, since the centrality of lesbian identities inform every aspect of the narrative. Fear, pleasure, pain, threat, and power are experienced in a distinctly not-modernist way. One advantage this has is to highlight how masculinist the standard history of modernism is, so that from a feminist criminologist point of view one might be tempted to follow Bruno Latour (1993) and wonder if we ever *were* modern.

Modes of interpretation tend to be unrelentingly self-reflexive, always refracted back through what it means to be a lesbian woman in an urban landscape. Comfort, consolation and solace are sought from other lesbian or gay friends. Hence we peel back the crime and find lesbian motives, lesbian victimization. The fears of the city which are metaphorized in the crime are not so much fears of the mass as fears of specific groups within it – misogynist men, confused women, anti-gay or anti-abortion lobbies. Other spectres loom large which are distinctly non-modernist: AIDS among gay friends, for example. The world is peopled by those affected by gay and lesbian issues, and the crimes against them. Thus the interest and importance of the lesbian crime novel is that it firmly reasserts the relevance of crimes against otherness, and the specific susceptibilities of those so designated *to* crimes, as well as crimes within otherness.

In transgressing the genre, the lesbian fictive voice renders crime more complex, and in many senses more human. Despite its allegiance to elements of hard-boiled style, the lesbian crime novel is up close and personal. As a methodology for reading crime it provides many challenges. The question, 'But is it crime fiction?' can clearly be asked. Yet, as I have argued above, we could ask this of any crime text. Is it about crime, or about being lesbian? But is crime about crime, or about being old, or young, or black, or powerful, or powerless? Crime is made to stand proxy for so many things that this is hardly a helpful question. One thing that is clear, is that lesbian perspectives on crime are very much lacking in most media cultures, being usually no more than the province of the sniggering *frisson* provided every now and again in the tabloid newspapers when it is suspected that lesbian jealousy may be the motive for murder. A consideration of transgression and crime, or indeed a transgressive criminology, become more possible once the prism on crime is shifted to a lesbian focus.

Can a crime novel thus be a political text, a transgressive text, a voyeuristic text, a text of place, an anything text? What does it mean to say that it is 'about' crime? This poses a problem for Christopher Gair (1997: 111), who, as noted above, found himself forced to ask 'When is a crime novel not a crime novel?' in reading the work of Barbara Wilson. The problem is that Barbara Wilson's work *cheats*. It sneakily eats away at the conventions of traditional crime fiction, 'seems only peripherally concerned with what has been conventionally defined as "crime"' and 'even then', he says, referring to Wilson's *Gaudi Afternoon* (1991),

> only as one strand within an infinite network of textuality incorporating not only novels and films, but also architecture, sexual politics, and the border between the cultures of East and West. As it explores such issues, the book blurs the oppositions – fact and fiction, self and other, male and female, mother and father, 'normal' and 'deviant' – upon which most other crime fiction and, more widely, Western rationalism has depended.
>
> (Gair 1997; 111–12)

Gair worries away at the problem of intertextuality; while the novel involves a repeat kidnapping the plot is 'often bewildering' (1997: 112), it seems more concerned with quotations from other crime fiction, and there is a lamentable absence of murder. He defines it as unequivocally postmodernist detective fiction. For him, it subverts the genre, adopts devices such as collage and pastiche, is deconstructive and fragmentary in its treatment of identity. Moreover, he notes, the concept of the self in the novel is 'primarily linguistic' (1997: 116), there is a confusing array of gender identities, Wilson makes constant references to architecture and thereby refers to the novel's own construction within the novel itself, and in general she decentres perspective. The function of the detective in *Gaudi Afternoon* does seem to be restoring a pre-existing order, concedes Gair, but at the same time making clear how that social order was constructed. The self is not unitary but a bricolage, and the aesthetics are transgressive.

Gair's experience of reading crime is quite dissimilar from that of Young. *Gaudi Afternoon*, he feels,

> stretches the genre of crime fiction to such an extent that it eventually implodes: the novel incorporates American popular

> culture, and arrives at a form of closure satisfactory to its
> American parent–protagonists, but refuses to privilege these
> values over the encyclopaedic allusions to global cultures
> which, like Gaudi's architecture, constitute the novel.
>
> (Gair 1997: 123)

One refers to a 'modernist' text, then; the other to a 'post-modernist'.
'When a crime novel is not a crime novel' is, when it is not modernist.
Otherwise it 'stretches the genre'. Nevertheless, what both readings do is
treat the fictive voice as an authentic social document about crime: about
fear, victimization, pleasure, pain, voyeurism, greed. This is the utility of
the fictive voice to the criminologist, and as such a voice it is neither more
nor less valid than criminological 'research' or policy pronouncement on
crime. That the fictive genre can be deemed to use crime as a metaphor
or a space, rather than be interested in crime for its own sake does not
invalidate this point either. Crime in everyday culture is a metaphor or a
space – for the end of dreams, for the passing of time, for the fear and
vulnerability which so often accompany failing faculties and the increasing certitude of death.

To illustrate this use of crime as a metaphor, I will give an example
from some ethnographic research I carried out with elderly people in the
northeast of England in the 1990s with a group of young researchers
(Brown 1994). Over and again we heard situated versions of Pearson's
(1985) well-known conceptualization of 'respectable fears'. As Pearson
famously demonstrated, crime is essentially about a 'structure of feeling',
since

> We know only too well the string of accusations . . . the break
> up of the family and traditional authority, the erosion of
> 'community' in place of urban rootless anonymity . . . the surge
> of irrepressible freedoms among the rising generation. These
> amount to a distinctive 'structure of feeling' with an emphatic
> post-war stamp upon them, which inclines us towards a dread
> for the future.
>
> (Pearson 1985: 15)

Explicitly, 'our' adults' accounts of crime and the decline of community culminated in a dread for the future:

I mean, I lived in West Terrace down there, and I lived in Louisa Street down there, and it was a good area, all the old houses, man, they've all gone. Everything is gone now, old pubs and everything, but I mean if you want to go anywhere, you want to go in the Newmarket [pub] and ask people in there about this area. It's getting worse. They break into the Newmarket all the time. They break into them shops over there . . . I don't think there'll be any bloody future before long.

(Brown 1994)

Ethnographic narratives which tell people's stories about how crime is situated in culture for them may be read in the same way as fictive texts; crime is both real and metaphoric, but so often it is metaphoric. The ethnographic narrative, like the fictive narrative, is an expression of voices, of selves, of the multiplicities of identities. Both arise out of the remembered or imagined, both depend for their grounding on the conscious or unconscious pains of modernity or its passing. Read as crime texts, they both situate crime in relation to memory and transformations of identity, and the same can be said of the historical record. This is not to deride the usefulness of field research to criminology, but rather to question the privileged claim of 'empirical' criminological research over the fictive voice. The fictive voice refracts the culture through its own generic prism. The research voice offers a different sort of prism, but it is still a prism.

In general, crime fiction has tended to remain the province of those working in literature and cultural studies, rather than that of criminologists. For criminologists, it has largely been treated fairly crudely or as a matter for content analysis. Sparks's (1992) sophisticated analysis of televisual crime fiction remains the most theoretically advanced treatment of the fictive voice (see also, for discussions of crime fiction, Muncie and McLaughlin 1996; Reiner 1997). In the discussion above I have attempted to show how crime fiction, treated as a textually mediated voice, offers a way of reading crime which is as valid as any other. The fictive voice, in other words, offers a particular modality or gaze upon crime. Emanating from the imperatives of modernism discussed in Chapter 1, it both refracts crime through modernism, and refracts crime back upon modernism, in Haut's (1999) term 'skip tracing the culture'.

More than just 'skip tracing' the culture however, it turns back upon the culture a particular knowledge form about crime, one that interprets crime and offers definitions of it. Often crime fiction works with crime as a metaphorical space, in a way that mirrors the kinds of metaphoric space occupied by crime in culture generally. In a mediatized culture, where knowledge forms about crime are all mediated in some way, all can be read as text; crime fiction works within the 'crime implosion' both to reflect and to challenge 'conventional wisdom' about crime. It also offers a unique way of experiencing crime, enabling both the pleasures and the pains to be vicariously pursued. At its cutting edge, it transcends the boundaries of the fictive, and this will be discussed further in the following chapter. 'True crime' stories, for example, and more ominously 'mondo' fiction and 'snuff' films, take the fictive voice to darker and perhaps more disturbing realms. The mainstream of crime fiction, however, is primarily important for its popular cultural voice, and the next section pursues the importance of mediated crime as popular culture through law and film.

Reading law film

If crime fiction offers a unique perspective on crime, then, it also does something more profound. As part of a knowledge implosion, it questions what we take to be valid knowledge about crime, and indeed what we take to be crime, as well as how we react to it. Reading law through film can have an equally subverting effect.

The elision of 'fact' and 'fiction', the subtext of much of this book, has a long pedigree in films depicting law and lawyers, which, in their quest for 'legal realism' frequently take real cases as the basis for dramatic lawyering (Greenfield and Osborn 1996), or address principles of justice in which the legal system is seen to fail. This opens up some complex areas of thought about what relationship media culture bears to law, as discussed more generally in Chapter 1. As an aspect of popular culture and of media representation, what does the fictive voice 'do' to law?

The 'suitability' of justice and the law for dramatic representation is clear, and operates at a number of levels. First it is metaphysically satisfying; 'natural justice' constitutes an ideology of first principles which remains an enduring source of human endeavour. Second, modernist western systems of justice, however flawed they are seen to be, are frequently assumed within hegemonic discourse to be features of post-Enlightenment rational governance, embodying principles on which the legitimacy of authority depends. They are therefore de facto legitimate and desirable focuses of public debate. Third, the law makes good movies. This has been framed nicely by Greenfield and Osborn (1995: 108) as a question of 'why do we (and film makers) love the law?' The innately dramatic properties of the courtroom, as they point out, were eloquently demonstrated by Pat Carlen in the ethnography *Magistrates' Justice* (1974). In brief, all films that address issues of legality and justice appeal to a strong and vocal 'popular legal imagination'.

'The Law', taken as a popular concept, provides an endless fund of ethical articulations. The 'law film' – which is defined here not just as film with a courtroom drama at its centre, but more broadly as a film that centralizes the law – is compelling because just as 'everyone' has a view on crime (what it is, its causes, and its consequences for victims) so 'everyone' has a view on the law – by which I mean what the law is, what it is for, and what it should be. The 'black letter lawyer'[5] is a rarity in everyday life; rather social life is peopled by jurisprudential subjects, and framings of the law are articulated constantly in popular consciousness. Why law and popular culture? My response would be that this is the grounded theory of the law, for as Smart (1989: 68–9) notes in relation to the 'quest for a feminist jurisprudence',

> the overarching problem that I have with the quest for a
> feminist jurisprudence which takes the form of constructing a
> general theory of the law, is the question of whether it is worth
> the effort of merely replacing one abstraction of the law with
> another . . . feminist work has a growing affinity with the idea
> of analysing the micro-politics of power . . . the last thing we
> need is a feminist jurisprudence on a grand scale which will set
> up general principles based on abstractions as opposed to the
> realities of women's (and men's) lives.

The law is not a set of abstractions, but a process of ongoing debate; moreover it is a question not just of what *is* the law, but of what is *outside* the law, and this is a process that occurs in the public, in the popular, domain. If law is a site of power, then conversely it is also a site of resistance, a characteristic of any discursive domain, as Foucault (1977) has demonstrated. Hence popular culture is as valid a source for reading law as are formal legal texts. Thus as Sherwin (1996: 71) argues, 'law is both a co-producer and a by-product of mainstream culture. The stamp of the latter continually falls upon the meanings the law produces'.

A frequently used example of this has been the film adaptation of Harper Lee's novel *To Kill a Mockingbird* (first published in 1960; film adaptation 1962). Here the 'story of law' unfolds as an ideological battleground for the structural and cultural tensions of race, gender and class in the American South, as Atticus Finch, a white liberal lawyer, struggles to utilize the discourses of a supposedly impartial justice in the defence of a poor black man accused of raping a 'white trash' woman. The discourse of the law is shown to be precisely that, a text in which all the principal actors refuse to follow the script, for the strictly legal and technical applications of the legal code mean nothing in the face of the entrenched visions of moral and racialized justice embraced by the Southern code. The problem was that it seemed Mayella Ewell, the woman in question, had apparently 'encouraged' the black defendant; not only this, but he had refused her 'attentions' in a polite manner. The Southern code required that her reputation be vindicated. In the end, what counted were the divisions of white-dominated America, a racialized fear and loathing so deep and so institutionalized that any liberal notion of justice must fall before it.

Fundamental legal issues work so well on film that innumerable examples could be used; Greenfield and Osborn (1996) for example, cite among others *A Dry White Season* (1989) featuring a human rights lawyer in apartheid South Africa; *In the Name of the Father* (1993) which is loosely based on the miscarriage of justice involving Gerry Conlon and the Guildford Four; and *Let Him Have It* (1991) which is based on the case of Derek Bentley, sentenced to death and subsequently hanged on dubious evidence.

As a mode of reading law, moreover, the cinema, together with other popular cultural forms, is rich in intertextuality. Its references to cases 'in reality' have already been mentioned. More than this, debates surrounding cinematic representations of justice find reverberations not just among its lay audience but are framed as relevant within legal debate itself, as we shall see below, and further, frequently form the basis of contention within the 'effects' debate, as discussed in Chapter 4. The popular legal imagination, or pop law (Redhead 1995) is arguably the most predominant form of law in culture. While everyone's lives are circumscribed by the discourses of the law, even defined by these discourses, it is mediated discourses that figure most prominently, and within this the fictive voice of the law is a strong one. Focusing here on the criminal law, we need to conceptualize 'the criminal law' precisely *as* a field of discursive practices. Lacey *et al.* (1990: 1) suggest a modernist critique of the law as social construction:

> We conceive criminal law very broadly as one way in which a society . . . both defines or constructs, and responds to, 'deviance' . . . if we understand deviance to mean behaviour which departs from social norms recognised by criminal law, the notion is circular: criminal law claims to respond to deviance, yet deviance (for the purposes of criminal law) can only be defined by looking to criminal law itself. Evidently, we have to look outside criminal law to get any grip on its nature and significance.

Popular cultural forms such as the cinema are both informed by and transformative of discourses of the law. This is not about how the law is practised in 'real' courtrooms, or how 'real' judgements are made in 'real' cases, but a question of how the law is publicly talked about. This is not simply a matter of 'popular opinion' about the law; it is about how discourses of transgression become spectacle. Law and spectacle become indivisible. The notion that 'the law' exists outside of the popular imagination becomes difficult to sustain, for the essence of critical socio-legal studies that explicate the law as a social construction, then mean that it is inevitably a mediated construction. The role of the cinema in this is to present 'cinematic parables of (in)justice' (Greenfield and Osborn 1996).

In this sense, the cinema by definition provides us with powerful readings of out-laws, and thereby of legal critique. To explore the implications of this, I will take the example of Ridley Scott's *Thelma and Louise* (1991). The film depicts two women who are 'thrown' outside of the law. A basic reading of the plot line is as follows (see Spelman and Minow 1996, for numerous reviews). An unhappy waitress, Louise (Susan Sarandon) and her friend Thelma (Geena Davis), a housewife in a loveless marriage, decide to go away for a 'girls' weekend' fishing to get away from their everyday existences. On their way to the cabin they decide to stop and have a drink. Thelma has a few drinks too many in the truck-stop bar and ends up dancing and flirting with a redneck. The man gets the wrong idea and does not take Thelma's refusal of him lightly. As he begins to sexually assault Thelma, Louise points a loaded gun at him, but instead of backing off meekly he insults the women, and in a momentary transportation of rage, Louise shoots and kills him. Thus 'accidentally' ending up on the run they find themselves heading for Mexico. Initially Thelma wants to do things by the book, but Louise quickly makes her see that, since everyone in the bar saw her dancing and flirting with the man in a highly drunken state, she would not stand a chance of fairness at the hands of the legal system. Things go from bad to worse. They initially get money from Louise's boyfriend (Michael Madsen), but Thelma loses her head over a handsome young man (Brad Pitt) with whom she has her first decent sex for ages. He steals the money and they are left broke. Thelma robs a convenience store and this confirms them as outlaws and fugitives. After this a buddy/road movie unfolds against glorious scenery with Thelma and Louise, knowing there is no going back, relentlessly executing natural justice against the men who stand in their way or attempt to subordinate them. This includes locking a highway patrolman in the trunk of his car (having thoughtfully shot air holes for him to breathe); and more menacingly, blowing up a petrol tanker driven by a lewd trucker who repeatedly harasses and sexually insults them. They are finally tracked by the police after Louise talks to a detective (Harvey Keitel) on a pay phone for too long explaining that 'this whole thing is an accident'. Knowing that there will be no recourse to justice for them in a male-dominated legal culture, they make a choice at the end of the film. In a burst of exhilarating freedom they join hands and drive their T-Bird into the Grand Canyon – better the jaws of death than the arms of the law.

As well as being acclaimed as the first feminist road movie, *Thelma and Louise* intrigued because it highlighted the sheer impossibility of legal justice from a feminist perspective. For our purposes it is an interesting case study in reading law, because of the legal debate that it generated and in particular, the huge response it evoked on several levels: first, its box-office popularity, second, the wide coverage it received in the popular press, third, the kinds of academic and popular debate it generated especially on the Internet, and not least, the way in which connections were made between it and 'real life' cases, of which I shall later use the example of Lorena Bobbitt.

Linda Lopez McAlister (http://www.mith2umd.edu/WomensStudies/ FilmReviews/thelma+louise-mcalister/(accessed 9 August 2002)), reviewing the film, on its relase in 1991, for The Women's Show WMNF-FM in Tampa, Florida proclaimed:

> Feminists! If you don't go and see another film all year, you're going to want to see 'Thelma and Louise' . . . it's . . . a philosophical film, one that existentialist feminist Simone de Beauvoir would love, for it depicts two ordinary women living under patriarchal domination in small-town Arkansas who actually succeed in achieving their liberation . . . as they become outlaws they are outside not only the civil laws but also the Laws of the Father as well and they begin to discover and express their own potential, their own feelings, their own strength . . . they achieve what the existentialist philosophers call transcendence . . . and it is a stinging indictment of society that the choice they make [to drive off the cliff] is the sane and reasonable one.

The C.G. Jung page on the other hand, took a slightly more psycho-analytic perspective. Despite its 'liberating achievement', we are told, 'the film confirms the old premise that women can never disentangle themselves from men – except in death' (Williams, D. http://www cgjungpage.org/films/tandl.html (accessed 9 August 2002).

Thelma, according to Williams, is a study in 'learned helplessness' whose internal world is peopled by male 'psycho killers' and conversely, for her, all men are 'psychos'. This explains her disastrous encounters and also explains driving off the cliff, the only way to get free. Clearly the C.G. Jung page constructs a different legal subject than does the above 'feminist' reading; certainly the aspect of responsibility is different. Rather than the structural inequalities of patriarchal law which propel Thelma and Louise into outlaw status, from Williams's reading it is internalized oppression that prevents autonomous 'rational' reaction to men's actions.

Whichever reading of the many proposed and preferred Internet post-ings is taken poses a methodological question about law and popular culture. The debate, however tongue-in-cheek or scurrilous some of the contributions, shows that reading law is a multifaceted process. Inter-textually, this crossed over into debate amongst academic lawyers; Spelman and Minow (1992) argued that:

> *Thelma and Louise* provoked widespread and intense public debates. The film gives us an occasion to explore not only what it means in our society for women to be outlaws, but also: (1) how different kinds of viewers might perceive and judge outlaw women; (2) how class and race, along with gender, may influence viewer understandings of outlaw figures; and (3) what the world and moral reasoning might look like from the perspective of the women characters cast as outlaws.

Spelman and Minow emphasize the role of *Thelma and Louise* as an example of popular legal culture, particularly commenting not just upon general public reaction, but that of the mass media, which they note often framed public reaction as a matter of gender warfare. What is this articulating? Ultimately, they conclude, since the law has done little to protect women from violence, rape, and sexual abuse, on one level Louise's act of murder is quite explicable, since 'law's centrality does not mean its utility'. The film is central to popular legal culture because, they argue elsewhere,

> It does seem clear that some viewers who love the film greatly admire the outlaw qualities of Thelma and Louise, while many viewers upset by the film are worried that it glorifies an ignoble kind of lawlessness. As Callie Khouri [who wrote the screenplay] has suggested, perhaps both reactions mistake the film for a kind of political treatise. But even if the film is not such a treatise, it is naïve or disingenuous to think about it and the reaction to it in isolation from a volatile political climate in which those clamouring for 'law and order' rarely join protests against the everyday forms of the abuse of women on exhibition in the film.
>
> (Spelman and Minow 1996: 266)

In an online discussion and study forum, Spelman and Minow took the issue further by linking the case of *Thelma and Louise* with the real-life case of Lorena Bobbitt. Whereas the former raised issues of serious legal debate from fiction, the latter case was treated by many with as much seriousness as if it were a fictive artefact of popular culture. In 1994, Lorena Bobbitt was brought to trial for castrating her allegedly abusive husband John Bobbitt. Having genitally mutilated her husband she discarded his penis, but then alerted police and the medical profession. Emergency surgery was performed and John Bobbitt's penis was reattached. The irony of the case was that in a mirror image of *Thelma and Louise*, it was not treated seriously at all in much popular debate. The *Chicago Tribune* (19 January 1994) headlined 'Bobbitt Tale Needs Happy Ending After the Bobbitt Salute':

> I hear reporters covering the Lorena Bobbitt trial are placing side bets on whether the two will get back together again after all the fuss has died down . . . Stranger things have happened. Beaten wives have taken their husbands back . . . Raped dates have dated their rapists again. It doesn't make the original charge any less valid . . . Besides, it will make a much better movie, won't it? Everyone speculates on how much money the two can make selling their stories to the networks . . . And what better ending for the story of an allegedly abused wife who cuts off her husband's penis, drives it out to the country, throws it out the window, tells police about it and doctors sew it back on and she goes on trial, than to have the two kiss and make up in the end? Hollywood loves a happy ending . . .
>
> When CNN interrupted live Bobbitt trial coverage to pick up live coverage of President Clinton's European trip . . . CNN's switchboard was inundated with telephone calls from angry viewers . . . It was left to a level-headed CNN anchor to assure viewers in tones that could only be described as apologetic that coverage of the fate of the Ukraine's SS-19 nuclear silos would not prevent the network from broadcasting the Bobbitt trial 'in its entirety'. Every moment of The Trial had been videotaped and the network would not rest until all of it was aired.

The Washington Post (11 January 1994), while treating the legal issues more seriously, still could not resist the pop culture element:

> But what's unfolding in the courthouse and rising up through all those media transmission towers is more potent than Howard Stern, Jay Leno, and David Letterman – it's a new

myth in a canon of female retribution fantasy as recent as
'Thelma and Louise' and as ancient as Greek mythology. Put in
another pop culture context: 'Touch her again and you're dead'
sings Juliana Hatfield, whose current hit album is part of the
wave of aggressive young female performers decrying violence
against women. The song, 'Dame With a Rod' envisions a gun-
toting heroine rescuing an endangered woman from a date-
rape scenario.

Somewhere, a young woman is writing a song about Lorena
Bobbitt.

While all the furore over the movie-turned-legal debate *Thelma and
Louise* and the legal-trial-turned-made-for-TV-movie of the Bobbitts was
taking place, a much lesser-noticed English film had been released in the
United Kingdom. It fails to make it into many movie guides; *Dirty Weekend* (1993) is almost entirely about natural justice. In it the protaganist,
Bella, escapes to find solace and peace by herself in a Brighton flat. From
this point onwards, she is beleaguered by a peeping Tom, or more seriously, a menacing voyeur, who torments and frightens her with his surveillance of her most private moments and his phone calls. 'One day', the
film narrates, 'Bella woke up and decided she'd had enough'. Based on a
novel by Helen Zahavi (1991) which was condemned in some circles as
amoral and pornographic, the film was described by one reviewer as a
'moral tale for the 'nineties' (http://www.futuremovies.co.uk). Bella (Lia
Williams) commences to execute natural justice. In her process of
'reclaiming the night' she breaks into the voyeur's flat and violently murders him. However, once inspired, she doesn't stop there, and begins to
avenge all acts of masculinist oppression. The casualties include a sexual
fetishist delegate to a conference and a misogynist and sadistic dentist.
Bella's spree of death and mayhem is never punished; in fact it is portrayed as immensely pleasurable and cathartic. Finally she is able to walk
along the beach at night. The book's author is quoted as denying that she
is anti-men, but asserting that society is anti-women. She wanted to let
Bella do

> what women are not allowed to do. In the final chapter she
> walks along the beach, and I long to do that in the middle of
> the night, but I knew that if I did that and I were attacked the

judge would say 'she asked for it'. Why am I not allowed to do that?

(Zahavi, quoted on review site http://www.futuremovies.co.uk)

Zahavi's rhetorical question, as with many of the issues raised in the *Thelma and Louise*/Lorena Bobbitt debate, could be approached in legal terms from a perspective offered by McColgan (2000) in an academic text entitled *Women Under the Law: The False Promise of Human Rights*, whose fact-list on women and violence makes impressive reading and deserves quoting at length:

> The true level of women's victimisation is probably considerably higher than that suggested by government statistics . . . Recent figures published by the British Medical Association estimate that one in four women has been the victim of domestic violence. Every week in the US, around 2,500 women are raped by current or former male partners and a further 90 are murdered, nine out of ten of the latter by men. The bulk of violent assaults by women are carried out by men known to them. In the US for example, 75 per cent of single-offender violence against women fits this category and, although women are only two-thirds as likely as men to suffer violent attack, six to ten times as many women as men are attacked by someone known to them . . . In 1994, more than 50 per cent of homeless women and children were fleeing violence and, according to FBI statistics, five women were beaten up by men every minute of every day and over 1,400 murdered by male intimates that year. And in the same year, 'between 50 and 85 per cent of the over 4 million women receiving AFDC [Assistance for Families with Dependent Children] have recently experienced or are currently victims of physical and emotional violence at the hands of the adult men in their lives . . . a 1991 US Senate report recorded that '50 per cent of women do not use public transit after dark and 75 per cent of women do not go to the movies alone after dark due to fear of rape'.
>
> (McColgan 2000: 193–4)

It is not my intention here to enter into a debate on the adequacy or otherwise of such statistics; their import is that figures like these form the fulcrum of a weighty legal debate over women as 'subjects of criminal law' (McColgan 2000: 192). Her point is that 'women have no constitutionally protected rights not to be beaten and raped by their husbands' (McColgan 2000: 198). Legal anomalies follow; women may not be able to mobilize a self-defence plea (in US law) if the threat to which they respond does not appear to have been 'imminent' (McColgan 2000: 201) despite a recent history of continual abuse; moreover, McColgan claims, even where the response is to direct threat, self-defence pleas are 'frequently rejected' (2000: 201); she concludes that 'women who have been the victims of domestic violence have gained little from the rights entrenched in the US constitution' (2000: 216).

Similar points supported by numerous case law examples are made in Nicolson and Bibbings (2000). That women stand outside the law in many respects is a tenet of feminist legal studies (Smart 1989; Nicolson and Bibbings 2000); what these films do is posit a feminist legal ethical discourse which by clear implication subverts the law and renders its language irrelevant, its hegemonic force impotent. This force, when women seek to be served by the law rather than stand outside it, is seen in *The Accused* (1988) a story, drawing its plot from a real case, which depicts a working-class young woman's battle for justice within the legal system after she is gang-raped in the back room of a bar. Much less fictional in tone than either *Thelma and Louise* or *Dirty Weekend*, *The Accused* peels back the supposed impartiality of the law to display its relentless and destructive force on women, particularly those without economic status. That the protaganist eventually achieves 'justice' of a kind is overlaid by the punishments by other means – of threats to her person by the perpetrators and their supporters and humiliations by the courts – that she experiences along the way. The fictive voice proclaims her to be 'the accused' in a seething critique of the law. The dialectical relationship between cinematic representation and 'real law' is thus a powerful cultural dynamic which both articulates the practice of the law and refracts it through the fictive voice, while reflecting back upon the law and standing in judgement upon it. The quest for justice and the consequences of injustice, as well as questions of what comes before the law, can no longer be easily separated into fact and fiction. Cinematic representations of the law construct popular conceptions of it, and insofar as the law is part of public culture, they enter into the law (Strickland 1992).

It is however, not simply the message of the cinematic that is at stake here; to revert to the discussion in Chapter 1, it also the medium. The multilayered visual language of film lends itself peculiarly to a postmodern cultural edge (Denzin 1991) which enables and encourages an intimacy with the surface that may create popular law, but at the same time reduces the law to, if anything, a play upon itself. It is here, I would argue, that the genre of the 'law film' by definition ends in the 'death of law' (Redhead 1995). Thus *Natural Born Killers* (1994) utilizes this quality to render itself 'a-law'; it simply has no statement to make about the law, for its only statement is self-referential with reference to a mosaic of self-generated intra-textualities. Its concerns are aesthetic and narcissistic, and outmoded concepts such as 'justice' are no more than imagic fragments of its superbly meaningless humour. There are no subjects, no objects; its violence is everything and nothing, since the 'violence' is everywhere but at the same time constantly rendered impotent by its mindless syntheticity. 'Micky and Mallory' never were; as soon as they are manufactured they are demanufactured as the events in the film are mediatized into and out of existence. Any externalities the film has are only to other surfaces which equally stand outside of any narrative framework. It is 'Baudrillardian' to the point of being heavily laboured; its transgressions transgress nothing except other images. This is why the media effects panic over the film (Harbord 1997) was so ludicrous; not so much that the supposed 'copycat' killings bore little or no resemblance to the film's violence, but that there was really nothing to resemble, nothing to imitate. Thus Redhead (1995: 88) reverts to the novel form to read crime and law:

> In what is increasingly being seen by cultural critics as
> 'postmodern' culture – 'post-literate culture to many other
> writers – in which . . . a visually-oriented mass media loops
> soundbites, public opinion survey results and news-as-
> entertainment for a global audience glued to television and
> video screens . . . the novel form is still a tempting style to use
> for the interrogation of 'rough justice' cases and real-life crime
> incidents.

The intentionally meaningless postmodern cinema is post-law; since by definition a 'postmodern jurisprudence' must be a contradiction in terms, unless it counts as 'what the law is not', in which case films like *Natural Born Killers* would of course represent whatever it isn't

(Redhead 1995: 79). Even then, this would suggest a binary opposition between the real and the imagined, an already dead project in post-modern culture. In this case a certain resonance may be found in the idea that postmodern film could be seen as a way of comparing law to 'other ways of imagining the real' (Santos 1987; cited in Redhead 1995: 79). In the end, postmodern cinema may serve to remind us of the vistas beyond the law; more importantly, it may be read as a portent of the death of law in a postliterate, visual, non-discursive world. These debates, however, are more relevant when related to the cyber than the cinematic, and will be discussed further in Chapter 5.

Reading the fictive: doing the culture

In the discussion above, I have provided some examples of the way in which attempts have been made to read the fictive of crime and the law, either through the predominantly linguistic, as with the novel form, or the predominantly dialogic and visual, as with cinema, and have drawn a line under postmodern cinema as of limited utility in reading crime and the law. In this section I wish to address more methodological problems; having argued the importance of the fictive as a mode of interrogating the social, one is left with the question of how to 'do the culture'. Popular culture by definition belongs to everyone; I am refuting an approach, therefore, which requires the application of particular academic techniques deriving from literary studies, cultural studies, or indeed 'formal' law or criminology. Instead I am suggesting that reading the fictive is a social activity that may be informed by all or none of the paradigmatic requirements of specific 'disciplines'. If it is anything, it is a uniquely archaeological, anthropological, biographical and personal journey into crime and law.

It is *archaeological* in the sense that the text of novel or film may be seen as artefactual in its relation to a culture or cultures. To this extent it does not just bear one relationship to culture, but many; and how that relationship is read will depend upon what questions of utility we wish to address. Reading the fictive is also archaeological in the excavatory sense; in scraping away at the layer upon layer of significations in the text we build up an increasingly detailed picture of the questions of meaning that we might wish to answer. Within this our journey is also historical, the text being, while in the present, also a relic of time past.

It is *anthropological*, because we are journeying into cultures of crime and law, not simply addressing them from the outside. We are not merely reading the text as ethnography; we are the ethnographers. The text itself constitutes, as well as represents, a cultural world which we become part of, and alter, through our participation in it. In doing this we face all the dilemmas of the anthropologist. We must address questions of difference – the difference between the world we are leaving and the world we are entering. The language, the customs (genre or conventions), the rituals and practices of the text are not those of our native culture. At the same time, we can never 'go native' in the text since we may share its life-world but not be ultimately of it. This requires a constant reflexivity in our activities of reading. We cannot carry chunks of its culture away as trophies; we cannot adequately describe its culture.

However carefully, as archaeologists, we scrape away, label, file, arrange, the question of difference always remains. Within these twin field exercises of archaeology and anthropology, we must constantly address the biographical and the personal. The latter are what we bring into the text with us; what has made us what we are. The contrasting and yet on some levels comparable interpretations of Haut (1999), Vanacker (1997), and Young (1996) in relation to the crime novel show this, as do the numerous Internet debates on *Thelma and Louise*. Our memories, experiences, selves, immersed in the text, act as a prism on the text, and at the same time, we are altered by our experience within it.

What does this kind of textual journey give us? Certainly not a unitary meaning, or set of unitary meanings. Nor, in the empirical sense, an 'answer', but perhaps more of a history. To explore these questions further, I use as an example a reading not of crime or law, but of the male body; a choice made for methodological and not substantive reasons. Joanna Bourke, a lecturer in economic and social history, took upon the task of interrogating the male body in the First World War. She writes:

> The body was the subject of both imagination and experience.
> Men could be able bodied: fortified, vigorous. Yet, their bodies
> could also be mangled, freshly torn from the war and
> competing for economic and social resources with civilians.
> Although men might possess useful bodies capable of
> performing their allotted civic and military functions efficiently,
> they might choose instead to malinger by refusing to
> acknowledge their duties in the workplace and in the armed

forces. For some, theirs was the beautiful physique, adored by
other men . . . yet commonly offered to women. They
expressed their freedom through their bodies, but were
besieged on all sides by military, medical and educational
disciplines which were governed by different aesthetics,
economic objectives, and moral economies. The corporeal male
would eventually become a corpse on some battlefield or
mortuary slab, inviting reconstruction through the memories of
beloved ones. All men's bodies were endowed with signs and
declarations of age, generation, class and ethnicity. It was
within this socially constructed 'frame' that bodies lived, were
imagined, and died.

(Bourke 1996: 11)

However distant this seems from the universes of crime and the law,
the problems of reading culture are similar. What faces Bourke is an
immense task of almost indefinable proportions, for war and the male
body, like crime and the criminal, occupy both a factual and a metaphorical space; one of definition (what is the male body in war?) and
utility (why do I want to know? What do I want it to tell me?). In the
context of the Great War, she is concerned with 'the values applied to the
body and the disciplines applied to masculinity' (Bourke 1996). She is
faced with a vast array of potentially illuminating cultural texts: literary
genres (war poetry and literature), popular literature, including
children's fiction, newspapers, war cartoons, war propaganda, medical
and military photographic archives and military and medical records,
diaries and letters . . . Indeed, some of her subject matter is not in fact so
distant after all from the study of crime and the law; on the exposing of
malingerers seeking to avoid their war duty, she notes:

Exposing malingerers was an important business: indeed, as
one army surgeon responded when asked if he was a doctor,
'No . . . I am a detective'. This metaphor was widespread, as
attested by Dr Henry Cohen's admission that it was 'tempting
to compare the methods of diagnosis with those of crime
detection.'

(Bourke 1996: 89)

It should not be surprising of course, that the excavation of one site of modernism should parallel that of another. War and crime, as Haut (1999) suggests, are not so far removed. Bourke faces the same interpretive puzzle as the reader of crime and law through cultural texts, in one sense taking the text on its own terms while in another altering it. What she does not do, and cannot do, is choose between her texts as 'more' or 'less' truthful, 'more' or 'less' useful; they are all cultural artefacts. In her own particular archaeological and anthropological expedition she delimits the mutilating of bodies, the malingering of bodies, the bonding of bodies, the inspecting of bodies, and the re-membering of bodies. All of these male bodies differently constituted and represented and refracted through the cultural resources at her disposal, she regards as crucially indexical to the construction of masculinity and the masculine through the Great War. In turn the war itself is constructed by the male body. What she arrives at in the end is a cultural collage through which she weaves an interpretive warp. Perhaps if anything is missing from Bourke's traverse, it is Bourke herself. The anonymous documentarian, her (presumably) femininity is apparently absent (yet of course it cannot be) from her reading of the culture, as is her epoch (though clearly it is highly visible through the application of terms like 'masculinities'). It is this cultural specificity of reading which if anything, needs acknowledgement.

Like any cultural text, the texts of novel and film may be treated not as reflecting, nor necessarily as self-consciously interpreting, but as interrogating and refracting, as indexically linking 'reality and representation'. That there is no one reading of crime and the law should be treated as axiomatic, the corollary, that the fictive voice can be as creative and useful as any other in that reading process, is also true. While the good ethnography may offer properties of systematic reiteration or more 'direct' access to a wide and complex range of experiences, its own form of mediation also clearly operates. I have sought to demonstrate this elsewhere in relation to youth and crime (Brown 1998). In relation to a classic example of youth culture research such as Willis' *Learning to Labour* (1977) for example, I have noted that:

> Despite a sensitive ethnographic study and an excellent account
> of the development of oppositional subcultures . . . his
> attempts to theorize the complex relationship between the
> boys' own perceptions of their culture and its structural
> significance leads Willis to the conclusion that they have a

'partial penetration' of class relations which finds expression in
their focal concerns . . . ultimately youth are made to stand
proxy for yet another series of adult longings and
preoccupations.

(Brown 1998: 35)

Thus to reiterate, I am not suggesting for a moment that good ethnographies are replaceable by fiction; the two offer quite different modalities. It is that given the highly problematic relationship of *any* account to
'fact', the fictional text can provide a particular and provocative set of
readings. 'Doing the culture' as a questioning and reflexive process must
include, in a mediatized society, the fictive voice. This is not to fall into
a nihilism of 'nothing can be said', but to expand the scope of what *can*
be said. Fictional forms offer a particular opportunity for the inclusion
of 'textual outlaws', for the discovery of transgressive voices and deviant
voices.

4 ■ DOES SPLATTER MATTER? REPRESENTING VIOLENCE, REGULATING CONSUMPTION

In this chapter I shall return to the 'effects debate', which has proved such an 'obligatory passage point' (Callon 1986) in media criminology and within the media more widely. By this, I refer to the sense in which meanings have become so closed around certain representations or images – particularly those defined as 'violent' – that it has become virtually impossible to confront or interrogate them without reference to their possible effects on audience behaviour or attitudes. The history of popular culture and concern over violence is already long and exhaustively documented and is touched upon in Chapter 1 of this volume. Here I intend instead to commit a heresy by questioning whether the effects debate itself is either valid or useful (or, indeed, interesting), and by disputing the common-sensical notion that 'effects' must be central to academic, policy, and public concern. The beast seems to be double headed, facing in one direction toward calls for the regulation of consumption, and in the other toward liberalization, ostensibly on the grounds of evidence for or against the harmful impact of 'excessively' violent images and language. As a result of a constant and contradictory babbel over very narrow definitions of violence (particularly 'sex'n'violence') far more interesting and disturbing questions regarding the mediated practices of violence have been stymied by the politics of media effects, and the seemingly inexhaustible resources of 'reservoirs of dogma' (Murdock 1997) which supply them. It is these latter questions which this chapter seeks to highlight.

A passionate cause: the splatter effect

It seems that one only has to throw enough 'gratuitous' violence or transgressive sex into a book, television programme, or more commonly a film, for it to be debated, denounced and defended until it is either censored or guaranteed a lucrative celebrity and notoriety. Furore follows furore, the examples seem endless. The twists and turns of policy and academic attempts to research and 'prove' effects of media exposure are dizzying in their volume and frequently circular or self-defeating enough to induce migraine. The title for this chapter came from a conscientious student who, having painstakingly gone through his litany of catharsis effect, syringe theory, desensitization theory . . . (see Kidd-Hewitt and Osborne 1995 for a succinct account) and arrived at the stunning conclusion that 'they might all have a bit of something in them', wearily admitted to liking 'splatter' movies and wondered if it mattered? Privately, I wondered too. He seemed reasonably well-adjusted.

As Harbord (1997: 139) points out, 'academia and the media (mis)inform each other, spurring themselves on to suggest or assert a causal link between film and aggression which can never be proved'. Surely in any sane empiricist universe, if 2500 academic studies of screen violence have failed to reach a conclusion (Pearl *et al.* 1982; cited in Harbord 1997: 139), then the wrong question is being asked. Fowles (1999: 20) puts the problem neatly:

> It is widely believed that empirical research has absolutely demonstrated the perils of viewing televised entertainment mayhem. There is good reason for this belief: it is affirmed everywhere, creating a tight discursive skein of conventional wisdom.

In a comprehensive chapter on 'violence, viewing and science' Fowles does us all a great service by braving a comprehensive review of the literature, temporarily taking it 'entirely on its own terms' (1999: 25). I have no desire to repeat the exercise, but readers are highly recommended to view the detritus of the debate as presented by Fowles, wherein they will also find full references to as many studies of 'effects' as they are likely to want to research for themselves. For those remaining unsated, further competent reviews of 'effects' research may be found in Pearl *et al.* (1982) and Howitt (1998). (I am not here distinguishing between study of film, video, and television 'effects', since the 'science' itself is paradigmatically constant, and is what is at issue in the first instance).

The sense of ennui generated for those who do not buy into the claim for media effects on behaviour is recorded neatly by Martin Barker and Julian Petley in their recollections of the release of the Newson Report in 1994 (Newson 1994; Barker and Petley 1997). Barker recalls his assessment of the Newson Report as being 'a thin tissue of claims whose only virtue was that they were what every politician or newspaper wanted to hear' (Barker and Petley 1997: 1). Their edited volume, *Ill Effects: The Media/Violence Debate* provides a definitive collection of writing emanating from a conference which was organized as a critical response to the Newson Report. It followed 'the blank silence we met when we issued [a] counter statement to the Newson Report' (Barker and Petley 1997: 2). The overarching question, it seemed to them, was one of why decades of deeply flawed empirical research and vacuous policy generalizations should continue to have such resonance, and why it was so difficult to make their doubts about such research, doubts shared by at least 23 'leading researchers', heard in the national press (1997: 2).

For Barker and Petley, and the other contributors to the *Ill Effects* collection, what is perplexing is why despite 'bad science' and inconclusive findings, 'effects' has so long remained the dominant research tradition (Murdock 1997). This is an important question and merits some further exploration.

The historical grip of 'effects' hysteria partly has its roots in the hegemony of the notion of 'proper' science (Murdock 1997: 69). As mentioned in the earlier discussion of the 'effects debate' in Chapter 1, Vine (1997) provides a good critique of the 'bad science' of the effects debate. My concern here is even more fundamental. The imagery of controlled experimentation, statistical correlations, and causality exerts a powerful, popular, political and academic force in creating an obligatory passage point through which, it seems, all debate must flow. It is a myth of modernity that the high priesthood of science, promoting a science of causes which may stand apart from other forms of knowledge, is therefore in a position to postulate elements of social life as objectively definable and measurable. An excursion into the social studies of science provides an even more basic questioning of the assumptions behind the effects literature than the well-founded 'bad science' critique.

Real science (that is, the activity of science) contradicts the 'science myth' on a number of levels. I have argued elsewhere (Brown 1991) that the ordering of representations into a relatively coherent formation may be defined as the basis of knowledge. As we decode 'messages' in the 'real world', we produce knowledge. The production of knowledge representations is always a corollary of practical activity, not a result of any necessary correspondence with truth. Knowledge, 'scientific' or otherwise, is, as sociologists of science have long argued, 'the correlate of the historical development of procedures, competences, and techniques relevant in various degrees to the ends or objectives of cultures or subcultures' (Barnes 1977: 6).

Microstudies of science in practice, such as laboratory ethnographies, have consistently shown this to be so (Barnes 1977; Law 1986; Latour 1993). The way in which representations are produced from scientific data are governed by interpretive conventions which are irrefutably social in origin. This is true of criminology (Maguire *et al.* 1997), but it is also true of X-ray crystallography or any other 'scientific' activity, and the question of whether 'social science' can be said to be scientific can be legitimately replaced by one of whether *science* is 'scientific' (Law 1986). The search for any direct correspondence between representation and reality is therefore flawed; what is at issue is the adoption of certain conventions of representation over others. Insofar as actors or groups successfully impose their conventions and conceptions on others who seek to challenge them, then the effect is one of power, not truth. 'Science' is in fact an *effect*, if we are to have an 'effects' debate. As Latour (1986: 273) puts it, those who are powerful are 'those who practically define or redefine what holds everyone together'. In studying the work of scientists, science has been reconceptualized as a product of the closure of controversy around definitions of reality, a process through which certain versions of data and the meaning imputed to it is made to 'stick'.

Callon (1986) has framed this as a four-fold process. First, *problematization*, in which the 'definers' establish themselves as the obligatory passage points through which all messages have to be channelled; second, *interessement*, which forms an alliance between these definers and others involved in the negotiations by placing devices to block out potential challengers; third, *enrolment*, which extracts compliance from other actors (compliance may be gained through physical force, seduction, or simple capitulation); and fourth, the *mobilization of allies*, a 'cascade of intermediaries or spokesmen' [*sic*] who, because they are purportedly representative of others, are taken to stand by proxy for the consensus of countless others (for example, 'society', 'the public') (Latour 1986: 216). Insofar as this process, which Latour terms 'translation', is successful, then 'science' is achieved. These strategies may be thought of as methods by which 'actors and collectivities articulate conceptions of the natural and social world and attempt to impose these on others and the extent to which these are met by success' (Law 1986: 3).

It is symptomatic of the success of the science of 'media effects' that controversy has in large part been so closed around it. To express incredulity that research so 'flawed' could have been accepted so apparently unthinkingly is therefore to misconceive the problem. The truth or otherwise of the knowledge claims made by the discourse of 'effects' is not the issue; rather the 'empirical' question should be one of the elements of successful translation of the world into a universe where 'violence' is successfully defined as an entity in a certain way, where 'variables' are defined in a certain way, and where 'outcomes' are defined in a certain way.

The 'effects' orthodoxy, like any other scientific orthodoxy, is neither more nor less than the successful outcome of a power struggle, the elements of which can only be understood with reference to the processes of the achievement of victory. To understand this fully would require a careful excavation of the archaeology of 'effects knowledge', to examine how successful translation has been achieved. This would include microstudies of the inception and processes of specific research projects, as well as of the politics and policy of funding, the social contexts of dissemination and public legitimation, and the cultural contexts of belief. In one sense it is a shame that this has not to date been undertaken, since a detailed research study of the tradition in the manner of other social research into scientific orthodoxy would probably prove highly illuminating. As things are, victory has tended to be accounted for by reference to the cultural contexts of belief such as is suggested by 'an archaeology of popular anxieties' (Murdock 1997: 83):

> The dominant 'effects' tradition has proved so resilient partly because it chimes with a deeply rooted formation of social fear, which presents the vulnerable, suggestible, and dangerous as living outside the stockade of maturity and reasonableness that

the 'rest of us' take for granted. 'They' are the 'others' 'we' must shield ourselves against.

This draws broadly on the well-known work of Pearson (1983) on 'respectable fears' and usefully situates the success of the strategies of 'effects science' against an analysis of generalized anxiety and the pains of modernity (Pearson 1985). Even more broadly, the 'effects' tradition may be located within a frame, which includes a theory of 'the violence of censure and the censure of violence' in late modernity (Sumner 1997). In an epoch where unreason has been denied legitimacy, it is easy to mislay the fact that censure itself is not particularly 'rational', but

> in practice, as we know from everyday life, very often the facts of the case are more complex than they first seemed, our ethics are rarely consistently and abstractly applied, our implicit explanations are structured more by our desire to condemn than the facts of the case, and the context in which judgement is made can colour all.
>
> (Sumner 1997: 3–4)

That there are elements of our culture that require the rationalization of censure does not make censure necessarily rational. The success of the 'blaming strategies' that attribute powers of malevolent and pernicious influence to media violence is not, from this perspective, so strange after all. 'Science' has typically been extended elastically throughout modernity to contain unreason, or the fear of unreason, as the history of madness and mental illness so eloquently demonstrate.

The passion of the 'effects' debate must derive to some extent from the necessity to blame, and in order to blame, the 'problem' must be named. Unfortunately, 'the problem' is far from easy to define. For what are the acts depicted in the media, acts of 'splatter' such as shootings, stabbings, beatings, and sometimes burnings, being blamed? It seems they are being blamed for inducing other people 'in real life' to behave in like manner; for presenting such acts as enjoyable, or necessary, or legitimate; for giving ideas about techniques of successfully accomplishing such acts; for inuring people to the true brutality of such acts by making them seem as everyday occurrences, blunting the sensibilities by progressively reducing the ability to shock; for corrupting young and malleable minds; for celebrating violence. To consume representations of violence causes violence; this can only raise the question as to what violence is. Yet the

intricate and ineluctable nature of violence, to which media representations actually do far more justice than the 'effects' debate gives it credit
for, is never addressed by those hotly demanding its regulation in the
media.

Decades of feminist research and theory has by now rendered it clear
that 'violence' is a contestable category (Smart 1984, 1989; Stanko
1985; Bibbings 2000), and that the body is not the only site of violence.
This opens up an enormous space for violence which the 'effects' debate
cannot address with its narrowly instrumental definitions. To correlate,
one must count. To count, one must be able to measure content (Sparks
1992). Lacking concreteness, how can equivalence be established
between, say, linguistic and physical violence? Between the violent and
the therapeutic? To wreak upon the psyche the havoc of uncertainty
which may constitute 'therapy'; is this, then, violence? To bring a human
being to a condition where they voluntarily seek the mutilations of
medical intervention, or to annihilate the psyche to the point of willing
submission to pain and death; is this, too, violence? The expurgation of
the soul, or the purging of the body of perceived impurities, or the felt
need to self-mutilate the body as the last resort in a search for autonomy?
If young girls seek to emulate the skeletal thinness of supermodels
through self-starvation or cocaine, should this be included in the search
for media 'effects'? Coercion alone cannot stand proxy for the term,
since the elimination of the will can itself be constituted as violence, as
can cultural forces which turn the will upon itself.

In her novel about the 'violence' of anorexia, *Life-Size* (1995), Jenefer
Shute's character Josie, busy starving herself to death, but incarcerated in
a clinic, dreams of once more being able to survey her body in the mirror:

> In the body, as in art, perfection is attained not when there's
> nothing left to add, but when there's nothing left to take away.
> If I had a full-length mirror, I could go through my posing
> routine: naked except for underpants . . . I bend over to touch
> my toes, seeing, in profile, the scalloped verterbraic crest. Then,
> facing the mirror, I reach upward to examine my arms, as
> streamlined and schematic as the elastic-jointed wooden figures
> that artists use. I can see every fiber of the small, perfectly
> defined deltoid, below which the upper arm reverts to bone.
> Traveling up and down like an elevator on its cable is the
> mobile, compact, biceps – a muscle I'm proud of, responsive,
> nervous, ready to flinch like a small mouse, its namesake.

The parts I like best are the shoulders, sharp as wings, and the collarbone, which I can wrap my hand around. Their names, *scapula, clavicles,* are poetry to me. Across my chest, the body's infrastructure is most obvious, and I even like the ugly violet maze of veins which traverses it: like the Visible Woman (that lurid kit I couldn't bear to look at in the toy store), I'm approaching transparency.

But today, if I continued my routine (inhaling, counting the ribs, clasping my hands around the waist until the fingertips touched), all I would feel would be thick, rubbery fat. No wonder they wouldn't give me a mirror: I'd kill myself . . .

It was clear to me that she [Josie's mother] – occupying so much space already, gobbling up so much more than her share, so crassly exceeding bounds – did not have the right to eat; nor did I, so long as a single fat cell remained.

(Shute 1995: 117, 122–3)

Josie dreams of swallowing glass: 'like shaved ice or sugar crystals . . . perhaps it would score me going down, scarring my throat so I would never have to swallow anything ever again. Open wide. There's a good girl' (Shute 1995: 219).

If the 'effects' debate does anything, it reveals the use of science to blame, to rationalize and account for one of the most irrational and hard to account for elements of modernity. It creates a narrowly delimited set of representations, nets them down as 'violence', and seeks to articulate blame. Thus to go beyond the 'effects debate' is to shift the grounds of how we read media violence on to a completely different terrain, one that *uses* instead of blames media texts, to read, and so to better understand, violence. The media culture of violence is part of, not logically prior to, the violence of culture in general. In a mediatized society, it makes no sense whatsoever to attempt to disentangle 'media violence'. Only when this is acknowledged is it possible to debate with any clarity the question of regulating consumption.

Representing violence and the body

In this section I wish to continue in my quest, not for a *definition* of violence, but for an appreciation of the many faceted ways in which violence is inscribed within media representations. The body, it seems, is still the primary surface on which violence is to be etched, but at the same time as defining violence, this throws its definitions into question. I shall thus focus on, but not necessarily limit myself to, the body; moreover, it is not at all clear to me where the body ends and the mind or spirit begins. In Josie's anorexic world, I would argue that violence is being inflicted upon her body. Yet a number of things are perplexing about this. First, the source of violence, its perpetrator, is not clear. Nor, even, is the violence itself. Is the violence upon her body the force-feeding by the clinicians, or the self-enforced starvation of Josie – or both? Surely, it must be both. One act of violence derives from the violation of Josie's will: forcing her to eat which is tantamount, for her, to torture: 'no wonder they wouldn't give me a mirror: I'd kill myself'. But a second act of violence derives from a society which has so mutilated Josie's sense of her right to occupy space that she does not have the right to eat, 'so long as a single fat cell remained'. Other parts of the book describe in a chilling manner the relentless sneering and leering which she suffers at the hands of her father; the suffocating desire of her mother that she fulfil her mother's desire for social status through conventional femininity; a society that constantly makes her feel foolish and people who chide her for her inability to meld into the world of Barbie and Ken, which disgusts her with its mindless obsession with consumption ('we are overeating as we slowly starve ourselves to death on American junk food'; Shute 1995: 106). Josie's search for the ultimate aesthetic, the antidote to the violent ugliness of the society around her, leads her to the quest for the ultimate transcendence; it is not death that she seeks but the exquisite state of transparency, of taking up no space in a world gorged and stuffed full. Yet this book would typically be seen as a psychological fiction, a personal story of someone who is ill, disturbed, not as a story of violence likely to incite violence. Featherstone *et al.* (1991) to the contrary show the body to be a question of social process, in the context of which Josie makes perfect sense.

Thus any theory of 'media violence' will require a theory of the mediatized body. Indeed, it suggests to me a whole shift of the packaging up of 'violence' as related to specific genres such as the 'video nasty'. Hence we are bombarded with images of youthfulness, slenderness, the possibilities of cosmetic enhancement through mutilation (surgery), and so on, which are profoundly implicated in self-harm and damaged personalities in consumer culture. A recent reality TV programme covered 'facelifts from hell', rivalling anything which could be offered by the film *Hellraiser*

(1987), yet remarkably less funny as people whose lives had been ruined in the search for the ultimate image-management were paraded before the viewer. Then again are documentaries covering 'cultural' issues such as female genital mutilation, hospital reality TV programmes, trauma reality TV programmes, an endless loop of embodied violence, either presented as aesthetically pleasing in themselves or legitimated by aesthetic or 'health' objectives. *Fat Club*, a reality TV programme following the live progress of a group of clinically obese people through boot-camp regimes of diet and exercise invited us all to share in the pain and humiliation, and the supposed ultimate joy, experienced by the participants. These examples demonstrate much more clearly than perhaps 'slasher' movies do, the extent to which bodily violence is subtly and not-so-subtly implicated in everyday life, but always already media-created. As Stone (1996) put it, will the 'real body please stand up?'.

The above examples contrast sharply with another search for the ultimate aesthetic, the space occupied by the serial killer, but this does not mean that the question of media violence posed should necessarily differ. 'Often gross, always fascinating, Brite's romantic vision of serial killers in love, using the male body like a communion wafer, is certain to disturb' is how *Time Out* characterized Poppy Z. Brite's (1996) novel *Exquisite Corpse*. 'Sometimes', ponders its protagonist Andrew Compton, 'a man grows tired of carrying everything the world heaps on his head. The shoulders sag, the spine bows cruelly, the muscles tremble with weariness. Hope of relief begins to die.' (Brite 1996: 1). Compton's salvation lies not in the obliteration of his own body, but in the obliteration of his self in the flesh of dead boys. Brite moreover challenges us to deny our involvement in the violence. We are not incited to emulate, because we are already participating:

> I had never savoured the decay. Handled it, yes. Conquered it, yes. But never had I revelled in it.
>
> Never, until now.
>
> As Jay stood smiling, I savaged the headless body he laid out for me. I gripped its rigid shoulders as I fucked it. I slashed its bloodless flesh with knives, scissors, screwdrivers, everything Jay put in my hand. When I had reduced it to little more than a smear on the ancient bricks, I wallowed in its scraps . . .
>
> Horror is the badge of humanity, worn proudly, self-righteously, and often falsely. How many of you have lingered

over a rendering of my exploits or similar ones, lovingly
detailed in its dismemberments, thinly veiled with moral
indignation? How many of you have risked a glance at some
wretched soul bleeding his life out on the highway shoulder?
How many have slowed down for a better look?

(Brite 1996: 159)

More than this, the 'victims' ultimately are not victims, but collabora-
tors:

When they discover how much their bodies are capable of
hurting, they're astounded. When they realize it isn't going to
end quickly, they crumble under the weight of their own fear.
The ones who have known pain are terrified from the start. But
either way . . . after you've been going for a while, after they've
begged and screamed and vomited and realized none of it's
going to make any difference, they pass into a kind of ecstacy.
Their flesh becomes like clay. Their insides cleave to your lips.
It becomes a kind of collaboration.

(Brite 1996: 178)

In the assortment of review extracts on the back jacket, in addition to
the *Time Out* review, Brite's book is described thus: 'Its strength [is] the
result of Brite's shocking, vivid prose; of the colour and texture of her
writing; of her wit, intelligence and the complexity of even her most
heinous characters' (*The Times*); 'Brite's prose style is subtle and evocative' (*Independent*). Clearly, the award-winning author has the approval
of the 'quality' press. What happened to the pornography that is
'poisoning our culture' so castigated by Germaine Greer in the *Observer*
(24 September 2000)? Is it that this sexually transgressive desecration of
bodies is not violent? Or that we are not being invited to be voyeurs?
Neither of these appears to be the case on any obvious reading. Is it that
male rape, murder, and necrophilia are intrinsically beautiful? Does
Brite's crafting of prose render the viciousness of the attacks on young
Vietnamese boys 'art', akin to 'opera, ballet, theatre and fine art'? If
transgressive violence, violence so physically extreme that it destroys
flesh unto flesh, exhibits a cultural aesthetic so fine that it is 'art', then
does the violence cease to become violent? Or, and perhaps more disturbingly, is it that we should be travelling beyond debates of 'taste' and

'decency', and beyond issues of essentially moral condemnation, to some understanding of the annihilating of bodies as an intrinsic and prominent part of modernity of which media culture, whether we denote it as 'art', 'pop', or 'trash', is yet one more indexical part?

In a fascinating survey of 'death film' Kerekes and Slater (1995) examine some of these issues in a way rarely contemplated in the kinds of relatively anodyne murder and bodily violations which concern the 'effects' literature. In *Killing for Culture* (1995) they set 'snuff' film within the broader media context, asking some provocative questions. 'Snuff' films are allegedly the filming of real death for entertainment. Kerekes and Slater point out immediately 'the enigma of snuff films, in which the *filming* of a killing would seem a greater atrocity than the act of murder itself' (1995: VII). Contrary to what the censorious panics surrounding the postmodern slapstick of *Natural Born Killers* might seem to suggest, death film has a long history and needs to be placed in context.

In their history of mondo cinema, Kerekes and Slater (1995: 81) point out that

> The mondo film has roots throughout the history of cinema. Almost as soon as the medium of moving pictures was established, Thomas Edison was filming *An Execution by Hanging* and individuals unknown were producing the first hardcore sex reels towards the end of the 1890's . . . and on kinetiscope machines in penny arcades, people could see actual newsreels of the beheading of a Chinese criminal outside Mukden, the guillotining of four French criminals at Bethune, and the hanging of a man in Missouri.

In retrospect it seems unsurprising that, taking the interlocking of the medium and the message, film makers should seek to produce images of the distant and the hidden, the exotic and the ostensibly taboo, simply because they *could*. The developing contours of modernity contained in the shrinking of the world and the domination of nation-states were studded with the humiliations of the flesh. The fascination with the notion of the 'exotic' so redolent of Victorian England for example, no longer required the physical transportation of bears in cages and genetically mutated or mutilated bodies, or the importation of 'live savages' for popular entertainment on the stage. Although the spectacle of the travelling circus of animals and human anomalies continued to be popular as carnivalesque, the cinematic technique expanded hugely the possible scope of vicarious violence, sexual or otherwise. Thus the 'shockumentaries' of mondo film coexisted with, and frequently mixed, depictions of fictional and 'real' violence in a discourse of the exotic and the hidden made available and visible, a discourse both misogynist and deeply racist. As Kerekes and Slater note, the 'dark continent' (as the publicity posters for the films phrased it) became 'a staple setting for both fiction and nonfiction films' (1995: 80).

While it seems plausible, as Kerekes and Slater assert, that the mondo film was, and is, primarily about exploitation and enlightenment (citing the example of 'educational' justifications for a certain genre of sex films; 1995: 82), the mondo is also more than pure entertainment or titillation. Although publicity for mondo films frequently cites 'thrills' or 'secrets revealed', they are also vehicles for the symbolic commodifications of domination and resistance. On the one hand, while mondo has covered a gamut of subject matter representing 'anything remotely deviant' (Kerekes and Slater 1995: 82), the purely visceral is not its only reading. As well as witchcraft, black masses, and voodoo, suitably sexualized, mondo also purveyed propaganda films. Here fact and fiction were blended to produce images of military and cultural victory during times of war, turning the embodied violence of war into symbolic and moral tales of victory and heroic suffering. The atrocities of the 'other side' were sold to the public through newsreels and war 'documentaries' as well as feature films, censuring one pursuit of violent means and simultaneously justifying another. Again, while this tactic of war is as old as war tales themselves, (for example Napoleon allegedly eating babies) the cinematic medium lent immediacy and credibility to propaganda.

Hence the Nazis produced anti-Semitic propaganda to prepare the German public for the mass extermination of the Jews. A film entitled *The Eternal Jew* included 'footage of a grinning Jewish butcher pulling out the entrails of a writhing cow', which was used to reinforce the message that 'just as it dealt with this cruel slaughter [a supposed depiction of kosher butchering], so the Germany of National Socialism will deal with the whole race of Jewry' (cited in Kerekes and Slater 1995: 186). On the other side, footage of German death camps was used to condemn the atrocities of the Holocaust: 'Let us never forget Nazi atrocities – The Real Truth'.

The subsequent release of previously suppressed 'death footage' of war, however, brings the war documentary nearer to Kerekes and Slater's claim that mondo film is principally exploitative; for example film of Hiroshima and Nagasaki confiscated by the Americans and not released until 25 years later in 1970, raises the question as to its place in the symbolic order of the post-war era. I have recollections of being shown some of this footage in undergraduate history lectures, and at the time thinking of it as unquestionably sick, but nevertheless an important record of the full 'real' horror of nuclear genocide. At the same time as they were confiscating this footage, the Americans were releasing anti-Japanese 'propaganda which depicted Japanese soldiers being burned alive as a narrator remarks "By this time we had shot, blasted, or cooked 600 of the little apes"' (Kerekes and Slater 1995: 188).

The release of the confiscated footage can thus be read as a reflexive realignment of post-war values, but this reading is thrown into ambiguity by a further mondo phenomenon. Death footage repackaged has been issued on video with unclear aims that suggest entertainment rather than education. Feature films have incorporated actual death footage, with a rash in the 1970s in post-Vietnam culture (Kerekes and Slater 1995: 178) of napalming and gang rape. To put a slightly different gloss again on the subject matter, as 'subversive art', on-film death has included footage of the rape and torture and execution of children as well as more general genocidal sprees. This fits of course with the late 1970s punk era of 'transgressive anything and the more the better', a kind of nihilism-for-fun which is angry for entertainment.

This latter development once more coincided with the development of the medium itself, a move away from archival film footage towards the immediate autonomy of the hand-held Super-8 video camera without which punk film would be difficult to imagine. While the Super-8 on the one hand expanded the possibilities of home-movie violence/sex/death, revealing a punk penchant for 'amateur realism' style violence, pornography, and taboo of considerable proportions, a more complicated development is seen in the 'Cinema of Transgression' genre (Kerekes and Slater 1995). Suicide film was a significant subgenre, along with the more familiar staples of rape, fear, and humiliation, sadomasochism, and other 'perversions', which attracted and encouraged the development of a thriving fanzine base. 'Transgression' however, was to provide the theme for a more 'artistic' reading of violence and death of the body, notable for example in the work of the late artist and film maker Derek Jarman.

Watson (1996: 33) describes Jarman's Super-8 work in the context of the latter's 'archaeology of soul'. The technology melded well, he argues, with Jarman's orientation towards his work, for 'there was no hard and fast distinction between personal life, his homosexual campaigning and his art, nor between the different artistic media and contexts in which he worked' (Watson 1996: 34). Watson notes Jarman's observations that the autonomy and effects of the Super-8 heralded something 'completely new'; 'the Super-8 camera is free. 35mm is chained by money to the institutions . . . economics have gutted mind from the format', and 'the home movie is bedrock . . . In all home movies is longing for paradise' (Jarman, quoted in Watson 1996: 36). The deinstitutionalization of movie-making in the 16mm format was further developed through the potential of video. Personalization and 'realism' acquire different meanings when divorced from large scale commercial film-making, in Jarman's case often a journey into the queer body. Transgression becomes represented as an art which effects a continual intertextuality in cross-referencing theatre and painting with film. Anti-establishment while engaging with the conventions of 'high art', visceral and at the same time abstract, deviance and violence are presented as both immanent and the stuff of pastiche, personal and also political and spiritual, on some readings, ego-driven and pretentious. Thus the multitextual and symbolically layered nature of his 1970s and 1980s films (a comprehensive survey can be found in the collection *Derek Jarman: A Portrait*; Wollen 1996) make the difficulties of reading violence and bodily deviance very clear.

Despite their bodily transgressions, it seems somehow that Jarman's work is not 'violent', while to return to Shute's (1997) work violence that is inflicted on the body can seem not to be 'about' the body but 'about' the mind. 'Death' film, however, particularly in its mondo and snuff genres, depicts violence in multiple complex ways, inscribed both on and through the body yet operating in different ways in relation to different producers and consumers, or sometimes combining the world of producer and consumer, and uniting the producer and consumer in that whether to make or view such representations is to partake in the culture of violence. But then, none of this meets the case either, since we are still left without a clear definition of violence; I have treated these representations as if they are self-evidently violent. Townsend (1998: 9), writing on photography, suggests that since there is no 'singular content' to representations, then perhaps we have arrived at a 'crisis of looking' which thus derives not so much from the singular content of the image as the multiple uses to which it is put. And it is this plethora of possibilities, contained within the photographic image, that is the cause of an uncertainty, a hesitation, even of panic, when we view it.

Since it is not possible to regulate the 'plethora of possibilities' within representation, then the 'effects' debate is killed stone dead. While on the one hand it is true that

in Western culture we seem to have a problem looking at certain images of the human figure, represented photographically. The nature and scale of this problem may be appreciated from the various 'scandals' that have attached themselves to particular photographers . . . Joel Peter-Witkin and Andres Serrano, publicly vilified in the US Congress; Sally Mann, the subject of stinging attacks over her representation of her children and the target of censorship by British authorities responsible for child-protection; Richard Sawdon-Smith, whose prize-winning photographs of a friend with AIDS related illnesses were deemed as too disturbing to print by the national newspaper that sponsored the prize; Sue Fox, receiving hate-mail after her pictures of the dead were shown in exhibition. Clearly these are photographers confronting significant taboos and being punished for doing so.

(Townsend 1998: 8)

At the same time it is clear that the sheer variety and scale of representations of the transgressive body, of humiliation, domination, pain, suffering, torture, rape, murder, genocide, bestiality, and self-mutilation render violence so much a part of our representational culture that the notion of taboo is also suspect. The 'news' media themselves are one of the main purveyors of violence, both in their coverage and the nature of that coverage. The 'overrepresentation' of violent crime in the 'conventional' sense (murder, especially of children and the elderly, street robbery, 'mindless thuggery', stranger-rape) is argued from within criminology (Reiner 1997), and at the same time the proliferation of more broadly violent news stories could be seen to include coverage of war, corporate crime, state crime, 'guerrilla' crime, violence within institutional sites such as child abuse and neglect, and global contexts such as economically produced famine, amongst others. In sum, the imagery of violence is rarely absent from screen or newspaper, in an increasingly immediate, global, and intertextual mode which makes fact–fiction divides daily less relevant. Violence as spectacle and violence as normal news are everyday frames through which we enact culture. Kerekes and Slater (1995), indeed, find an easy juxtaposition between death film and violence 'news', citing among many other examples the assassination of John F. Kennedy, R. Budd Dwyer's televized press-conference suicide, the Heysel stadium disaster in Brussels in 1985 and the Hillsborough stadium disaster in 1989. One might just as easily add the destruction of the World Trade Center in 2001, and numerous instances from 'reality TV' footage, the latest boom industry in prime time TV. The divisions are barely even ones of genre any more, as Kerekes and Slater demonstrate, since the elision of death and violence into entertainment is almost complete.

In the end it seems that media 'violence' may most usefully be viewed from two perspectives; first as a contested discursive domain, and second as an integral part of a violent culture, where far from being taboo, violence is endemic. 'Taboo' relates only to those areas of representation where definitions are successfully closed around the notion of the forbidden or the (un)desirable, which eventually must be instances of classification systems (Douglas 1966) and of the kind of processes described by Callon (1986) as moments of translation, representative of the social questions of distinction (Bourdieu 1984). Similarly 'cultures of violence' – whether formally sanctionable 'violent crime' (Levi 1997) or 'violence' more generally, whether criminalized or not – are also contestable. The 'media violence' debate does not lose all meaning, but rather becomes the site of understanding the contestations of violence and violent crime, and thereby also of understanding the fencing off of some areas of violence as public and/or criminal focii of censure.

Contestation and cultures of violence

That 'violence' is indubitably a category of language and image does not reduce it to a question of semantics or etymology, although it is both of these (Goodman 1997). Its inscription within the body and the sensory experience mean that it is a discursively constituted representation of some experience of powerlessness, pain, and suffering, a mode of giving expression to the 'seeing' which comes before words (Berger 1972). Sometimes it seems more accurate to abandon the attempt for an academically impeccable definition of the world; certainly Goodman's (1997) conclusion that we were 'at the close of a particularly nasty century' has a user-friendly resonance. It is a difficulty that 'the more one thinks about "violence" the more it means' (Goodman 1997: 159). Coercion must surely be a necessary element, but not necessarily a sufficient definition, of the term. Probably the best that can be achieved is to map some of the areas of contestation mobilized in the name of violence and to consider their implications.

Violence, very generally speaking, might be said to involve the successful attainment of power over the other through the application of successful coercion, but even this must be fenced around with the caveat that the destruction of will (thereby rendering the achievement of 'power over' non-coercive: surrender or 'giving oneself up') might itself be classed as violent. These questions are undoubtedly crystallized by 'the most horrifying manifestation of that murderous process of modern history, that orgy of technologized killing that occurred in the Third Reich' (Craig 1997: 29). That there should be a market at all for mondo footage of death camps for thrills and even pornographic use (Kerekes and Slater 1995) must make reference to something of chilling importance in modern culture. The frequency with which the Holocaust is part of a culture of denial suggests an orientation toward murderous annihilation riven with ambiguity. It has prompted a perceived need for some form of understanding that goes deeper than the conscious and reflexive sociological categories of modernity, an engagement with the categories instead of the psychoanalytic. While I do not intend in this book to enter into the discourse of psychoanalysis per se, since I am engaged with the more public domains of representation rather than a search for aetiologies, it nevertheless is crucial to recognize that

> there exists an aetiological myth of Western civilization based on a morally elevating story of humanity emerging from a pre-social barbarity. The myth enables an explanation of genocide as a failure of modern civilization to contain the morbid predilections of man's [sic] nature, i.e., not enough civilization . . . Such reasoning . . . fails to comprehend the ambivalent nature of society.
>
> (Craig 1997: 51)

In seeking a definition of violent cultures, it must be recognized that the lack of *conscious* perception of coercion does not necessarily rule out violence. This means that forms of psychic trauma that render people compliant to acts which inflict pain or death upon them may render violence publicly less visible, and means that any delineation of violent cultures or cultures of violence must always be somewhat provisional. What the susceptibility of cultures to the mass sanctioning of genocide, whether through psychoanalytic processes or active and conscious approval, shows is that such mass violence may be on any moral or spiritual level horrific, but cannot be regarded as abnormal in the strict sense of the word. This ambivalence to levels of violence which involve the sadistic destruction of populations infuses the whole of our media representations of violence, and our attitudes towards them. In other words, as Rubenstein argues,

> civilization means slavery, wars, exploitation and death camps.
> It also means medical hygiene, elevated religious ideas,
> beautiful art and exquisite music. It is an error to imagine that
> civilization and savage cruelty are antithesis.
> (Rubenstein 1978: 92, in Craig 1997: 51)

'Savage cruelty', albeit often in a technicized and bureaucratized form, actually provides one of the major cultural aesthetics of modernity. The pure enjoyment taken in the spectacle of pain, in particular of the humiliation of autonomy through the destruction of the flesh – particularly 'wanton' destruction finding no legitimation in rational discourse – is commonplace. It forms the basis of many sexual fantasies, and is the stuff of 'high culture' as much as 'low culture'. Racism and misogyny are two manifestations; in general the pleasure of reinforcing a sense of power through the infliction of violence go hand in hand. Thus we inhabit a culture of violence; our rational and civilized, yet 'particularly nasty century' which recently ended was studded with wars, mass murder, brutal repressions, institutionalized hatred, and individual sadisms finding expression through our allegiance to their representational texts.

This is only surprising if we assume an identity of consciousness and thought, and a belief in rational thought beyond its artefactual presence, an assumption thrown into question by Derrida (1978, 1981). Our ambivalence manifests itself in a simultaneous censure of the conventional crimes of individuals while sanctioning the generalized violence of the era. It involves the frequent rounding up of hostages to fortune, sacrificial icons who are made to stand proxy for our consciences, while at the same time we devour voraciously as many media images of violence as we can get our hands on, either overtly or covertly. Censorship forms the institutionalized production of cultural scapegoats which soothes our need to feel civilized. Its innate contradictions as a process reflect not the inadequacies of the machinery of censorship or its definitions, but the necessity of leaving most of the violence *in* the culture; it is not so much a hypocrisy as a morally justified sleight of hand.

Aesthetically and practically, the duree of social life is dependent upon violence. As Foucault made clear in relation to sexuality (1981) 'repression' was a heightened concern in an era where sexual discourses proliferated, constituting a squeezing out of spaces of difference. The proliferation of violence, which may in one sense be defined precisely as the attack upon difference, is endemic within a modernism that centres upon the myth of rational thought, a dynamic requiring in equal part the condemnation of violence. Thus when Durkheim formulated his famous notion that 'crime brings together upright consciences and concentrates them' (1969: 102) he was describing an effect produced by the ambivalences of reason in relation to classifications of otherness.

'Violent crime' occupies a specific discursive site within this historical formation, in any epoch representing the historical moment at which censure operates to delineate and name a resolution of ambivalence. This accounts for the difficulty of any empirical endeavour to quantify 'how much' violent crime there is (Levi 1997), and consequently, 'how many' instances of violent crime are presented in the media. Such definitional questions can only be answered with reference to definitional categories themselves. Since the latter are historical products of the victories of translation (Callon 1986), then the high profile criminalization of some actions as violent, the ambivalence toward others, and the non-recognition of other categories of action as 'violent crime', charts only the politics of discursive formation. That all violent crime is violent, but not all violence is crime, is a quite comprehensible outcome of the general constitution of difference and censure in 'modernist' thought. Levi identifies numerous spaces of ambivalence in relation to the production of the categories of violent crime. As he notes, it becomes clear when these are examined that 'culture shapes the conditions under which we attribute responsibility and blame to those individuals whose acts result in harmful consequences' (Levi 1997: 844). Placed in this context, 'labelling perspectives' in criminology (Becker 1963; Lemert 1972) reveal a potential for insight of which simplistic treatments have robbed them. The question to which the notion of the moral panic addresses itself (Cohen 1971) lacks an 'ultimately satisfactory' answer, since the accounts characterizing the debate 'are insufficiently grounded in historical *process* to demonstrate why things turned out that way, and, moreover, historical processes themselves are not wholly determinant' (Levi 1997: 845).

It is a far easier matter to describe the apparent contradictions in the apportioning of censure than it is to account for them. Despite this, Levi remains committed to the optimism of rational discourse in a search for explanations of violence:

> The frequency of violence and its social distribution, and their stability over time and place, tell us a great deal about the relative plausibility of biological/personality-based explanations for violent behaviour, on the one hand, or subcultural/cultural explanations, on the other. This, in turn, helps us to assess the justifications offered by politicians and the media for their policies, for though policies driven by popular appeal and/or retributivism may need no validation by research evidence, we can only hope that rationality imposes *some* constraints, at least on populist 'law 'n' order' movements outside the United States.
>
> (Levi 1997: 848)

For me, the flaw in Levi's cautious optimism lies not so much in the first part of this extract as in the second. We may learn about the social distribution of the *plausibility* of explanations, which may help us to assess the *justifications* (legitimatory discourses) of politicians and the media, but the hope of 'rationality imposing constraint' implies that rationality is a discourse that emanates in any necessary way from phenomena. The contrary is probably the case: that the discourse of rationality requires an equal discourse of unreason but that this latter is a domain of representation that bears no *obvious* or *necessary* relationship to any intrinsic properties of action. The rhetorical demands of the 'justice for James' campaign, as we have seen, are 'rational' neither in prevention terms (they would not 'logically' ensure the prevention of further violent attacks on children) nor in terms of the application of social disapproval (they would not sate the desire for, or public expressions of desire for, retributive force as a bedmate of moral sanction). That policy or justice could be logically predicated on improved aetiological comprehension is to 'magic away' the history of aetiological discourse as a tactic of power. Levi, in other words, is invoking an effect of power to cancel out an effect of power, but is presenting this as a question of invoking a better correspondence of discourse with the 'truth' to deal with a question of power. That truth (to which we have no unmediated access) could dissolve power seems contradicted by the very processes of history to which Levi alludes.

This question of the correspondence of media representations of violence to levels of actual violence will not go away. It is a quest of reason, which is eminently understandable from within the confines of rational thought. The problem is not that the actions which are (or are not) denoted as criminally violent can be ignored as linguistic categories, since clearly the inscription of pain and suffering upon body and psyche are real in their effects. It is rather that mediated experience is treated as if it is separate from the 'real' and not part of the practices of the 'real'. The struggle that Levi faces is thus one of mobilizing his measurements of phenomena in such a way that will render them acceptable as manifestations of violent crime which the currently popular discourses of censure can accommodate within their own terms. To step outside of these constraints would be to render himself a 'textual outlaw' (Young 1996). This is not to say that Levi's enterprise is irrelevant, but to understand it as part of, and not a solution to, the struggle over definitions and censures of violence in culture.

Hence the selective processes of violence and its censure as represented in the media of 'news' or 'entertainment' or 'art' are cultural practices which forge a certain landscape of violence predicated on its appeal; it makes little sense to divorce the 'producer' and 'consumer' in any clear way, since the producers are also consumers and vice versa. The work of representation is done by everyone embraced in the representation–reality dyad and as such, violence and censure are constantly replicated. The pleasures of violence are aesthetic; 'thrills' and 'shock' are sensual pleasures that derive from the vicarious enjoyment of violence censured and taken out of context, so that it seems an abrogation rather than a mundane aspect of coherent tradition. That people would act violently *in imitation* is to ignore culture as praxis; that people

would adopt the vocabularies of media violence in their everyday practices of violence is a sine qua non of a culture where meaning is based on
language, a point made in a different way by C. W. Mills (1959) in his
discussion of 'vocabularies of motive'. What remains of interest however, is, as Sparks contends, the necessity of attention to 'the continuity
between the spheres of the political and the aesthetic' (1992: 63).

The political and the aesthetic: gendered violence

The aesthetics of seduction and desire slide easily into those of domination; domination elides into coercion. The intertwining of these aesthetic conventions with the politics of gender constitute one of the most
complex and pressing questions of the practice of power in contemporary 'civilized' societies. The confusions and contradictions embedded
in legal discourse reveal how enduring and profound are the cultural and
material expressions of gender/power (Nicholson and Bibbings 2000).
These confusions and contradictions surround the legal categories of
rape and sexual assault, offences against the person, and prostitution. As
a corollary they run through the whole of criminal law, notably its 'general principles' of intent, consent, responsibility, provocation, and self-
defence which in the very assumption of generality suppress the specific
differentials of power and identity upon which gender categories are
predicated (Lacey 2000). Feminist argument has thus tended to be
directed at the normative support that the language (and thereby the
practices) of law provides for violence against women. Moreover,
feminist discourse analysis has also pointed up the domain of the legal as
actually constituting women and men 'as legal and social subjects'
(Lacey 2000: 96). If one accepts the latter proposition, then the law does
not merely support or legitimize gender inequality and male violence
against women, but also produces it through active collusion. It is then
unsurprising that the 'power of [patriarchal] law' has generated resistances from a radical feminist perspective which fundamentally refutes its
predicates and concepts. In their purist form, these oppositional discourses have relied on an unproblematic identification of the representation–referent relationship. Thus Mackinnon can assert that 'male
power produces the world before it distorts it' (Mackinnon 1982: 542;
cited in Smart 1989: 77). The whole of culture is thereby an expression
of patriarchal power, of which the law is one field. The only *real* woman,

upon which a non-patriarchal rule of law could be based, is pre-cultural, so that the field of cultural practice is a series of ideological obfuscations serving principally to perpetuate women's material subordination and to secure their 'consent' to it (Mackinnon 1982). The only value of the 'law' therefore, is the extent to which it can be utilized as a strategy to recognize the 'wronged woman'. My intention here is not to enter into this debate as such, but to highlight the political framework within which representations of 'violence against women' and its aesthetic status may be framed.

Somewhat dismissively, Kerekes and Slater describe the mythic 'snuff movie' ('live murder' film for entertainment) as being, for feminists, the 'ethereal byword for "the ultimate in woman hating" ' (1995: 243). For Kerekes and Slater their critique of the feminist attack on 'snuff' is that it is unsubstantiated in its claims that such films actually exist rather than exist as a myth, and that it conflates violent pornography with other forms of violence such as support and/or enjoyment of the literature of Nazis or the Ku-Klux-Klan (1995: 243). While they are correct to point out that there clearly *is* a difference between really killing someone for aesthetic purposes, and making a highly plausible 'mock up' of doing so, they overstate the case if the feminist perspective is to be taken into account rather than merely brushed away. The feminist point is surely that if 'snuff' *were* to exist, it would be only the far point on a continuum. That men seek out ever more violent representations of woman killing is evidenced by the market in mondo and death film; that 'reality' can be successfully used as a marketing device whether or not it is true attests to the point that men do indeed find a great deal of sexual pleasure in the violent death of women, and the more 'realistically' presented the better. Kerekes and Slater also dismiss the notion of 'transgression' as merely a catchphrase. It would seem a reasonable word to use in that it denotes violation and the crossing over of boundaries that are conventionally and publicly delineated in certain ways. 'Transgression' also implies a journey or process, rather than a simple distinction between a mythical 'normal' and 'abnormal'. This attempt to dismiss feminism undermines what otherwise would be an insightful observation when they refer to the 'moral paradox' at the core of the snuff phenomenon:

> It is evident that the outrage and furore over snuff reveals a
> tacit desire – indeed – a *need* – for it to exist, if only as an idea

. . . death forms a large and integral part of our collective unconscious. Just as modern man [*sic*] is compelled to incorporate ritualism and symbolism into his everyday life, so must he experience – and exorcise – the primal.

(Kerekes and Slater 1995: 246)

It is the 'emptying out' of the 'snuff' phenomenon of historicity and gender power that renders this assertion so anodyne. Postulating 'universals' of 'man' and 'history' leaves us precisely nowhere. 'Snuff' emerged in a specific form in a specific historical period; that its representations of power are largely gendered is also clear. The 'tacit desire' and the 'need' relate to the desire and need of masculinist sexualities. Consider the following:

The Samurai administers a drug to the girl and picks up a pair of shears . . . he then cuts through the victim's clothing. The scene fades upon him reaching her underwear . . . the Samurai raises a bradawl and plunges it into the girl . . . with intermittent edits to the face of the Samurai and the victim, dazed and delirious . . . the Samurai turns his attention to the lower extremities. He saws off one leg, lifts it to his face and caresses it longingly . . . drawing up the sheet on the limbless, still living body, the camera avoids the genital area by focusing upon the victim's navel . . . The Samurai incises the torso with a scalpel . . . As he prods his hands into the wound, a cutaway reveals a red trickle running down from the girl's mouth. When he thrusts his hand deep inside the wound, the girl vomits a mouthful of blood. Her head rolls sideways and she dies. The Samurai pulls from the abdomen a handful of intestines and organs. He raises a machete and, in slow motion, hacks off her head. It flips through the air and comes to rest on the floor. The Samurai props it up on the bed and enucleates an eyeball with a dinner spoon. He sucks on it, cross-eyed with delight. Finally, in a clichéd post-coitus gesture, the Samurai smokes a cigarette . . . The scene fades to reveal the city once again. Ahead is another girl.

(Kerekes and Slater 1995: 174)

This is a description of a sequence from a film called *Guinea Pig 2:*

Flower of Flesh and Blood. Kerekes and Slater say 'many think *Flower of Flesh and Blood* to be a genuine snuff film' (1995: 173), and this is perhaps more important than their textual analysis of the film and its techniques, which suggests that it is not. Caputi, in a radical feminist reading, places such material within a framework of 'crime formulas'. Such films, she argues, constitute a formulaic genre of 'slashing, chopping products' which 'articulate the larger ideology of sex crime' (Caputi 1988: 63). Within this she conflates a range of films and novels, from *Psycho* (1960) and *Halloween* (1978) to *Snuff* (1976). The complex and internally differentiated history provided by Kerekes and Slater does reveal a difficulty with this conflation. *Snuff*, the film which gave the name to the mythic genre, despite being a scam, was specifically promoting the *idea* of real sexualized slaughter of a woman on screen:

> The thumping of a heartbeat swells onto the soundtrack. Upon the blade reaching the crotch, the director sinks his hand deep into the wound. A posthumous fist-fuck provides him with a handful of entrails. Moaning softly to himself, he then sinks his hand back in for more. Deeper, this time, deeper, pulling out her heart. Orgasmic shuddering on his part. He dips his hand in once again, clawing around . . . The frame blurs into a washed out umber, then runs into leader-tape. A voice punctuates the blackness and whispers: 'Shit, shit . . . we ran out of film'. Another voice, again whispering: 'Did you get it – did you get it all?'
>
> (Kerekes and Slater 1995: 21)

'Death film' is clearly not all the same, unless one wishes to enter into the kind of discourse which conflates heterosexual penetrative sex with rape (Dworkin 1981). It is the immediacy of snuff, whether fake or not, that provides the thrill, which brings the forms of domination that it portrays nearer to a field of lived experience. Caputi's formulaic rules (of which she cites seven) clearly do not apply to all films depicting the violent and sexualized killing of women (see Caputi 1988: 64). 'Mother hatred' is identified as a major internal dynamic of such films, a mythic pattern that 'dominates and directs the actual cases of sex crimes as well' (Caputi 1988: 71).

Actually it is the sense of intimacy with the image that renders 'snuff' so powerful, particularly later versions shot on 16mm Super-8 or camcorder technology. Caputi's reduction of the medium and the message to a generic formula of psychological typology can say little about the complexities of aesthetics, desire, and power that drive snuff. That 'death films' represent men's fear and hatred of women and their paradoxical symbolizing of danger is an interesting but incomplete-feeling notion in relation to the nature of the violence of these texts. It also ignores the growing involvement of women in discourses of violence against men. Feminist 'revenge violence' has become quite a popular theme in film and literature, as noted in the previous chapter. Hollywood's *Thelma and Louise*, the English film *Dirty Weekend* based on the novel by Zahavi (1991), and a much earlier low budget offering called *Born in Flames*, a sort of feminist-meets-punk-revolutionary movie about the takeover of patriarchal society by women (1983), as well as novels such as Jennifer Shute's *Sex Crimes* (1997) and Laura Kasischke's (1997) *Suspicious River* are examples. In *Sex Crimes* the woman protagonist gouges out the eyes of her male victim with her bare hands; in the acknowledgements at the back of the novel Shute includes women's self-defence manuals (for the uninitiated, the latter usually offer sound advice on attack to the eyes and/or genitals of a presumed male assailant, but would undoubtedly be useful for any woman seeking satisfaction from violence against men). Then of course, the genre of the serial killer novel has on numerous occasions been adopted by broadly feminist writers, so that while the perpetrator of violent crime is typically male, the resolution is female (see for example Val McDermid's *The Blood in the Wire*, 1997).

For me there are two major gaps in the kind of argument mobilized by Caputi; the first is the oversimplification of the equation of representations of sexualized violence with 'misogyny', an inevitable and obvious product of 'patriarchy'. The second problem is the avoidance of the feminist adoption of violent tactics against men in mediated representation, a violence that has an aesthetic content and is not simply about 'self-defence' or 'provocation', unless the latter is taken to mean the provocation of masculinist culture in general.

On the first issue, it is questionable how much further the concept of 'misogyny' takes us in reading violent representation. This is because it provides an embarrassment of riches; it is used to account for the discourses that render men rational and women 'mad', for foot-binding, female 'circumcision', sadomasochism, rape, and pornography, as well as sexual violence (Ussher 1991). 'Misogyny' becomes a discourse that is

> prevalent in different contexts and cultures [and] contains a
> number of common elements, which seem to transcend the
> normal divisions of nations or history, or of academic
> discipline. It is simultaneously pervasive and perverting.
> Women are objectified, associated with danger and temptation,
> with impurity, and with an uncontrolled sexuality. They are at
> the same time to be worshipped and defiled, evoking horror
> and desire, temptation and repugnance, fear and fascination.
>
> (Ussher 1991: 21)

Sexual violence is thereby rendered as an instance of a pervasive form of misogyny 'exemplified by rape, sexual murder, prostitution and the glorification of sado-masochism' (Ussher 1991: 31). 'Misogyny' is thus tautological, defining of and defined by, violence. Conventions of violence as the cultural expression of a response to 'otherness' and to 'irrationality' by a perpetually fragile sense of identity, an irrational space representing ambivalence towards the rituals of pollution, taboo, and secular defilement, are well-documented anthropologically (Douglas 1966). They can be applied equally effectively to the representation of Jews in anti-Semitic discourse, to the mad (in general), to the inhabitants of the 'savage' cultures of the 'dark continents' (Kerekes and Slater 1995). Feminism may thus provide an interesting theory of the violent text, but does not go nearly far enough in its explanation of the general seduction of violent power in the 'age of reason', while at the same time falling short of accounting for specific representations of the violence inscribed in the female body for spectacle. Without resort to the pre-cultural or attention to historical specificities and contradictions, it has often lacked a theorization of masculinities (Connell 1995). The latter is probably needed to deal with the multiply structured masculinities that exert tactics of power and coercion over other men, over boys, by boys over other boys or infants, over animals, between ethnicities, and even against no particular 'other' but as an expression or extension of masculine identities as with the 'hardware violence' of the action-thriller (Sparks 1992: 137). Thus hegemonic masculinities are successful outcomes of attempts to exert power requiring a theory of the subordinated as well as the hegemonic (Connell 1987, 1995; Messerschmidt 1993; Jefferson 1997). That meanings are not closed around masculinities, but instead constitute an ongoing terrain of negotiation and struggle, suggests that outcomes are uncertain and the unitariness of notions of 'misogyny' and 'patriarchy' mean that they are insufficient to account for representations of sexual(ized) violence.

This in turn relates to the second gap alluded to above. The growth of representations by women writers and film makers of specifically gendered violence towards men may be part of a 'waning of female complicity' (Giddens 1992; Walklate 1995) which include in their discourses of violence an implicit questioning of the law. These must be seen as oppositional moments in the contested terrain of gender/power signifying broader cultural processes of late modernity, whereby concepts of the self and of the legitimacy of an increasingly wide range of gendered practices and meanings are thrown into question. Snuff pornography, as a particular instance of the symbolic assertion of a white, western, over-determined masculinity given its particular shape by technological developments in cinematic media, is already contestable and residual as an exercise in cultural power. Its aesthetics of violence are already yesterday's vestments, redolent of the louche misogynist underground 'artists' of the 60s and early 70s, rednecks, sweaty heavy-metal bikers and other archaeological remains, and contemporary post-punk cultists.

Does splatter (still) matter?

The new wave violence of mediated representation points in two directions: to the surface ironies, the meaningless non-narrative, non-subjective 'play' violence of, for example, 'postmodern' cinema (Denzin 1991); and the globalized prosthetic violence of the cyber (Featherstone and Burrows 1995). In this sense 'splatter' probably no longer matters, but in the end that would be too glib a statement. Insofar as cultural representation constitutes cultural practice, the 'postmodern' moment has not eclipsed the effects of late modernity. Violence still occupies a huge space and cannot be theorized away as virtual in a mediatized society. Its representation and the celebration and censures attached to its aesthetics are as real as the subordinating practices and legitimations of which it is a part. The formations of gender/power, nation/power, race/power, religion/power, however complicated they have come to seem, and however sophisticated the media technologies which partly constitute them, have not evaporated. Mediatization has not rendered power virtual; rather globalized virtualization has rendered power more pervasive and subtler than ever, while coexisting with local and highly physical power–violence narratives that may render the twenty-first century even 'nastier' than the twentieth. What has been annihilated is any meaningful censorship debate, as the politics of regulation increasingly acquire a fragmented and dispersed character which, thankfully, at least might consign the 'effects' debate to the archives of modernism.

5 ▪ (S)TALKING IN CYBERSPACE: VIRTUALITY, CRIME AND LAW

Cyber has now become the current ultimate in mediated social life. Along with the exponential growth of global communication networks comes a wave of social theorizations, which are, for want of a better phrase, post-postmodern. Even to label the genre 'social theory' sounds antiquated in relation to its referent, which in some senses is a post-social space. This leads to a considerable problem of language on a number of counts. First, the available vocabularies to describe and conceptualize the cyber are already outmoded by the nature of that space. Cyberspace has its own syntax, which is only partially comprehensible by those outside its cultures. Second, existent languages of social theory typically engage with notions of discourse and narrative that are not generally speaking the primary axes along which cyber is 'structured' (indeed the cyber is very much anti-structure as we might apply the term to social formations in the 'real' world). Third, 'earth' language attempts to formulate knowledge discursively in some relation to real referents, whereas cybercultures have no direct referent. Its references to the real are artificial, simulated. 'The body' and the reflexive internally ordered self of modernity are only useful in describing what the cyber is not. To this extent, the cyber is divorced from reality and its theories of being and action. Categories of crime and law consequently prove notoriously hard to apply to the cyber. To an extent it is an unregulated and unregulable space. This is not science fiction however, and (currently) on the other side of the screen there is a person and a people-constituted social environment, so however much it may seem that the cyber is separate, it exists within a very real social, economic, and political context. In squaring up to this contradiction, without attempting to resolve it, interesting areas of debate are opened up to those concerned with the domains of crime and law which may, in their difficulty and challenge, provoke some healthy rethinking of the traditional concepts of criminologists and lawyers. This chapter therefore seeks to resolve nothing, but it does try to begin a process of thinking about crime and law from a cyberperspective. From talking in cyberspace to stalking in cyberspace, the frameworks of the 'real' are therefore applied, often metaphorically, to the prosthetic, while at the same time taking the latter partially on its own terms.

Cyberspace and cybercultures: approaching the prosthetic

The work of William Gibson, previously mentioned, has to be considered in any discussion of contemporary media culture. This in itself illustrates the theme of this book, since Gibson, the 'cyberpunk' novelist (1984, 1995) – or even the 'father'(!) of cyberpunk – has latterly been feted as a sociological theorist. Burrows (1997), in an essay on Gibsonism, suggests that the novelist has superseded the recent high priests of social theory. In a comment on the processes of sociological '*passeification*', Burrows (1997: 235) writes:

> It is not just technology which appears to be accelerating towards meltdown, so are our cultural and sociological understandings of the world . . . The recent literature on things 'cyber' is a case in point. Reading it makes the latest pile of books on the postmodern, globalisation, reflexive modernisation (last year's model?) and the like appear mellow and quaint. Never mind who now reads Marx? Or even Foucault? Who now reads Baudrillard?

Of course the irony in this is that even when something as allegedly theoretically different as the cyber is concerned, we just seem unable to resist the elevation of someone (male) to the status of 'founding father'.

Surely it is partly the addictive allure of Gibson's writing style that makes him preferable to the dry or obfuscating discourses of 'social theorists proper'. Who would you rather spend an evening with, the author of *Das Kapital* or the author of *Neuromancer*? William Gibson is just more *fun*. We need a caveat on Gibson, because allocating him the position of social theorist extraordinaire reduces talking about 'the cyber' to blinkered, linear and elitist (and male-dominated) modernist epistemes. This is the antithesis of the Gibsonian 'vision'. Amongst all the other things that the cyber may be 'about', one of them is the proliferation of voices, which are not particularly amenable to filtering, regulation, or hierarchical orderings of the status of knowledge. It is an interesting shift, which turns to fiction as social theory, and a long overdue one, since as Burrows (1997: 235) also notes

> Our inability to account for our changing world in sociological terms has led, not just to an ontological insecurity but to ever more frantic attempts to provide some sort of sociological frame for a constantly moving target. In the recent conceptual scramble some analysts have begun to turn to sources of inspiration beyond traditional social and scientific discourses.

Cyberhype has been widely criticized for its dystopia, or more commonly utopia (Weinstein and Weinstein 2000), but this hardly seems important since all literatures (whether 'fictional' or not) about the social world have contained dystopian and utopian elements reflecting the difficulty of comprehending change in which we are immersed, (for example, Marx and H.G. Wells). 'Futurology' and 'doom' have been endemic in accounts of technological change and the accompanying transformations of the orderings of the social. This is merely an inherent danger of trying to see the world, any world, from the over-and-aboveness that only the sleight of hand available to historians, with their conventions of narrative re-orderings, can really do more or less plausibly. In dealing with the cyber, therefore, it simply has to be accepted that what is said about it must be constantly provisional. Thus I am seeking, as Bell (2000: 1) puts it, to 'understand the ways in which cyberspace as a cultural phenomenon is currently being experienced and imagined'.

'Cyberspace as a "peopled" and "people driven" environment is intricately connected with human agency; yet as we sit in front of the computer terminal we are "simultaneously . . . relocating ourselves in the

space behind the screen, between screens, everywhere and nowhere" '
(Bell 2000: 3). The nature of cyber*space* is different from the physical
spaces of the built environment, and given that the language with which
we attempt to delineate it is metaphorical (cf. Lakoff and Johnson 1977)
we need to be reflexive about the adequacy of those metaphors. McBeath
and Webb (1997: 250) argue that we are prone to adopt 'false analogies',
and 'the language we use to try to grasp the structure of cyberspace . . .
trades equally on notions of radical difference and sameness'.

Four main analogic strands are important to this chapter: community, city, body, and identity. The 'virtual community' has been a
term associated with the cyber since (and even before) the growth of
cybercultures. Paradoxically this usage has frequently been a case of the
imaginary aping the imaginary. Rheingold's (1993) *The Virtual Community: Homesteading on the Electronic Frontier* is a case in point. Virtual communities are envisaged as parallel to 'real' communities, a
notion that can only be problematic since the fragmentation of 'community' (if it ever existed) has been well charted in the theorization of
modernity. Loaded as it is with ideological baggage, not least its
mobilization of unity as a legitimation of the suppression of otherness,
and intertwining historically with the extreme violence of racism, it is
difficult to apprehend what a 'virtual' community might be. As
Bankowski and Mungham (1981: 86) observe, it is largely a term used
to obfuscate, through connotations of oneness and togetherness, the
real divisions in society. 'Community' is a politics of location, implying
physical proximity and/or affective or spiritual proximity. Shared interests in a particular mode of social organization are presumed. It is an
image notoriously difficult to locate empirically, a projection of resistance to alienation. Thus McBeath and Webb (1997: 256) are probably
correct to argue that

> the structure of projection of virtual community is a double
> movement of alienation both from the 'real' everyday world of
> objectified culture into the atomised private life-world and then
> to the 'virtual' community world, an illusion as humanly rich
> as the ideals of community in the everyday world.

At the very least, such a notion of the virtual community would imply
a flight from the ontological insecurity of late modernity (Giddens
1991), a

planet converging . . . virtual community seems a cure-all for isolated people who complain about their isolation. Locked in metal boxes and on urban freeways, a population enjoys socializing with fellow humans through computer networks . . . Pierre Teilhard de Chardin, the French Jesuit palaeontologist, envisioned the convergence of humans into a single massive 'noosphere' or 'mind sphere' . . . This giant network would surround earth to control the planet's resources and shepherd a world unified by Love.

(Heim 1998: 39)

In its most utopian formulation Heim (1998: 41) refers to this idea as 'nerds in noosphere', or 'the Teilhardian internet is optimism gone ballistic'. For Heim community, if anything, results from a struggle with everyday realities. This is certainly borne out by the contemporary policy-practice usages of the term. In the UK for example 'community regeneration', which for well over a decade has been the urban language of postindustrial regional governance, represents precisely this. Allocate scarce resources to deindustrialized urban spaces, and consult 'the community' on how they should be deployed. Anyone who has worked or researched or lived in these environments will know the power struggles which ensue over the notion of community. In the name of 'rebuilding the community' the old want the young suppressed, the young want more ownership of public space, 'problem families' are to be purged, allotments are to be revamped, microeconomies are to be fostered, wasteland is to be reclaimed and crime and fear are to be minimized. Solutions are hotly debated; resources contested; scapegoats are sought; in-fighting between residents of localities can reach fever pitch. Committees and forums are set up wherein battle takes place.

This is a long way from the 'virtual community', for in the real community, writes Heim, 'people throw their lot together and stand face to face in ethical proximity' (1998: 42). Precisely because the cyber is a human–machine interface, any notion of community in relation to it is inextricably related to questions of social order and division outwith.

Graham (1997) comments upon the failure of urban planners and policy-makers to understand city–telecommunications relationships in the postwar era; resources and actions have been concentrated on intervention in physical infrastructures. While his identification of the need for planners to take more account of the growing telemediation of urban life is surely valid, it does have a flavour of denying the materiality of everyday life. For most people, ironically largely *because* of their habitation in postindustrial landscapes, the local infrastructure remains a principal locus for, and focus for contestation over, issues of 'community'. Waiting for absent buses in the rain, gazing out of windows onto derelict wasteland, picking up the detritus of urban frustration (the trampled plants, the broken glass), needing to get to Iceland for the 2 for 1 offers, and not being able to get a job remain stubbornly present delineating features of the urban experience. If nothing else, it is for reasons like these that Net users cannot be united solely by a technology, although the affective attachment to technological embodiment may prove to be one ground of commonality.

However, the proliferation of racial hatred sites, 'terrorist' sites, paedophile sites, death sites, religious sites, campaign sites such as those soliciting support for revenge–justice, and so on, demonstrate clearly that 'virtual communities' such as they are, have one foot firmly in the real. If the Net is seen as 'rekindling the sense of family' (Robins 2000), it includes the families of worldly politics, worldly crime, and worldly law. The Internet has featured widely in the media as the meeting place for those supporting or perpetrating the attacks on New York City and Washington DC on 11 September 2001; it is also a trading post for prostitution and exploitation, for the selling of children, and for tactics of guerrilla attack amongst much more, and provides hang-out space for all sorts of people whose 'deviant' or criminal proclivities might make it difficult for them to place an ad in the local classified columns.

Thus there is no easy correspondence between virtual technologies and ideal communities; despite arguments that cyberspace produces symmetry of subjects, 'we must begin from the real world, which is the world in which virtual communities are now being imagined' (Robins 2000: 90–1). In this sense, 'virtual communities' as self-defined cause a difficulty. Taking them on their own terms is, too, a decision with political implications rooted in the real world. While *Mondo 2000*[7] sat 'squarely and safely on the postmodern fence, covering its postmodern ass' (Sobchack 2000: 139), the cyber continued to operate in a reciprocal relation to the real.

The dangers of 'playing the God-Trick' as Donna Haraway (1985) put it, are further instanced when the city, the body, and identity are considered. Of course the city in the modernist sense is transcended by cyberspace; physical location is unimportant, the 'urban', the 'conurbation', and the 'nation state' are replaced by the global matrix of the wires. In this sense the 'global village' is a truism. But what flows into the machine is still partially the sensibility of the urban, and, since cities have from their beginnings been metaphorical and imaginary spaces as well as material contexts (Westwood and Williams (eds) 1997) there is a continuity here. At the same time it must be acknowledged there is fracture. Cybernetworks, in their unquestionable dissolution of modernist structures of time and space, do constitute an environment of flexible reconfiguration, and time and space are no longer frames *inside* which events occur (Latour 1987).

Next I wish to consider the second dyad; as well as community/city, body/identity is transcended in the cyber. A large and growing literature on the cyborg (see Featherstone and Burrows 1995, and Bell and Kennedy 2000 for comprehensive surveys, Haraway 1985 for an early definitive discussion and Stone 1996 on the prosthetic) has identified the blurring or dissolution of the 'key analytical categories we have so long used to structure our world' . . . 'the categories of the biological, the technological, the natural, the artificial *and* the human' (Featherstone and Burrows 1995: 3). Along with this must come transformations of identities. This blurring is a continuum where 'at the one end we have "pure" human beings and at the other fully simulated disembodied post-humans which can only exist in cyberspace' (Featherstone and Burrows 1995: 11). The prosthetic of course is a feature of culture that is not limited to the cyber; as Featherstone and Burrows point out, we increasingly see the 'aesthetic manipulation of the body's surface' (1997: 11) which can be achieved through cosmetic surgery, through medical surgery, or through prosthetic additions (even a pair of spectacles would qualify as the latter). Even the most rudimentary of these manipulations is associated with some shaping of identity, as attitudes towards and of spectacle-wearers show. The popularity of the prosthetic alternatives, contact lenses, and more recently laser modifications, reflects not merely utilitarian ends but questions of 'who I am'. Cerebral implants, central to cyborg-films but also with a history in the 'treatment' of mental 'illness' go directly to the sense of self, creating a prosthesis out of the brain. The *principle* of the prosthetic then, derives from the dynamic created at the mind/body/technology interface. Stone (1996: 4) evokes this eloquently in her consideration of physicist Stephen Hawking, who is, in essence, a cyborg whose medical condition makes it virtually impossible for him to move anything more than his fingers or to speak. A friendly computer engineer put together a nice little system for him, a program that displays a menu of words, a storage buffer, and a Votrax allophone generator . . . he selects words and phrases, the word processor stores them until he forms a paragraph, and the Votrax says it. Or he calls up a prepared file, and the Votrax says that . . . So I and a zillion other people are on the lawn, listening to Hawking's speech, when I get the idea that I don't want to be outside with the PA system – what I really want to do is sneak into the auditorium, so I can actually hear Hawking give the talk.

But when she achieves this 'this thing' happens in her head, and she poses the question of 'exactly where . . . *is* Hawking? There is the obvious physical Hawking . . . but a serious part of Hawking extends into the box on his lap . . . Where *does* he stop? Where are his edges?' (Stone 1996: 5). Stone characterizes this dilemma as a 'boundary debate', and it lies at the heart of comprehending transformations of the cyber. To some extent any technological embodiment (cf. Featherstone and Burrows 1995) must transform identity; while cyborg genre films have extended this to include computer chips to replicate human emotions and create false memories, as in *Blade Runner* (1982; director's cut 1993).

While for most people the ultimate cyborg, including prosthetic identity and prosthetic memory, exists only in the world of sci-fi or computer simulations, the general point made by Stone marks the transformation of the merely human into the always-technology-mediated human. Of course this point was made by McLuhan, in his equation of technology with extensions of man [*sic*] (McLuhan 1997, originally 1964). Indeed, Latour's (1988, 1993) deliberations on networks and artefacts are consistent with Stone's further point that a dichotomy based on an assumption that humans ever are separate from technology is flawed; rather the two are constitutive of each other. In late twentieth century 'economies of meaning' she argues, nature is a:

construct by means of which we attempt to *keep technology visible* as something separate from our 'natural' selves and our everyday lives. In other words the category 'nature', rather than referring to any object or category in the world, is a *strategy* for maintaining boundaries for political and economic ends, and thus a way of making meaning.

(Stone 2000: 517)

Unlike the 'extension of man' implied by say, the light bulb, which alters social organization; cybertechnologies and the humanoid are inscribed *within* each other and thereby constitute each other. Body/identity/technology subject/objects are not 'humans' in the sense of 'nature'; the boundaries have imploded, so that the person-as-cyborg, the subject/object of the twenty-first century, is a fully mediatized being. The cyber is at the same time a means of 'decoupling the body and the subject' (Stone 2000). The assumption of virtual identities bears no necessary relation to the body in question; a Net user may be constituted by multiple subjects, none of which are consistent with the body/subject 'on the outside'. The only sense in which the virtual subject is necessarily connected to the body is that the virtual or imagined subject has its roots in the consciousness of the body/subject. This latter point remains an important one however, because the user must always return to the body when s/he logs off. Therefore we return to the real, to the body politic and politicized, the gendered body, the racialized body, the suppressed body, the dominant body . . . in which all virtuality is rooted *in the final instance,* for as Stone comments, no virtual body will 'slow the death of a cyberpunk with AIDS' (2000: 525).

Crime, law and the cyber

As cities and bodies vanish, and communities and subjects transmutate, so to the same extent does crime, to a large extent their twentieth-century historical correlate, also lose its familiar metaphorical significance. The spaces and places of the cyber are criminogenic, but not in the way that cities and the 'real' social are, and not in the way that 'real' bodies are.

The physical and material force of city crime, the aesthetics of fear in the built environment, is replaced by other forms of victimization. Victimizations of the body are replaced by victimizations of the virtual subject. This does not necessarily increase security, since the spaces of exposure in the cyber are much greater, the ability to find the security bubbles offered in metropolitan oases much less. Nor does it necessarily follow that 'virtual' victimization is less destructive in its effects; arguably, they are much greater and more pervasive. Further, in the power afforded by the human–machine interface, there is a 'value-added' edge to victimization. More people can be affected at once; the possibilities of detection are immeasurably reduced, as is the potential for legal regulation; the potential gains of certain crimes (fraud, hacking, etc.) are huge; and perhaps above all the potential to bring down infrastructures which now rely on the virtual, is no longer merely a sci-fi hacker fantasy. All the goalposts within which crime can be conceptualized are now irrevocably moved, yet with 'one foot in the real' these are hence not only 'new' 'crimes', but also enhancements of old ones (sabotage, stalking, robbery, and so on).

If cities were 'ungovernable spaces' then cyberspace is far more so (Lash and Urry 1994). Then again, given the alterations in the dimensions of space and the nature of the technology, the local is also transformed, raising a whole new series of questions about 'sub' and 'counter' cultures. The expansion of the matrix has not meant the death of the anorak! The sociologies of urban popular (sub)cultures have been in transformation for some time with the increasing globalization, intertextuality, and virtuality of music culture, for example, and the accessibility of the Internet has transformed the notion of the fanzine, with consequent far-reaching implications for law and popular culture (Redhead 1990). In this section I will explore some of these examples in more detail, from spam to (s)talking, gaming to hacking. I shall refer to forms of 'victimization' rather than 'crime', since the latter term is mostly inaccurate as applied to cyberspace. This itself, as I shall argue, raises complex questions for the notion of 'law'.

Spam

Stivale (1997: 133) defines 'spam' as:

> That unnecessary data transmission that one participant
> deliberately produces often simply to fill lines on the recipient's
> screens, but sometimes to communicate aggressive messages as
> well. 'To spam', then, means precisely to inflict such verbiage
> on other 'Net' comrades, alone or *en masse*, and is generally
> taken to be a form of online harassment.

Stivale proposes three levels of 'aggressivity' in spamming, using the example of the LambdaMOO (multi-object oriented) MUD (a multi-user dungeon), a site 'structured like a large house with nearby grounds and community' (1997: 134). Participants in the site are guests in the house and can move around the rooms of the house, engaging in communication with around 8000 other 'guests'. Participants register, choose a character name, a gender, and a personal description, and are then on the road to their virtual identity. The highest level of aggression, 'pernicious spam', is of most relevance here, in that it often 'consists in virtual imitations of "real life" practices of harassment', using sexually explicit verbiage to 'spam unwitting participants in ways that might well be legally actionable in real life' (Stivale 1997: 139, 140). In one instance Dr_Jest sent homophobic and sexually violent spam to victims, which spurred a debate as to the status of 'words' as weapons, and whether they 'contain the force of "acts"' (Stivale 1997: 140).

The problem here is that if virtual names are spamming virtual names, then technically there is no 'real' aggressor or victim. The only sanction here is the exclusion of the user from the site, or his or her suspension. A rather different complexion was put on the matter in a case cited by Stivale where a male student was accused of using a female student's real name in a sexual fantasy involving torture, and posting it to a Usenet group. This case came to court on federal charges of transmitting a threat to kidnap or injure by electronic mail, but the judge gave priority to the First Amendment and dismissed the charges (Stivale 1997: 141).

The particular nature of cyberlinguistics poses further problems, since the language of the LamdaMOO MUD, for example, operates at different communicational levels: to 'say' is to talk directly, to 'emote' is to express a feeling or action indirectly, and to 'whisper' is a private communication between recipients within the same room (Stivale 1997: 141). These levels may be seen as having different relationships to the equivalence or otherwise of the virtual with action, and are therefore contestable textual domains. In addition, spam culprits can reappear in different identities, and the virtuality of identity also calls into question action. For example, in spamming a virtual identity, does it make a difference if misogynist spam is directed towards a female identity yet the 'real' holder of the identity is a man? (This of course is unknowable anyway unless the victim reveals their 'real' gender in complaint).

It is not just the question of whether the 'virtual' harassment counts as an act, but one of whether the practices in question are regulable. The contrast with the – still mediated – 'real' is clear when one considers that telephone harassment, which is highly actionable, is criminalized, and carries potentially stiff penalties. Spamming thus raises issues that reappear over and over again in the cyber: defining victimization as such, apportioning seriousness, and regulating cyberbehaviour. The seriousness of this difficulty is revealed if one considers Appardui's characterization of the imagination 'as social practice' (1990: 5).

MUD *wars: virtual practices of violence*

If Appardui's phrase is applied to the phenomenon of war games in MUDs, then we arrive quickly at a point of considering whether cyberwars constitute symbolic violence, and what the implications of taking such a position might be. Ito points out that to enter into MUD wars is to be already empowered, since it requires, as with any other cyberjourney, a certain material status in the 'real' world (Ito 1997), that is to say, ownership of or access to hardware and software, telecoms, and the possession of literacy and computer literacy, or cultural capital. However the virtual power struggles that take place in war gaming are, for Ito, as 'real' as the 'real' which enables the gamer to participate. Virtual characters are, he argues, 'alternative reembodiments' which generate questions of 'connection and accountability' (Ito 1997: 96). Pking (killing other characters) is a case in point, and follows the conventions which typically frame killing in the 'real'. MUDmurder would be killing someone, unprovoked, for pleasure or other motives. Self-defence however is MUDpking under provocation; then there is revenge pking for revenge. One of Ito's virtual respondents sees pking as 'almost like killing' in that it ends someone's *extension* of their real selves (1997: 97). Killing a virtual character is delineated from killing a monster because 'a monster is nothing. A monster is an extension of the game. It's not *real*. A person's *real*.' (Ito 1997: 97).

Cyber discipline and punishment represent a problematic not comprehended by Foucauldian discourse (Foucault 1977). Multiplicities of virtual identities, and the opportunities offered within the MUD for hiding make it very difficult to catch an offending MUDder. Punishment relies on the ability to banish an offender, which, because the MUDder can create new characters, is ineffective unless the whole site is banned; even then users with multiple access opportunities can simply re-enter from other sites. Although the 'sheriff' can confiscate properties of offenders (genitalia, physical strength), it does not solve the problem of multiple identities. Thus the dislocation of the virtual subject and the physical body permit the proliferation of offending. While all of this may seem trivial and even insulting to victims of 'real' crime (how could there be comparability between a 'virtual' rape and a 'real' rape?) it raises interesting questions of symbolic domination and violence which feminism has long been tackling in relation to other representational worlds such as fiction and film. The issues of disembodied identities, however, further complicate the symbolic violence of the cyber. In MUDrape it is the virtual identity that is being violated; the 'real' self of which it is an extension or projection is not necessarily embodied in the gender, sexuality, race, or any other dimension of identity of the actual user. Does this therefore make cyberaggression irrelevant (Wall 2001)?

S(talking)

These issues become more 'real' or more embodied when 'talking' on the Internet is considered. While spamming, pking, and MUDrape remain internal to the cyber, whatever their extensions into embodiment through their attachment to embodied identities may be, Usenet groups relate more clearly to 'real' people and would therefore conventionally be regarded as more serious. Frequently heated debates through Usenet groups can generate antipathies that have resulted in some users adopting the identities of others and placing postings in their 'names'. These may be of a pornographic or sexually explicit nature, transforming the identity of the victim into an aggressor. In many other cases motives are not clear, and may involve posting threats to the victim, distribution of defamatory 'information' about the victim, or invitations 'from' the victim, sometimes with details such as the victim's telephone number and/or address. Although this kind of behaviour is legally enforceable, and has resulted, for example, in jail sentences for perpetrators, the 'true' identity of the perpetrator is not always penetrable. Adam (2000: 216–17) cites one instance where the perpetrator did receive a six-year jail sentence:

> Angry that a woman has spurned him, he assumed her identity and posted personal information about her, including her address, in Internet sex chat rooms where he claimed sadomasochistic fantasies in her name. As a result of this a number

of men tried to break into her house. The man thought his identity was preserved on the Internet. He was eventually caught after the victim's father spent hours on the Internet posting messages that he hoped would attract the stalker. When the stalker eventually made contact, the woman's father turned the case over to the FBI.

In many more instances, however, the capabilities for hiding real-world 'identities' in the cyber result in non-detection, and in any case, not before the damage has been done. Thus there are two somewhat different scenarios here. While the most obvious one is the case where offline details about another user are revealed, opening them up to embodied threats of victimization, the other, while more contentious, is clearly, under most definitions, threatening behaviour. Even where both perpetrator and victim are anonymous, the symbolic and emotional violence may clearly have 'real' consequences for the online user not dissimilar to those experienced by victims of embodied crime: fear, anxiety, shame, anger, violation, humiliation, and so on. To dismiss stalking where offline details are not revealed is to assume that the victim herself (for most stalking victims, as in embodied reality, appear to be women (Adam 2000) sustains an unproblematic dissociation of her virtual and actual identities, or that because the threat of embodied violence is not likely to be actualized, then the psychological injury is less.

'Imposture' and power

The complexity of defining virtual victimization is further revealed when one takes into account that the identity of the perpetrator may also be in disjunction from their embodied identity, creating a 'false' situation of trust. Stone's (1996) account of the 'cross dressing psychiatrist' is interesting in this context. As noted above in the example of gaming dungeons, role-playing has long been integral to the cyber, at least since 1972 and the invention of Dungeons and Dragons, the original role-playing game (Stone 1996: 68). Stone's tale concerns a male psychiatrist who opened an account on a CB chat line on CompuServe in 1982. Having been mistaken for a woman, he was attracted to the different, deeply personal and textured ways in which women interacted, and decided to go online as a female. As 'Julie' he impersonated a mute paraplegic neuropsychologist, severely disfigured, who never saw anyone in person.

The impostor developed a whole identity around this 'person', started a women's discussion group on CompuServe, and doled out advice. 'She' was even active in detecting men masquerading as women on the Net, and warned other women of the dangers of things not being what they seem (Stone 1996: 70–2). All of this, if disturbing, might not be surprising if Lewin Sanford, Julie's creator, had been remotely like her; but in his 'real' personality online, Sanford was a flop, being a 'devout Conservative Jew' to Julie's atheist, a non-drug taker and almost a non-drinker, compared with Julie's penchant for getting high online, a sexual innocent compared to 'Julie's erotic virtual prowess . . . and fully able-bodied' (Stone 1996: 77). Yet he convincingly inhabited and projected the persona of a severely disabled woman.

One obvious conclusion of this is that to be multiply identitied is not necessarily to be pathologically disturbed; Lewin Sanford consciously and knowingly imposed a 'false' (something of a misnomer, clearly) identity in order to gain the confidence of women online and to be able to communicate with them, his anonymity protected by the system. The only way s/he could be found out was through carelessness.

Was Sanford victimizing women, whether or not he used his insights for gain or to inflict pain? In his (her) erotic adventures, was s/he committing sexual assault? The question of imposture, of course, has since become a highly publicized issue in relation to paedophilia as well as gender. 'Impersonation' of children in order to gain access to 'real' children in chat rooms seems in common-sense terms an obvious form of victimization, even if offline contact does not occur. But *is* this impersonation, in a culture where multiple realities are an acknowledged normal part of social life? The splitting of the body and identity creates an enormous problem for conventional paradigms of harassment and assault. If it is that our bodies give lie to our identities, as typically seen in the case of transgendering in 'reality', then only the surgical alteration of the body (in the case of gender at least) can create 'fit'. In the virtual this requirement is eradicated, freeing up a whole range of identities across ethnicity and the life course which, it could be argued, are no less authentic for their disembodiment. That this process could be a conscious *choice*, that people can choose rather than be innately driven to, achieve virtual cross-dressing through identity-manipulation, makes clear the deeply contradictory nature of attitudes toward transidentification. On the one hand multiplexing identities is normal and conventional; on the other it raises the problem of consensuality, since those interacting with the multiplexed identities have not knowingly consented to expose themselves to all of those identities. If the multiplexed identity is normal, however, then how can it be imposture?

Gaming and the embodying of the virtual: what can we learn from Lara?

Virtual embodiment poses as many questions for crime and law as does virtual disembodiment. Computer gaming, a highly elaborate cultural universe, illustrates this. In its PC/online crossover, it also highlights nicely the human/technology interface. It is both isolationist and fantastical, melding the individual, embodied PC user with an imaginary world of her or his choosing (the alter-ego world of the nerd in the bedroom); and highly social (crossing into the online world of disembodied global interactivity). In this section I will use the example of Lara Croft, also known as the Tomb Raider heroine, to look at what kinds of dilemmas arise when, in embodying the virtual, the crossovers between the virtual and the real occur in several directions at once.

> Lara Croft, created by [UK] based Core Design for gaming software publishers Eidos, has emerged as the first digital pin-up heroine . . . Core Design estimates that Lara has generated in excess of $300m. Lord Sainsbury has suggested that she should be an ambassador for 'New Britain'.
>
> *Design: The Journal of the British Design Council*, Spring 1999

In 1997, UK-owned companies involved in the 'interactive leisure software market' had a revenue of around £1.2 billion, £417 million of which came from exports. Lara has appeared in 'depth' and 'lifestyle' articles in *Telegraph* magazine, *The Face* and *FHM* (UK) and *Newsweek* and *Time* (US) among many others. Tomb Raider I, II, III, IV and V, the computer games in which the computer image Lara 'stars', have all topped the games charts and won almost every industry award in the UK. Tomb Raider was named one of the Design Council (UK) Millennium Projects. At last count, the AltaVista search engine found many thousands of web pages with 'Lara Croft' in the domain name. An 80-employee company in Derby, a small nondescript UK town, originally created Lara Croft and Tomb Raider. Tomb Raider rapidly became the cult favourite in the gaming community. Core, the creators, described the games as 'third person perspective action-adventure games offering a mix of exploration, puzzle-solving, and combat' (*Design* 1999, as above).

The iconic tidal wave which subsequently washed Lara into cyberspace was something of a shock to its creators. The managing director of Core Design, interviewed in *Design* (1999), said 'It's quite astounding. I'd like to say it was all a master plan, but I'd probably be struck down by lightning'.

The following discussion examines the way in which the icon of Lara Croft, one of the most important recent UK cultural exports to the US, has run head-on into legal discourse. Much of this centred around Core's wrath over 'misappropriation' of the product: fans either manipulating images of Lara or setting up their own editors and/or web sites using the Tomb Raider name. It is interesting that the attempt at social control was largely levelled at 'fans' rather than commercial sites. The highest profile case, in which a lawsuit was actually pursued to the tune of $1.1 million, was reported in the UK broadsheet newspaper the *Independent* on 19 March 1999. Headlined '$1.1m to keep Internet heroine's clothes on', the article described Lara as the 'improbably pneumatic gun-toting cult heroine of the Tomb Raider computer games'.

When Core Design found out that an American website called nuderaid.com featured hundreds of images of Ms Croft in pornographic poses, it decided to sue. The technology editor of the *Independent* found 14,600 web pages in a search combining 'Lara Croft' and 'naked' (my own estimate would be much higher). However, the difference in the case of this particular site was that nuderaid.com contained game players' *own* pornographic renditions of Ms Croft, although, reported the *Independent*, Core Design would like to rid the Internet of all images of Lara Croft. A spokeswoman for Core Design claimed 'we own the copyright on all forms of her image' and further,

> We don't want Lara to be associated with pornographic
> material. We have a large number of young fans and we don't
> want them stumbling across the pictures . . . or finding sites
> which are linked to other pornographic sites. It's completely
> irresponsible.
>
> (cited in the *Independent*, 19 March 1999)

The counterclaim from the site owner, reported as being one Joel Williams, was that since the site had been visited by at least 6.5 million web surfers since 1998, the writ represented an attempt to curtail freedom of expression. He posted a response on the web site which purportedly read (the site no longer carries the pictures):

> The site was created for fans to showcase *their* fantasy artwork
> . . . we provided the FREE ARCHIVE for the fans to express
> their love and fascination for their favourite fantasy woman
> . . . Yes, the artwork was of an adult nature and for mature
> audiences only; but the only people who visited this site were
> FANS of the GAME.
>
> (cited in the *Independent*, 19 March 1999)

Actually searching the Web on Lara Croft was a time-consuming business. It led into a massive labyrinth of sites, aptly named in one case 'The Universe of Lara Croft'. In this virtual 'Fannie' (fanzine), everything was covered, from Lara Croft's 'past', to hot tips on playing Tomb Raider, chat and news groups, what Lara does at Christmas, who is the man for Lara, links to other web sites, Geocities image imports, fan art, and, importantly in this context, the state of play in relationships with Core and their attempts to enforce international copyright over use of domain names and manipulation of images. With what appears to be a largely (though by no means exclusively) teen/early 20s following, Lara Culture is *big* on the Net.

Lara fans not only share an all-consuming interest in Tomb Raider gaming, Lara lifestyle, gaming in general, and Lara 'facts', but a sense of ownership over Lara and Tomb Raider. They believe that they should have the right to edit the levels of the game, to interact with it and determine the Universe of Lara. This goes much beyond, then, the swapping of 'hot tips' on gaming. The 'Tomb Raider Universe News' is subtitled 'What is Happening in the Tomb Raider Community?' Fans prepare their own web sites, invite other fans to join in constructing them, and mount their 'own' images of Lara as fan art. Lara Fan Fiction abounds:

> Have you checked out the latest in Tomb Raider Fan Fiction?
> Being Tomb Raider fans, I would like to invite you to check
> out WONDERS OF AN ANCIENT GLORY, my novel sized

Tomb Raider fan-fiction! It is currently being posted at *Tales of Beauty and Power* until I can get my own site up!

(fan site accessed March 1999)

The question of ownership (as Redhead, e.g. 1995, 1997b, has often explored in relation to soccer fandom) is central to Lara fans. They engaged in a continual debate with Core, occupying an ambiguous relationship toward the company; on the one hand they expressed themselves indebted to Lara's creators while at the same time resenting the company's continual attempts to enforce its ownership of Lara.

Despite Core's protestations of concern over pornographic content, perusal of 'innocent' fanzines suggests that Core were just as energetic in attempting to control the (non-'pornographic') activities of youthful fans, and are not above sending threatening letters to children and young people. Core's lawyer is dubbed 'The Big Stick Man' in *Tomb Raider Universe News* (*TRUN*). Domain names and image manipulations are the usual battlegrounds.

Chris, 'a teenager', got into particular trouble and a very heated debate ensued. Core instructed Chris that they would take legal action if he insisted on creating his own level editor:

> CORE's BIG Lawyers take on a teenager and WIN!
> Chris had been helping with the level editor. Chris and his parents received a nastygram from Core's lawyers. Chris has/had the web sites Lara's Cyberworld and Tomb Raider 3 the third beginning and he was helping with Tomb Raider Unity . . . Well, Chris' parents are furious. Core says he has to shut down all his web sites. Core says that tombraider.net infringes on copyrights so they are taking that away.
>
> *Chris:* I'm really sad . . . I will close all my sites, Lara's Cyberworld and Tomb Raider 3 the third beginning and I will stop to help the Tomb Raider news section and I will stop working on the level Editor project . . . I will not be able to talk to you because my parents are really furious and they will stop my internet connection. I will be able to surf and mail for the next few weeks and then my cyberlife will stop. Why? Because Core is not happy with what I have done so far. I have received a letter this

morning from Core, Core lawyer says: 'Within 14 days you must write a letter to us in which you promise and agree that you will not alter any Tomb Raider product (Level Editor) and that you must abandon the name tombraider.net, because its unfair competition and taking unfair advantage of Core products is not allowed'.

Editorial: OK Core Design. Chris is standing up and taking a grown up attitude on all of this. I hope Core does the same and does what is right!!!! If Core considers the demographics of your fan base and the competition such as Trespasser, Indiana Jones, Prince of Persia, you will also realise that you are kicking yourself right smack dab in the pocket book with this controversy (somewhat toned down from yesterday, when I was more upset).

(excerpts from *TRUN*, October 1998)

Just as teen magazines both make pop stars unreal, by iconizing them, and then immediately make them real again by detailing their 'fave foods', 'fave football team' etc., so the Lara Croft fanzines make Lara real by telling us about her 'past', and speculating about 'who is man enough for Lara' and Lara's 'fave foods'. Virtual Lara is as 'real' as virtual Bill Clinton.

The crucial difference between the icon/real person interchange in the teen magazine, and the virtual/real in cyberspace, is that in the cyber universe, all is interactive. The interactivity of the cyber is essential to an understanding of its special relationship to 'reality'. The fans make Lara, Lara makes the fans, the fans interact with each other to recreate Lara, so that Lara embodies the multiplicity of negotiated identities of each and every fan, and at the same time fans collectively share an identity through Lara.

Thus for Core to contest that Lara is 'their' image makes no sense in relationship to the virtual world of Lara's Universe. At this point the fans are able to interact with Core to contest Lara. Thus the (re)invention of Lara becomes a battleground which for the fans goes far beyond copyright, in which 'copyright' seems not only trivial, but also an insult to them and to Lara. It is as if Core were crying, 'But she was *our* idea', a stance to which the fans, aficionados and passionate defenders of cyberculture can only react with bemusement. Without interactivity, the Lara Croft controversy could never have arisen. It is the *changing* of the images that is at stake, and it is the interactivity of the technology that enables global fans to protest at Core Design's attempt to preserve copyright over the icon. As Levinson (1999) notes in his discussion of the relevance of McLuhan's work to the digital age, the cyber marks the definitive move from 'voyeur to participant'. In 2002, Tomb Raider was reported as having sold 28 million copies, described by *PC Gamer* magazine as 'one of the most successful gaming franchises in the modern gaming world' (May 2002: 46), and Lara Croft as 'the single genuine icon of gaming not owned by an international console manufacturer'.

The 'fan' in the cyber, then, is a rather particular kind of fan. The fandom of the Tomb Raider followers is not the old fandom of the football terraces, and not even the new fandom of the satellite TV sport-watchers. It is neither fandom, nor postfandom (Redhead 1995) but a virtual fandom of allegiance to – well – virtuality! It is not 'rooted' or 'communal' in any traditional sense of the word, nor is it necessarily artefactually based; it has no place and no necessary material existence. Yet it is passionate, articulate, and bound together by the focal concern with virtual Lara Croft. Interestingly, it seems Core has caught up with its own ethos and accepted the marketing potential for the ownership of Lara in the form of some limited concessions to fans: Core's Operations Director, Adrian Smith, extols the virtues of the sixth Tomb Raider game (Tomb Raider: The Angel of Darkness) in offering more role-playing potential so that 'you can make her feel more like *your* Lara than anyone else's' (quoted in *PC Gamer*, May 2002: 50).

Cyber subcultures

The struggles over 'who owns Lara Croft', over the identity of Lara Croft, and the virtual body of Lara Croft, highlight the broader question of ownership in the cyber. The 'virtual embodiment' of celebrities, of political institutions, of money systems, involves the transmutation of 'real' people, 'real' objects, and 'real' structures' into virtuality. This has laid them open to contestation, a possibility that has been exploited to the full by hacker culture.

The definition of hacking needs to be seen as multilayered. 'Hacking' can embrace so many different virtual acts of sabotage, intrusion, infiltration, and 'theft', or 'fraud' that a unifying definition is not immediately apparent. One predominant theme taken up by many commentators, and promoted in early media representations, has been that of hacking as a counter-culture, or 'a rebel with a modem' (Ross 2000: 256). 'Property (information) is theft' has been the clarion call of the pro-hacker. It is the basis of an *ethical* position (exhibited by the Lara Croft fans) which asserts the 'right of users to free access to all information' (including embodied images). In the 1990s, argues Ross, 'the cybernetic counter-cultures . . . are . . . being formed around the *folklore of technology* – mythical feats of survivalism and resistance in a data-rich world of virtual environments and post-human bodies' (2000: 258). 'Hacking' also constitutes diverse forms of online strategies, which more broadly are about a particular attitude toward the human–machine interface. A hacker interviewed by Taylor (1999: 16) in a fascinating research study, opined that hacking is not just about computers:

> [It] pertains to any field of technology. Like, if you haven't got a kettle to boil water with and you use your coffee machine, then in my mind that is a hack. Because you're using the technology in a way that it's not supposed to be used . . . So, for me it's not only computers it's anything varying from locks, computers, telephones, magnetic cards, you name it.

Ingenuity and the kick arising from it are the *expressive* dimensions of hacking. The skill, and its exhibition, are *performative* dimensions. The beauty of hacking, the art of the hack performance, only truly capable of by either other hacks or those who originated the system, might be configured as the *aesthetics* of hacking. I would argue that all of these dimensions – the ethical, the expressive, the performative, and the aesthetic – cohere in a cultural politics of hacking, which has richly diverse virtual manifestations. Perhaps more than this, I would add the dimension of the *subversive*, since hacking consciously seeks to subvert the technology, its originally intended 'functions', and/or the individuals or groups whose interests it represents. These pertain whether or not particular instances of hacking are successfully defined as 'criminal', but are, indeed, common dimensions of many forms of criminality.

I use the phrase 'cultural politics' of hacking to indicate a number of positions which the hacker may inhabit. To an extent hacking has a

'Robin Hood' image, implying robbing the information-rich to pay the information-poor, but this would be to oversimplify hacking motivations. Hacking is far from being solely an idealized demand for cyberdemocracy, as it has often been characterized. The latter characterization of hacking has on one side a dystopian vision of the information society in which the information elite exercise an omnipotent power over the populace, on the other, the hacker-as-hero who retrieves democracy and privacy by alternative means and restores the autonomy of the individual.

This is exemplified in the film *Enemy of the State* (1999). In the film the US 'National Security Agency' kills a US senator to get a bill through Congress which will essentially destroy all rights of privacy. The killing is accidentally taped by an ecologist carrying out a study of bird-migrating habits and through a series of twists and turns, ends up in the possession of a young lawyer, Robert Dean (Will Smith). Every available piece of information technology is brought to bear on the problem by the NSA, from highly advanced bugging and surveillance mechanisms – particularly the use of satellite technologies, which are omnipresent as they home in on Dean's every move – to the manipulation of the news, ('framing' Dean as a fraudster, a Mafia puppet, and an alleged murderer), and the dismantling of Dean's private life (attempting to wreck his marriage by setting up a supposed sexual liaison with an ex-girlfriend who just happens to be his link to the cyber counter-culture, disabling his credit cards, and so on). However, the cyber counter-culture contact, a rejected ex-NSA expert who has taken to private surveillance work, saves the day through his superlative hacking skills. For every infomatic strategy employed by the NSA, Brill (Gene Hackman) has a counter-strategy, developed in his secret computer lab. The film develops into an action thriller based on hack and counter-hack, with Brill and Dean in a quest, not just to save Dean's life (in every sense) but to preserve the freedom of democracy. Based on the premise that being paranoid doesn't mean they're not out to get you, *Enemy of the State* elevates the hacker to the status of the saviour of the free world in the ever-encroaching grip of the virtual and corrupt megalomania of the state. With convincing special effects and believable technological weaponry, a less overtly 'Hollywood' presentation would leave the Internet TV market decimated. 'If nothing else' commented one reviewer, 'it'll wear out the anoraks' pause button when the video comes out' (review by Ceri Thomas, *Flicks*, January 1999).

While it makes great movie material, this idealized view of the hacker is highly mythic. Aside from the pitfalls of the 'paranoid position' (Ross 2000: 264) itself, which formulates a 'totalizing, monolithic picture of systemic domination' (Ross 2000: 263), I have already suggested that hacking must be seen as comprising numerous dimensions, which are by no means simply political. Moreover, hackers' own accounts of their motivations are much more complex than that of the information revolutionary (Taylor 1999). Taylor aggregates the expressed motives of the hackers he interviews under six headings (1999: 46). Of these, I will focus on three which seem to be interrelated: feelings of addiction, curiosity, and enjoyment of feelings of power.

Addiction to the technology interface is as fuelled by the advertising industry as is consumption of alcohol, cigarettes, chocolate, and other cultural stimulants and narcotics. Its chemical component is probably adrenaline. Hackers, notes Taylor, often use the language of addiction and obsession to frame their activities.

> We are addicted to information and knowledge, and our drugs
> are withheld from us. We are forced to seek our precious
> information and knowledge elsewhere. We have to find
> challenge somewhere, somehow, or it tears our very souls
> apart. And we are, eventually, forced to enter someone's
> system.
>
> (Toxic Shock Group 1990, quoted in Taylor 1999: 47)

The moral panic over the alleged addictive qualities of computer games for example, focusing on children in particular, have paralleled those over television – as in 'Computers Turned My Boy into a Robot' (*Daily Mirror*, 18 March 1993, cited in Taylor 1999: 49). A fictional example of addiction is found in Sinha's (2000) novel *The Cyber Gypsies*, whose principal character, an advertising writer known as 'Bear', finds his marriage, family, and entire conventional existence being destroyed by his addiction to roaming the cyber in the company of Jesus Slutfucker and others.

However one of Taylor's respondents takes issue with this projection of addiction onto the technology; he contends that hackers are not necessarily compulsive or addictive; that *some* are is, he feels, a quality of the person and not the technology (Taylor 1999: 49). Basically, a nerd is a nerd. Thus when I asked my students to define a 'hacker', one of them said brightly: 'Spotter, innit!' Nerds, (train)spotters, anoraks: all conjure up images of introverted addicts/obsessives, compelled by the poetics and mystery of intricate masses of information which to many would seem downright irrelevant. Sitting on a bench on a miserable train platform one windy, rainy day, a small herd of boys and men rushed past me, led by the excited cry of '37 on Corby wires!' I looked at the man next to me. 'Rare haulage', he explained. On other train journeys I have seen similar figures, solitary, murmuring train numbers into dictaphones for transcription later. (Anyone who has transcribed tapes longhand knows how long this takes).

A crucial difference is that hackers *intervene* in the system which produces the information. The challenge lies partly just in breaking the codes, an ineffable curiosity to know if it can be done, how, and what lies on the other side, testing the limits of the technology and the system.

The discourses surrounding hackers, while portraying them as dangerous, also, through the nerd imagery, embody them as inadequate, physically unattractive, and as Lupton (2000: 481) points out, sharply contrasted to 'the idealized, clean, hard, uncontaminated masculine body of the cyborg as it is embodied in the *Robocop* and *Terminator* films'. The hacker metaphorically might exchange his anorak for a dirty raincoat, envisaged as a sexual inadequate and social misfit whose only relationship is with his computer.

The hacker, however, participates in a very erotic activity in cyberspace. Both obsession and curiosity are elements of desire; the hacker seduces the system, attempting to transform it from part of the other to part of the self; and is seduced by the system, its mysteries holding both the promise and threat of unconquered terrain. Inextricably related to feelings of power, hacking represents the dialectics of domination and control, access and penetration. The hacker can bring down systems, endanger individuals and corporations through the publication of 'private' or 'classified' information, and threaten infrastructures. It is hardly surprising that it is a male-dominated world (Taylor 1999); perhaps, like most crime, it requires above all a theory of masculinities (Jefferson 1997), an irony considering the transgendering or de-gendering of identities which occupies such a large place in the cyber. Net women are more likely to engage in women's work or the culture of the feminine, or for expressive and communicative relationships to gayness. Clerc for example, reports that online fandom is highly gendered, and to some extent she supports the generalization that 'men communicate for status, and women communicate to maintain relationships' (Clerc 2000: 221). However, lesbian and homoerotic sites are highly popular; and women generally are highly active users of the Net. Therefore cybercrime and cybervictimization require a prioritizing of gender as an analytical category.

Viral victimization

Unlike flaming, which refers to a war of words (Millard 1997), the metaphor of the virus is more sinister. The bogeyman of the virtual world, anyone who has been the victim of a virus attack will know the sense of horror and helplessness as the screen crumbles before them. The sensation of the sender of the virus must be akin to that of the arsonist watching the beauty of a burning building. As apparently random and uncontrollable as an arson attack, ever more sophisticated viruses are an endemic form of attack in the virtual world. Firewall after firewall may be erected, only for the user to discover that they are about as effective as window locks in preventing burglary. The market in viruses ensures their effective circulation, as does their ability to self-replicate. In the age of AIDS and HIV, such metaphors carry a resonant message of menace. This not only includes the connotations of the inability to find a cure, but also of contributory negligence. As Lupton (2000: 479) says,

> there are a series of discourses that suggest that computers which malfunction due to 'viral contamination' have allowed themselves to become permeable, often via the indiscreet and 'promiscuous' behaviour of their users (in their act of inserting 'foreign' disks into their computer, therefore spreading the virus from PC to PC).

Some viral threats are even emailed warning of retribution for carelessness. During the writing of this book, I received a warning that the university's computer systems were going to be brought down by a virus which would collapse all the information systems upon which its functioning depended (including, unhappily, the payroll system). This was to be a 'punishment' for 'your laughable security systems. Your firewalls are pathetic and your anti-virus systems come out of the dark ages'. The warning was either a hoax (although it was clear from information given in the email that the 'attacker' had penetrated the university systems as they alleged), or the rapid upgrading of the firewalls and virus scanners succeeded in repelling the onslaught.

Perhaps the scariest thing about viruses, apart from what they can do, is that the discourses of motivation surrounding them are 'irrational', frequently based around notions of 'because I can', 'doing it for fun', or 'punishment'. Insofar as virus culture is linked to hacker culture, it is the culture of the 'terrorist' hacker. Rushkoff reproduces a typical example, Virus 23:

> WARNING:
> This text is a neurolinguistic trap whose mechanism is triggered by you at the moment when you subvocalize the words VIRUS 23 words that have now begun to infiltrate your mind in the same way that a computer virus might affect an artificially intelligent machine . . .
>
> The words VIRUS 23 actually germinate via the subsequent metaphor into an expanding array of icy tendrils all of which insinuate themselves so deeply into the architecture of your thought that the words VIRUS 23 cannot be extricated without uprooting your mind . . .
>
> When you have finished reading the remaining nineteen words this process of irreversible infection will be completed and you will depart believing yourself largely unaffected by this process.
>
> (reproduced in Rushkoff 1996: 251)

Viruses can also be mutated and co-opted, and subsequent mutations of Virus 23 quickly appeared. A 'war of the memes' is generated, essentially a war of the words, since memetic viruses are not about crashing systems but about implanting subversive ideas, or viral manifestos, into your system. Viral hoaxes can be as important as viruses because they are weapons in symbolic warfare, and mirror symbolic warfare in the mediated world generally, where dominant discourses are subverted by counter-cultural messages. Rushkoff (1996) details a number of these, as well as tactics which, like viruses that are launched by disabling the computer systems they wish to overthrow, use guerrilla warfare methods, create a sensation that forces the media to react, thus generating counter-reactions and thrusting the counter-cultural discourse into the limelight. Whether or not this kind of activity is criminal largely depends on how amenable it is to criminalization. Grabosky and Smith (1998) deal with the issue by translating cyberactivity into the language of conventional crime: 'electronic vandalism' including memetic invasion ('electronic graffiti'). This is a double-edged sword. By substituting a criminalizing set of metaphors ('vandalism'), they place the cyber within the comprehension of traditional criminology; in doing so, they also 'hide' the many difficulties of equating the cyber with the embodied world. This continuing problem is highlighted by the final category of victimization to be discussed in this chapter, that of hate 'crime'.

Cyberhate

This observation brings us back around to the construction of the Other in cyberspace, which finds its manifestation particularly in hate sites, whether misogynist, homophobic, or racist. For example, hatred and patriotism web sites in the UK include Skinheads-UK, White Aryan Resistance, Ku-Klux-Klan, Neo-Nazi, Nation of Islam, Jewish Radicals, Foreign Nationalism, and Antigay. Zickmund (2000) reports a proliferation of US-generated hate sites of similar persuasions. This of course immediately deflates the claims of those who see in the cyber a global community, for the 'community', as in the real world, is itself the focus of political and pathological hatred, as subgroups seek to promote the annihilation of other groups. While in the UK 'real' world, incitement to racial hatred, for instance, may be a crime, it is endemic in cyberspace. It is used to 'traffic' in hate to countries where strict hate-censorship laws exist, and Zickmund found that in America,

> members can be easily routed to a variety of groups through a clearing station, such as the Aryan Re-Education Link. This station is a linking service for thirty-four separate radical Web pages. The groups represented tend towards the skinhead spectrum, but white supremacists are advertised as well.
>
> (2000: 240)

She found that the 'dominant metaphoric association' used by group members was that of war, and particularly the iconic adoption of the Nazi era (Zickmund 2000: 241). Sites are also used to market Nazi products such as military paraphernalia and iconic devices like swastika stick-pins.

The objects of hate function to bind together the hate-community, being represented as contaminating and threatening forces, which require 'containment'. Homosexuals are represented as those who will bring about the collapse of family life, sodomize your sons, and destroy the Church. Third World immigration is described as 'killing our people and our way of life. GET INVOLVED AND STAND UP FOR YOUR WHITE RIGHTS' (Scarborough Skinheads, cited in Zickmund 2000: 243). Displacement (the reversal whereby the hate group see themselves as the dispossessed, robbed of their heritage by the Other) is usual.

The dimensions of cyberhate follow the dimensions of race hate, homophobia and misogyny in general; what is different is its accessibility, pervasiveness, and lack of amenability to regulation. A 'global underground', instantaneously linked through the wires, is hardly an 'underground' in the conventional usage of the term. Cyberhate sites also differ, though, in that they are vulnerable to retaliation, flaming and spamming. The interactivity of the Web means that target groups and libertarians can attempt to subvert the subversion directly. In an ideological and discursive war, this relatively disadvantages the hate groups, whose tactics in the embodied world would also include anonymous attacks on the person and the victimization of property. Conversely, however, Zickmund argues that the participation of oppositional voices provides members of hate groups with a platform, 'factors which increase the opportunities for the enactment of radical rhetoric' (2000: 251).

Although interesting, I find Zickmund's analysis disturbing in that she refers to hate groups as 'radical subversives', and those who confront them as 'antagonists'. Despite Zickmund's obvious oppositional attitude to racism, I find her usage euphemistic, and therefore legitimating. This underlines the dilemma that I have already raised: that the wars of the cyber are essentially wars of words. Policing discursive violence in a cyber environment must prove impossible, because interpretation and interactivity are far more flexible and abstract than with embodied violence. If language is social practice then the complexities of identifying or regulating taxonomies of hate are multiplied in the virtual world, while at the same time the effects of victimization are difficult to establish. The issue of control in general is an ever-present problem in any attempt to apply modernist discourses of 'crime' and 'law' to the cyber.

The virtual/real: where does it leave crime and law?

The dilemmas presented in this chapter seem not to present a problem for Grabosky and Smith (1998). They begin a chapter on 'electronic van-dalism and terrorism' (relating to hacking and viral attack) by saying that 'many forms of telecommunications-related crime are simply tra-ditional crimes committed with modern tools' (Grabosky and Smith 1998: 47). At the same time they admit that their use of the term 'van-dalism' is metaphoric (whereas they clearly consider the use of 'terror-ism' as merely descriptive!). However, 'the activities which are the subject of this chapter are distinctly modern' (Grabosky and Smith 1998: 47). As a result of this strange logic (the substitute of one metaphoric dis-course with another) they see it as unproblematic to simply apply con-ventional contemporary, or 'modernist' categories of crime and the law to the cyber. True, the law may need redrafting, but ultimately for Grabosky and Smith the definition of the criminal and the application of law as we know it are questions of reform.

The conclusion here must be to argue that their assertion takes no account of the cyber as a cultural realm which has contours quite incom-patible with such a position. The complexities of the articulation between the cyber and the embodied world render any discourses that rely on traditional notions of the body, identity, ownership, and copy-right demand a retheorizing, even a fundamental challenging of, Cart-esian formulations of law.

The cyber is the ultimate always-already culture; it has no history, no memory, and no future. In this sense it is global culture, not because it represents a unitary world culture, or a culture tied to a world state, but because it is all-embracing while being diverse; integrative while being disintegrative; divided not along boundaries of nation-state, time or place, with identities tied to these, but along many different and con-stantly shifting fragmentary planes (Featherstone 1995; Barker 1997). The (sub)cultures of cyberspace are the multifaceted allegiances to aspects of the cyber itself. As I have argued, this is not to take a naïve view that the cyber exists apart from the material. Clearly in economic and global political terms it does not.

The potted history of the cyber quickly reveals its origins in US defence systems, the Cold War and the development of satellite tech-nologies, the growth of packet switching and networking, and its rapidly developing commercial as well as defence potential. That any discussion of cyberculture sits within a matrix of the military and state interests of US domination, and within the imperatives of global capitalism, and therefore is bounded on all sides by these materialities, is (or should be) clear (see Kitchin 1998 for a good empirical overview). Such imperatives drive concerns with encryption and privacy (Loader 1997), and a continual tension between the discourses of privacy and democracy.

The decentralized flexibility that characterizes cyberspace and renders it 'amorphous, anarchic and global' (Raab 1997: 169) has, since the development of LamdaMOO programming allowed users 'to alter their surrounds and build new parts of the world' (Kitchin 1998: 35). A glance at graphs of the proliferation of hosts and networks show exponential growth between 1993 and 1996 alone (Kitchin 1998: 39). A mapping of differential rates of growth of the matrix in 1994 show dynamic spurts in the numbers of hosts in parts of East Asia (notably Hong Kong, Singapore and Taiwan), Eastern Europe, and Latin America as well as the continuing expansion in the already highly developed networks of the West, Japan, and Korea (Kitchin 1998: 42). The development and growth of VR (virtual reality) is proceeding with similar alacrity, and Kitchin predicts that immersive technologies will reach the same status as, and will merge with, the Internet in the next decade or two (1998: 53).

Attempts to comprehend these developments within modernist discourses of crime and the law face not only the complexities of devising frames of reference which can deal with jurisdictional, detectional, and enforceability difficulties, but also fundamentally fail to recognize the normative and cultural basis of law and crime, as if the interface between culture, economics, and politics never existed. That both the law and the cyber are linguistically and discourse-based systems is evident from the ongoing struggles with syntax and metaphor completely undermines such a position. The capabilities of the technology/human interface demand a prioritizing of the cultural.

Japanese entrepreneur Masayoshi Sun asserted that:

> There are only two numbers in my vocabulary – zero and infinity. The Internet encompasses both these characteristics. It has zero variable cost; there is zero decrease in accuracy as information is passed around. At the same time, it has infinite reach, infinite information, and infinite product range. Neither of these things – zero or infinity – were possible in the past.
>
> (cited in the *Independent*, 17 February 1999)

As shown in the Lara Croft example, and as suggested by the other studies of disembodied virtuality and virtual embodiment discussed in this chapter, there are profoundly disruptive questions for any equation of the cyber with the real, as if the cyber were merely a somewhat bent mirror of the real. These questions encompass those of ownership, definitional adequacy, policing, and enforceability. It is not enough to develop 'old law for new technologies' (email interview in Taylor 1999: 153) or to draw easy analogies between embodied crime and cybercrime, for 'cyberspace is the site of disjunction, where analogical production comes to find the limits of analogy' (Moreiras 1993: 198, cited in Taylor 1999: 144). Or, as Karnow (1994: 8, cited in Taylor 1999: 145) puts it:

> The battle of the metaphor always erupts in the face of new and powerful technologies. Our imagination is fired, but our stability is threatened; and we always seek the precedent for understanding. So we use the property analogy; the metaphor of invaded homes and goods when systems are attacked, the allusion to space and universes. But this is a category mistake.

Who owns Lara Croft? Is it the Big Stick Men? Clearly not, since 'she' is a product of cyberculture itself. But the notion of copyright is not only questioned, it is transformed by virtual embodiment. The inherent property of interactivity in the cyber renders all images manipulable by all users. This is not a case of 'copying' because a digital image has no inherent fixity. 'Traditional' legal language cannot comprehend the complexity of an interactive virtuality, however much it may attempt to do so.

The ubiquity of the cultural imagery of the cyber is also characterized by its fluidity. If the image of Lara Croft is changed, then is she/it any longer Lara Croft? Who owns she/it if she/it is no longer Lara Croft, but a different Lara Croft? Who, in any case, owns a cultural icon, particularly one that is continually mutating at the hands of its participant–consumers? Since Tomb Raider itself was designed to be interactive (the point of the games themselves is to allow interaction) the fluidity of the icon has already been set as a starting point. Likewise the disembodiment of the virtual identity, and the multiplexing of identities, transforms the notions of subject and agency, perpetrator and victim.

On hacking, Taylor (1999: 155) repudiates the analogy with the criminal act of theft or breaking and entering, because:

> Hacking intrusions do not involve the same threats of transgression of personal physical space and therefore a direct and physical threat to an individual. With the complete absence of such a threat, hacking activity will remain viewed as an intellectual exercise . . . rather than a criminal act even if, on occasion, direct physical harm may be an indirect result of the technical interference caused by the hacking.

Definitional adequacy particularly comes into prominence with the issue of pornography. While prosecutions have obviously been successfully brought, for example in the UK under Section 1(3) of the Obscene Publications Act 1959, which defines electronic transmission as publishing, this does not solve the problem of definition. Definition of pornography is already collapsing under the weight of its own contradictions in the 'real' world, despite repeated attempts to resurrect the issue. This is even more hopelessly entangled in virtual space. Is a naked Lara Croft a design icon or a pornographic image? Does this depend upon the eye of the beholder? Can a computer-generated image be pornographic? Nuderaider, a commercial porn site (not as in nuderaid.com), manipulated the Lara Croft images into hardcore pornographic scenes as a 'front end'; these then lead directly into general hardcore pornographic sites. These are not 'smutty jokes' on Lara Croft's image but invitations to join the 'Tomb Raider Ring' ('Click Here!'), containing the 'usual'(!) hardcore subsets, for example, Amateurs, Anal, Asians . . . Blacks, Blowjobs . . . Teen – through the alphabet, and 'special' tastes such as 'How Young Do You Like Them' ('Click Here'). The Nuderaider homepage protested against its critics:

> Do you think it's scary that there are men out there *fantasising* [Click Here!] over a computer generated character? No, because men will fantasise about anything. Compared to sheep or whatever I think Lara's quite a healthy fantasy. What's wrong with wanting to sleep with a computer generated character? She's got a perfect body after all.

The significance of cyberspace lies in the way in which, as a cluster of technologies, it offers the potential for human–human and human–computer interaction to take place at the level of the virtual; it is not the technology itself which transforms human interaction, but the entering into the technology of the subject, effecting a transformation of the subject into the virtual, of human identities into virtual identities, and conversely investing virtual phenomena with ostensibly (simulated) 'human' qualities.

In the cyberuniverse of Lara Croft the virtual becomes embedded in the real. This is the mirror image of the real-in-the-virtual; in other words, the Lara Croft phenomenon merely strengthens the case that in virtuality, the virtual/real *distinction* becomes somewhat meaningless. If men a la Nuderaider masturbate over a computer-generated image, does that make it pornography? Is virtual reality sex – the idea of the orgasmic sensation, which is not actually 'real', therefore pornographic? If something has no material existence can it be pornographic? The difficulty is not so much where pornographic images from the 'real' world are merely scanned into the machine – or at least this is no more difficult than definition in the 'real' world – but whether the notion of the virtual essentially undermines the discourse of pornography as transgressive. Lara Croft is not a person. Nor was 'Julie'. The rise of the virtual/ prosthetic undermines any legal control legitimated by a regulation of the body.

Many attempts have been and continue to be made to solve the enforcement 'problem' through congresses, directives, watchdogs, and committees, peopled by lawyers, international representatives, politicians, the police, industry experts, academics, and so on. Partial and temporary 'solutions' are sporadically found to tiny parts of massive questions. Where one stands on this is a matter more of cultural subscription to particular discourses and representations of law than one of demonstrable efficacy, since to date there has been very little demonstrable efficacy from any perspective. Extending legal approaches to pornography and obscenity on the basis of the contradictions which have dogged the US, home of the Internet, for decades leave an existing disjuncture between discourses of law and sexuality widening inexorably.

From the perspective of 'cultural criminology', the far more interesting question is one of the challenge to the theoretical and normative basis of regulation and law in the context of popular (cyber) culture. One important point of interest in the Lara Croft example is that it dissolves the paradigms within which we are used to thinking about the regulation of popular culture. Redhead (1995) has already convincingly argued that the late twentieth century sees the point at which law disappears into popular culture. The present discussion in a sense begins where

Redhead's argument regarding 'disappearance' ends (see Redhead 1995: Ch. 5). For Redhead,

> the regulatory regimes which are necessary to create surveillance of [cyberspace] can be envisaged as 'cyber-law', the policing of cyberspace and the dawn of the disappearance of the body-in-law . . .
>
> Virtual reality sex through interactive sex games and 'teledildonic' suits is threatening to make legal and social regulation impossible, a state of 'virtual law'.
>
> (1995: 59–60)

While being in general sympathetic with these statements (although unfortunately anyone has yet to present me with a teledildonic suit for Christmas), I would take the argument further. Ultimately, the virtual is not a place where law can be. The law does not so much disappear into popular culture, but rather popular cyberculture problematizes the law. Any concept of the law as moral arbiter, as normative representation, depends not only upon the body, but also on place, space, time, and the ability to impose discourses based in natural language. It depends upon memory, history, and a concept of the subject. 'Virtual' or 'cyber' and 'law' are in essence oppositional. In the universe of Lara Croft, there is no body, no space, no place, no history, no memory, no property, no subject, in any sense in which we understand these terms in the 'real' world. There is no nationhood, no boundary. Without these there can be no transgression. Legal transgression is only something that the regulators in the 'real' world can attempt to project upon the virtual. Resistances emanate easily and effectively from the virtual in response to attempts to police the cyber. This is not to say that the virtual is a-normative.

Rather, in cyberspace, the normative comes from within, only to the extent that its virtual inhabitants accept or reject it. 'Modernist' notions of law dependent upon conceptions of state, polity, rationality, contract, property – in essence most of what is taken as the basis of law – has little purchase in a virtual world.

This is of course why some argue that the cyber represents the ultimate 'democracy' (Levinson 1999). It dissolves the rule of law. From this one could conclude that the cyber is the safest haven for popular culture. One is of course left with some nagging modernist misgivings. What of the role of global economics and the power of the cyberindustries in determining the form and content of cyberspace? What of the fact that, despite the development of alternative languages ('pking' for instance) much net discourse still exists in 'real world' language, that net cultures relate to 'real world' politics, as with hate sites? Centrally also, cyberspace's social divisions of contestations over power have their roots in the 'real' through the human–technology interface; despite the multiplexed identity, gendering in cyberspace arises out of, and feeds back into, 'real' gender/power. 'Cyberspace' cannot be treated as a neutral space, or a definitively 'different' space; but neither can it be grasped by existing notions of crime and the law.

Poster (1995: 79–80) argues:

> For what is at stake in these technical innovations, I contend, is not simply an increased 'efficiency' of interchange, enabling new avenues of investment, increased productivity at work and new domains of leisure and consumption, but a broad and extensive change in culture, in the way identities are structured . . . if modern society may be said to foster an individual who is rational, autonomous, centred and stable (the 'reasonable' man of the law, the educated citizen of representative democracy . . .) then perhaps a postmodern society is emerging which nurtures other forms of identity different from, even opposite to, those of modernity.

More or less dismissing such theorizing, Robins (1995: 137), for example, counters with:

> These issues are not without interest. But, at the same time, there is the exclusion of a whole set of other issues . . . it is as if the social and political turbulence of our time – ethnic conflict, resurgent nationalism, and urban fragmentation – had nothing to do with virtual space. As if they were happening in a different world.

Are these arguments incompatible? Poster's position does not necessarily deny 'the real'. It is more that cyberspace fundamentally embraces and transforms the real to the extent that one cannot separate out 'the real' from 'the virtual'. Robins's position, likewise, is not contradicted by Lara's, or any other virtual universe. The range of computer games available certainly contains many that are explicitly based in disturbing areas of social conflict: 'Hooligans: Storm over Europe' for example, a pro-Nazi game, was regarded as too offensive by *PC Gamer* magazine to be given the 'oxygen of publicity' (*PC Gamer*, May 2002: 16). The interactive implications of the product make the term 'game' something of a misnomer, as the discussion of pornography in relation to Tomb Raider, and the section on cyberhate above suggests. The 'social issues of our time', in other words, have everything to do with virtual space, and the reverse is also true.

This issue will not go away; it will intensify with the increasing development of virtual reality and its interaction with the Internet (Heim 1998). Where would crime and the law be in an attempt to normatively configure or regulate the sensory world? The debates surrounding the cyber are not, for all sorts of reasons, amenable to resolution. Rather, they form one moment of a general complex of shifts, which demand a realignment of ourselves toward crime, law, media futures.

6 ■ CRIME, LAW AND MEDIA FUTURES

In presentation the map attains . . . *the level of discourse.* Its
discursive form may be as simple as a single map image
rendered comprehensible by the presence of title, legend, and
scale; or as complex as those in *The New State of the World
Atlas,* hurling multiple map images, diagrams, graphs, tables,
and texts at their audience in a raging polemic. It may be as
diverse as vacation triptiks, rotating cardboard star finders,
perspex-slabbed shopping centre guides, chatty supermarket
video displays, or place mats for Formica dinner tables.
Presentation is more than placing the map image in the context
of other signs; it's placing the map in the context of its
audience.

(Wood 1992: 140–1)

The criminological world could benefit immensely from Denis Wood's
(1992) explorations of representation in *The Power of Maps.* It is a revelatory work, unpicking the multiple relationships between cartographic
discourses and an imagined reality, between interests, instrumentality,
and the power of knowledge. In this closing chapter I will consider
crime, law and media futures, first from the point of view of cartogra-
phy, taking Wood's theoretical framework as a starting point, and

second asking whether the theorizations of the 'postmodern' can add anything to (or dissolve) this framework, and what might lie beyond or outside both the 'modern' and the 'postmodern'. Finally I shall return to questions of ethics that have surfaced repeatedly, in different ways, throughout the book, and to the question of crime, law and media futures.

Cartographic convolutions?: the media mapping of crime and law

The reality/referent, fact/fiction dilemmas which plague the theorizing about crime and the media paradoxically pose fewer dilemmas from a cartographic perspective. A map, explicitly representational, is not expected to be 'realistic'. Nevertheless it bears the burden of requirements of accuracy, a concept laden with unspoken entailments. Accuracy in respect of what? In respect of whom? The diverse contexts in which maps are produced and 'consumed' clearly have ramifications far beyond the Ordnance Survey. I have uncovered no better aid to conceptualizing the dilemmas posed by mediatization than Wood's thesis. Lacking in conceit, it orients itself towards culture in a way that expresses an acceptance of the ultimate unknowability of the real while being acutely aware of the kinds of jobs which knowledge does. Below, I use Wood's analytical dimensions in a retrospective application to the themes raised in the preceding chapters. Subsequently, I shall reject what I perceive to be the overdetermination accorded to instrumentality which I feel is present in his work. For the present, however, I want only to appropriate his writing in a positive sense.

Maps do not reflect order in the world, nor do they give order to the world. They *render* the world coherent, but only if you know how to read them. Moreover that reading depends in turn upon what you bring to the map by means of requirements. The range of modes of representation and interpretive conventions applied to the world through the process of mapping it are as diverse as the possible range of interpretive thought.

That maps are *rational* aids to the practical negotiation of spatiality, or relationality, is a notion only highly developed in modernity. As such they go hand in hand with Giddens's conceptual mapping of the epoch. The maps necessary for the early modern period were of course, aids to navigation and symbols of the power of colonization in the emergence and consolidation of the nation state (Giddens 1989, 1991). Throughout modernity, maps have been the essential underpinning of the rationalization and bureaucratization of the world. The transformations of information and the electronic media remain cartographically dependent, but change in emphasis from the mapping of physical terrain to electronic terrain: the maps of nodes and cables, electronic waves and digitized landscapes. Thus the language of the 'information society' is the language of maps; search engines are merely navigational tools. Our contemporary maps are frequently maps of matrices, of the disembodied virtual. We live 'map immersed in the world' (Woods 1992: 34). Maps become the interpretive and legitimizing tools of modernity. Through a series of complex transformations and displacements, we are placed within a frame which delineates the possibilities of travel and the limitations of being. To go outside the map is to risk madness; we may fall off the edge of the world, metaphorically speaking. Thus maps are representations of presence and absence, and the modernist urge to fill in all the blank spaces in all of the maps represents the colonization of the rational and the banishment of the Other:

> Power grid, population density, police coverage, land values – what's missing? . . . generations of accumulated culture [are] laid up and garnered here . . . It is this *subsumed and amassed cultural capital* that mapmaking societies bring to the task of making maps.
>
> (Woods 1992: 48; emphases in original)

However, this urge to encompass *all* of the world in maps is a self-delusion of the modern epoch, for what mapmakers systematically do is to create meaning, not just by the manipulation of what is included, but by its selection. The map is not, and by its definition never could be, a perfect analogon. It naturalizes 'the cultural *out* of existence', but to do this 'the natural content of the landscape must be culturalized *into* existence' (Woods 1992: 78; emphasis in original). As Woods argues, the trick of the map is to impute a *point* to the world by simultaneously creating an image of a correspondence to the reality it purports to represent, yet the world *has* no point, it is pointless (1992: 76).

Maps, in other words, are analogous not to the natural but to other media forms. Woods makes a very clear case for the McLuhan (1997) equation of form and content. His example is Tom Van Sant's 'portrait map' of the world. Created in 1990, this image exploits satellite technology to present a view of the world as if it were painted 'from life' (Woods 1992: 49). It is in essence a satellite-created map, a seeing that goes beyond the capability of the human eye, a reality that '*exceeds* our vision' (Woods 1992: 49). The satellite picture contains over thirty-five million pixels of information. Does this make it more 'true'? Not according to Woods (1992: 53), for

> This is less of a *dividing up* than a grinding or pulverizing of reality, done in this case with multi-spectral scanners. Scanners *scan* the land by virtue of a mirror . . . the mirror directs the light refracted from the earth through a prism onto a small array of photoelectric or other detectors. The modulated electric signal these generate – millions of bits of data per second . . . is then transmitted to earth and later computer-processed to produce photographs. Though elaborate, this process sounds straightforward. It's not. Each step not only determines a perspective through which to view reality, but also resulted from a choice that was (usually) bitterly contested. That is, the first intrusion into Van Sant's map of the society out of which it emerged occurs at the level of . . . the scanner.

Woods documents the conflicts of interest involved in producing the satellite images from which Van Sant's image was created: NASA, the Department of the Interior, the Department of Agriculture, and so on. The spectral windows chosen reflected the successful tactics of interests, and the subsequent manipulation of the quantities of data amassed, for budgetary reasons had to be highly selectively processed. 'Endless codes slither between the object and its image' (Woods 1992: 54). Take the filter in the scanner, which filters light over detectors tuned to different wavelengths, then there is a choice to be made between wavelengths, which were not chosen at random but because they corresponded to the existence of particular things on the earth. Crops were 'coded' spectrally in order to be able to differentiate them, by showing how much of each colour of light the plant reflects, thus identifying it as wheat, oats, etc. The refractive properties of the plant thus come to stand for the plant (Woods 1992: 54). Van Sant then hand-tinted the images to restore them to a 'realistic view'.

Thus the medium is the message, but the technological processes of mediation, however sophisticated, come no nearer to representing 'reality' than the maps drawn by children of their views of the world. The latter are not *bad* maps; they are maps based on different interests, signifying different priorities, and different stages of spatial development. This is not a continuum along which the child travels toward the ability to better reproduce 'the real'. It represents choices about information selection, its perceived relevance, the conventions, increasingly, of an educational system and perhaps an outcome of some sort of power struggle with parents or teachers over adequate representation. The child's map, resembling to the adult eye perhaps a scribble, is typically efficacious from the child's point of view. The more important things are usually bigger, for example, a convention often noted in the history of world maps. Woods's point is that *every* map is produced like this; a representation, which mobilizes skills and technological media, articulates them through meaning via selection, and is based on instrumental interests. A culture or a subculture can be read from its maps. Power and interests can be served and masked by maps. What maps *can never do*, with the most sophisticated technologies available, is communicate an external reality. In the end, it is simple. A pixel is not a plant cell; it is a pixel. This is not a world of signs and referents, but of signs standing proxy for other signs, an imagined or projected reality. Tolkien's maps of Middle Earth (Woods 1992) are not less 'map-like' than any other map; they indicate the necessary dimensions of the imaginary required by the fantasy. They allow his books to 'do their job'. Only cartographic hegemony lends the 'real map' its authority. So,

> it is easy but disingenuous to froth at the mouth over the flimflams of advertisers, or the falsehoods of Nazi propagandists, or the charmless fabrications of military disinformation specialists . . . the fact is that all of these more or less self-evident falsehoods owe whatever authority they have to the great national mapping projects, to the wall maps in the thousand classrooms, to the road maps the gas companies used to give away, to the plates in atlases, the cuts and insets in newsweeklies and textbooks . . . built from the *white lies* about which these maps are all but *entirely silent*. Because it is the cartographer and not the graphic artist or the political cartoonist who has first repressed the magnitude and significance of his intervention in what passes in the map for a

transcription of nature, it is in precisely the *cartographer's products* that the repressed experience – the interest represented, the point of the map – must be sought. This is not only because it is essential to understand what that interest *is*, but because it is its *repression* that enables the map to masquerade so effectively as truthful and accurate . . . Thus the problem was never '*how did this map fool me*', but '*why was I so inclined to wholeheartedly believe in the first place?*'

(Woods 1992: 77–8; emphases in original)

Using an encoding–decoding analysis broadly based on Barthes' *Mythologies* (1972), Woods argues that interests are effectively masked in maps by a semiotic process. Maps are not factual and the assumption, or judgemental criterion, of accuracy placed on them serves only to disguise their essence as semiological systems. 'The map proper – if we can refer to such a thing – . . . is more mythic precisely to the degree that it succeeds in persuading us that it is a natural consequence of seeing the world' (Woods 1992: 105). 'Map reading', for Woods, would thereby entail a reading of its value system. This reading in turn, depends not on formal map-reading skills but on cultural familiarity; the signs of the map are related to their place in an already-experienced context to which its relevance is related. Moreover, drawing on Eco (1976), he asserts that what is important is 'the notion that signs, or sign-functions, or symbols . . . are realized *only* when coding rules bring into correlation two elements . . . from two domains or systems (the one signifying, of expression, the other signified), of content' (Woods 1992: 110).

It is the self-evident nature of codes, that are so important in masking the map's true essence as a semiological construct. Thus even a state highway map is unavoidably '*a map of the state*: that is, an instrument of state polity, an assertion of sovereignty' (Woods 1992: 106; emphases in original). The presentation of the map clearly shows the state borders, the surrounding area is merely shaded yellow. There was no instrumental requirement to show the border thus, but 'from the perspective of myth this delineation of the states' borders is of the essence' (Woods 1992: 106). Why? For Woods, because not only is territorial control dependent on effective mapping, but

the repetitive image of the territory mapped . . . lends credence to the claims of control (and hence the extensive logogrammatic application of the state's outline to seals, badges, and emblems. Who would question the pretensions, the right to existence, the *reality* of North Carolina? Look! There it is on the map!

(Woods 1992: 106)

The importance of this apparently simple point is clear when we think what it signifies *not* to be on the map: it connotes remoteness, insignificance, unworthiness of attention, a lack of meaningfulness or importance. Other spatial metaphors refer to the symbolic importance of cartographic inclusion; it is 'in the middle of nowhere', a 'tiny insignificant little country'; how different to the 'majestic continent' of a colonized world.

The burning imperialist quest to name previously 'undiscovered' places produced a frenzy of cartographic activity. Currently there is a proliferation of 'uncharted continent' and 'lost continent' travelogue, notably in relation to Antarctica. The noble exploits of Sir Ernest Shackleton and his crew, mapping Antarctic territory for Britain, has been resurrected in television docudramas, the reprinting of journals and photographs, the retelling of the expedition of the *Endurance*. Now the map of Antarctica stands for 'the extraordinary spirit of Shackleton and his men, and their indefatigability and lasting civility towards one another in the most adverse conditions imaginable', as the book-jacket introduction to the reprint of Alfred Lansing's *Endurance: The Greatest Story Ever Told* (Lansing [1964]2000) says. While Britain was fighting the First World War on one front, the brave explorers of the Empire were fighting it on another, symbolic, terrain.

At the same time the map of Antarctica stands for scientific hegemony in the twentieth century. The writer Jenny Diski (1997: 7) muses:

> The scientists, it seemed, had wrapped up an entire continent for their own and only their own purposes. No-one could go there without their say-so, because their objectives were pure, and being pure they were entrusted with the last pure place on earth. The rest of us are frivolous despoilers who need to be controlled. A poet or a painter who wants to experience the emptiness and grandeur of the continent which, by treaty, belonged to no one and therefore I suppose to the poet and the painter as much as anyone else would not be able to go

without massive financial resources . . . Antarctica is in the control of the scientists as Mecca is under the authority of the mullahs.

The map of Antarctica for Diski is an emotional and spiritual map; she writes, 'I wanted my white bedroom extended beyond reason' (Diski 1997: 5), and she ironically laments, 'I wish I thought properly, like other people seem to think . . . Still. The thought was there. Antarctica. And along with it a desire as commanding as any sexual compulsion' (Diski 1997: 4).

Since Diski wrote this, Antarctica has been put back on the map in other ways; the tourist industry to the continent has expanded; it is now well and truly on the tourist map. Antarctica is no longer remote. The myths and legendary exploits are rekindled for the millennium, and the ships refitted to the highest level of tourist luxury.

Thus the extensive metaphoric lexicon surrounding maps is indicative of their power; a map exists far beyond its cartographic boundaries and extends deep into the social body. It represents aesthetics, desire, vicarious adventure, international rivalry and international cooperation; more recently it has come to represent a barometer for the proximity of the end of the world as maps are made of global warming and the distribution of wildlife populations. The physical delineations of scaling, shading, borders, contours, vegetation and other features of the 'natural' landscape (constantly being remoulded through human agency) arise out of these relations.

Woods's account of the power of maps, despite its richness, perhaps overemphasizes instrumentality. It suppresses the aesthetics of mapping, the desire reproduced in the idea of the uncharted, in the maintenance of the unattainable and distant, flying in the face of the time-space compressions of the electronic landscape. But then the latter too, have their own terrains of seduction: glimpses of the world in the wires, the sensuous and haunting eroticism of Gibson's matrix in *Neuromancer* (1984).

Thus it is with the contemporary mediascape; it is analogically comprehensible as a mosaic of maps. The maps of the actual, 'natural' physical world bear no more or less relationship to it than do media representations to social reality. The mediascape is at once more and less than the real; it could never correspond to it, and vice versa, because the media creates reality in the way maps create landscapes: partly in relation to the practical objectives and normative practices of institutions, partly in relation to the expressive signifiers of inexpressible lusts and longings, fears and hopes, hedonisms and nihilisms of cultures.

The practical consequences of this for the interpretation of the crime–media relationship are extensive. 'Empirical' or 'administrative' criminologies produce one set of maps, but they render crime no more comprehensible and law no more legitimate than do the supposedly 'fictive' cultural maps of detective novels, or the imagined justice of the courtroom drama, or the hybrid genres of news, docudrama and reality TV. A cartographical viewpoint enables us to abandon the discourse of distortion once and for all. Following from this, other dichotomies also dissolve: 'high' and 'low' culture; truth and falsification; fact and fiction; science and society. Instead it becomes possible to focus on crime and law representation as knowledge work, a mapping of contested terrain in particular ways within particular generic, economic, political, and technological contexts, all of which are inscribed within each other. This is not to assume that knowledge work is necessarily functional in any mechanistic sense; it can equally be anti-functional in that way. This is to recognize what the 'mass' media has long recognized: that crime is expressive as well as instrumental, seen in instances from the aesthetics of graffiti artists to the embodied practices of mutilation. It is also to recognize that crime maps culture maps crime; certain elements are scaled up, certain elements are scaled down, depending upon the cultural work it is being made to do. Neither an anatomical diagram of an arm nor an artistic representation of a mutilated body tells us 'more' about the world. The question is *what* they tell us about the world. This is interactive work as much as map-reading is. It is context-dependent (Barnes 1977) and relates commonly, but not inevitably, to the instrumentality of certain representations in certain contexts for certain actors or collectivities.

In this kind of scenario the traditional oppositions of producer and consumer, and representation and audience are also blurred. Increasingly the flexibility, the mutability, of knowledge representations is a matter for both (traditionally speaking) producer and consumer. This is seen most clearly in the case of digital technologies, where the constraints and possibilities of the medium frame both constituencies. Even the legal code loses some of its immutability through the mediatization of the legal, mobilizing and animating the popular legal imagination in ways that produce obligatory passage points in the public domains of censure and 'rights' to which 'the Law' must ultimately pay attention.

The metaphorical and mythical dimensions of crime are an integral part of the mediatized world; the search for descriptive adequacy at the level of category application is a red herring in that it is akin to the belief in the possibility of an objective taxonomy. Crime and law are words and images; their content and significations are plastic. The feelings and experiences of the everyday to which they relate however, are as real as breathing is.

What, if anything, postmodern theory has to say to this is still provisional. Either it tends to be mobilized at such a level of philosphical abstraction that it is hard to see how it can operate outside of its proponents, or its observations are, ironically, made at a meta-level which makes specific readings difficult. As such it stands accused of a nihilism and indifference to lived experience (the death of the real, the death of the social) which allegedly render it 'poisonous' or 'dangerous'. This is a misconception, since in order to be either of these things it would have to have a programme of some kind. Moral abstention is not the same as moral depravity. 'Postmodern' insights are amenable to appropriation. They can be plundered as can any other form of knowledge; indeed postmodernism could be appropriated to meet almost any ends. Its own abdication from ethics is consistent with its prioritizing of appearance over meaning; somehow, its opponents feel it necessary to swallow the beast whole. Surely postmodernist theory's only agenda is to have no agenda; it has severed itself from the essentially morally based meta-narratives of history and society, that is all. This aspect of postmodernism may well be 'voodoo semiotics' (Nichols 1994). So, to raid postmodernism, to steal its insights discriminately from within its project of meaninglessness, may be thoughtcrime but is eminently do-able. So what if such thievery undermines the essence of the nothingness that it is supposedly about?

The concepts of the simulacra, of the hyperreal, and of implosion in particular, are immensely helpful in grasping the things that crime becomes under conditions of mediatization. The postmodern focus on media forms and the collapse of structured systematicity remains interesting whether or not we like its (disingenuous) claims to represent only the death of meaning. Feminist theory has long been used to rifling through masculinist renditions of the world for the odd rich picking; why stop now?

Beyond and outside the postmodern

Retaining my cartographic vantage point in the face of the postmodern, I am looking now at what I have discarded: principally, the possibility of unmediated access to reality; potentially, that the concept of reality itself could be a linguistic prison. If as Latour argues 'we have never been modern' (1993) then the error lies in a failure to achieve symmetry of knowledge claims. Suspecting the latter to be a possibility, I would like to examine Latour's (1993: 94) argument in more detail.

> The first principle of symmetry offers the incomparable advantage of doing away with epistemological breaks, with *a priori* separations between 'sanctioned' and 'outdated' sciences, or artificial divisions between sociologists who study knowledge, those who study belief systems, and those who study the sciences.

Typically, we have engaged in asymmetric explanations of the form 'truth is explained by nature' and 'falsehood is explained by society'; that is, we have 'explained truth through its congruence with natural reality, and falsehood through the constraint of social categories, epistemes, or interests' (Latour 1993: 94). If we adopt the first principle of symmetry, beginning from the notion I have used above, that 'nature has no preference', then nature explains neither truth nor falsehood; 'truth' and 'falsehood' are both explained by society, so 'constructivist where Nature is concerned, it is realistic about Society' (Latour 1993: 94). This is not good enough for Latour, however, and roughly corresponds with my notion that reality (nature) may be a linguistic prison. Nature and Society, he contends, are 'part of the problem, not part of the solution'. A generalized principle of symmetry would therefore be required in which Nature and Society are to be explained (Latour 1993: 95). This cannot be achieved by 'cheating', in the sense of using Nature to explain Society and Society to explain Nature. What we are left with is a nature–culture. It doesn't make sense, in other words, for scientists to cross-dress as sociologists, or sociologists to cross-dress as scientists. This is only a problem, points out Latour, for the modernist episteme, which insists on dividing Nature and Society, according to one or the other priority. So, those who invent sciences and discover physical determinisms never deal exclusively with human beings, except by accident. The others have only representations of Nature that are more or less coded by the cultural preoccupations of the humans that occupy them fully and fall only by chance . . . on things as they are.

(Latour 1993: 99)

Importantly, other (non-western, non-modernist) cultures

cannot really separate what is knowledge from what is Society, what is sign from what is thing . . . For Them, Nature and Society, signs and things, are virtually coextensive. For Us, they should never be. Even though we recognize some fuzzy areas in madness, children, animals, popular culture and women's bodies . . . we believe our duty is to extirpate ourselves from those horrible mixtures as forcibly as possible.

(Latour 1993: 99–100)

Latour's argument frees us from the tyranny and confusion of having to presume a separation of nature and culture and of having to produce a theory of one which accounts for the other, often in a continuing process of assertion and refutation of explanatory primacy. The answer for Latour lies in a kind of non-exotic anthropology. 'Non-western nature–cultures symmetrically constitute humans and non-humans. Some cultures mobilize ancestors, lions, fixed stars, and the coagulated blood of sacrifice . . . we mobilize genetics, zoology, cosmology' (1993: 106). We inhabit a world of hybrids, which are produced through the mobilization of human and non-human resources.

Two examples spring to my mind, which may clarify this abstract formulation. In the film *The Hour of the Pig* (1994), we see the conflict of an emergent rational, modernist rule of law with a premodern nature–culture where animals can be tried and sentenced in a court in equal part with humans. The blank incomprehension with which a modern worldview confronts this phenomenon is potentially the basis of humour and absurdity, but the film is a serious exercise in the exploration of the formations of modernism and the creation of 'unreason'. Yet we can only confront the animal trial as an absurdity *if we assume the universality and supremacy of the modern episteme:* that is, its separation of nature and culture, reason and unreason. Contextual information provided on-screen tells us of the estimated number of animal trials, which took place historically, indicating that the plot was not dreamt up in some drug-induced hallucinogenic moment. They actually *did* that? How barbaric, how uncivilized. Certainly, but if one wishes to argue about the ethics of the civilizing process, that is a different issue (and would anyway throw the superiority claims of civilization into doubt, since at least animals were accorded legal rights as well as responsibilities). The questions we ask are too literal, too preclusive: 'how could a pig abduct a child?'

If we ask a different sort of question, namely, 'how are human and non-human resources mobilized in the law of this nature–culture and to what ends?' then we arrive at a quite comprehensible analysis of the operation of knowledge and power. Unless we accept Latour's principle of generalized symmetry, however, we can never reach this point, because we will always be trapped by the false dichotomy which accords primacy to a mode of thought we call 'rational'. To take the latter route is no more than an exercise of power in itself; we are mobilizing human and non-human resources differently, hierarchically, to achieve an answer that accords with our approach but does not enhance the understanding of the particular nature–culture which puts pigs on trial. Why should not a pig be mobilized in the organizing of order and rule-systems? There is no inherent property of animality, which prevents a pig from being a criminal. This is *not* to say 'all is permitted'; that is the easy way out. The film shows precisely how the role of animals in the ordering and functioning of this nature–culture makes its appearance in the crimino-legal domain comprehensible. It is only our arrogance, which accords priority to our own nature-culture. Of course it would be unthinkable for us to assert that 'the pig is the guilty party'. This does not make our nature–culture *better*. Ethical decisions arise out of particular constellations of nature–culture and the different ways in which mobilizations of humans and non-humans produce different power–knowledge formations. All is not relative, which would suggest that there is 'nothing to choose', but all is context-bound and context-productive.

My second, nearer-to-home example, is that of the cyborg. What is the cyborg if not a mobilization of human and non-human resources? *This* is why the law as it stands cannot cope with the field of the prosthetic and the virtual. The Law is based on a division between 'nature' and 'society', where 'human' and 'inhuman' are framed according to asymmetrical principles. No surprise that the ethical contestations of the law arise in relation to human–nonhuman articulations: life support machines, dead men's spermatoza, genetic cloning, and virtuality. What *is* Dolly the Sheep if not a creation of nature–culture?

Mediatization stands as part of the nature–culture mobilization. Crime and Law are at its heart because they are axes of ethical and normative contestation. 'Postmodernism' in the end is a stepping-stone to an appreciation of the kind of formulation offered by Latour. Beginning with a thought-provoking assessment of Baudrillard's work by Rex Butler, I want to suggest that Latour's deceptively simple formulation can help to 'rescue' Baudrillard's (deceptively complex) dilemma. Butler (1999: 17) writes:

> If we look at the various systems Baudrillard analyses throughout his career – the organization of domestic objects in *The System of Objects,* consumer society in *Consumer Society,* Marxism in *The Mirror of Production,* simulation in *Simulacra and Simulation,* the social in *The Shadow* and the work of Foucault in 'Forget Foucault' – we discover that Baudrillard is not simply comparing them to some outside real which they exclude, but implicitly agreeing with them that there is no outside, that the real can henceforth only be defined in their terms. The problem these systems set for their interpreter is that, after them, there is no other measure by which they can be judged; it is only by applying their own criteria that they can be assessed. But Baudrillard's argument is that, even in their own terms they fail . . . There is always a kind of internal limit – that paradox of the sign . . . which means that if the system is able to expand forever and nothing is outside of it, it is also never entirely closed, something is always left out of it. And it is this internal limit, this difference that makes resemblance possible, that Baudrillard calls the *real.* Thus . . . there is that real which is brought about by the system and that real which is the absolute limit to the system . . . his problem is how to think the real when all is simulation, how to use the real against the attempts by various systems of rationality to account for it.

While Baudrillard's formulation of 'internal' reality is helpful in appreciating the way in which the media constitute crime, it is the sense in which the concept of the simulacra seems to leave him hoist with his own petard that proscribes the limits of his analysis. What he does with the signifier–signified, representation–referent problem is not all that dissimilar to Latour, in that he opposes the notion of opposition. However in clinging to the categories of modernity, in the final instance a reality 'out there', which cannot be resolved by the internal reality of the system, we are left with a topography of internality of a formation and nothing more. He throws aside the constructivist, cartographical insights that help us to understand how reality is mobilized in certain ways to produce certain representations, patterned by forces of power and interests, but he does not replace them 'with' anything. Having announced the death of the social, the real 'outside' becomes incomprehensible at the same time as the real 'inside' becomes superficial.

While incomplete, constructivist approaches at least have the advantages of the first principle of symmetry. In describing the mediation of crime and law according to the first principle of symmetry, we are able, as Woods has done for maps, to consider *why* crime and law are imbricated and represented as they are in contemporary globalized media-culture. In maintaining an assertion of *social* reality, constructivism has been able to produce illuminating studies of language-as-practice, of how mediations of crime and law at the level of internality are shaped by the broader knowledge formations and structures of feeling prevalent in a culture. Constructivism is able to account for the ways in which raced and gendered ways of seeing crime and law, for example, produce and are produced by media forms. In banishing the notion of the determinate Nature, it lends equivalence to crime and law texts, taking our possibilities of reading crime beyond the formal requirements of 'empirical social science' without sacrificing the notion of the experience of crime and law as *real* and *important*. It leaves the door open for alternate readings, and for policy and ethics, that is to say, for the continuing contestation of power and censure.

Constructivism does not really attend to Baudrillard's problems at all, contenting itself with a largely ethical critique of his work. Latour's thesis, however, has the promise of going beyond both approaches, in requiring a complete overturning of modernism, not by positing a post-, but a non-modernism. Discarding the term 'society', Latour refers not to the *death* of the social but the never-existence of the 'social', *if* by the latter is implied a divide between Nature and Culture. He replaces the social with nature–culture, a shift that retains the analytical concern with power, but poses a completely different question of how nature–culture mobilizes quasi-objects (Latour 1993). Baudrillard has abolished the 'internal great divide', but retained the 'external great divide' (Latour 1993: 99). Latour puts it thus: on constructivism, 'are you not . . . tired of those sociologies constructed around the Social only, which is supposed to hold up solely through the repetition of the words "power" and "legitimacy" because sociologists cannot cope . . . with the contents of objects or with the world of languages that nevertheless construct society?' (Latour 1993: 90). On deconstructionism,

> Are you not fed up with language games, and with the eternal scepticism of the deconstruction of meaning? Discourse is not a world unto itself but a population of actants that mix with things as well as with societies, uphold the former and the latter alike, and hold on to them both. Interest in text does not distance us from reality, for things too have to be elevated to the dignity of narrative. As for texts, why deny them the grandeur of forming the social bond that holds us together?
>
> (Latour 1993: 90)

Nature and Society exist in networks that produce hybrids, entailing the mobilization of human and non-human quasi objects (Latour 1993: 133).

Finally we have something that enables us to break free of the limitations of modernist assessments of the crime, law, media, culture relation (without falling into a postmodern trap which is continually forced to engage with modernism or casts itself adrift completely from the possibility of explanation, understanding, and action). We can see the false premises on which the 'media effects debate', the 'media and fear of crime' debate, the 'primacy of science and empiricism' debate, the 'media as ideology' debate and the 'realism' (left or right) debate, are based: the premises that reality and representation exist as strata organized in some sort of hierarchical relation, however recursively, that nature and culture are separate, and that the latter re-presents the former.

Crime and law in media culture

In stepping outside of any particular disciplinary affiliation, and by broadening the scope of my inquiry beyond the traditional concerns of criminological analyses of crime and the media, I have sought to refract crime, media and the law through a number of very different prisms. There is no one 'answer', because there was no one 'question'. What I am concerned with is a process of *reading* crime. I do not treat 'the media', 'crime', and 'law' as discrete entities, as separable knowledge–objects that can be related one to the other in any kind of causal or hierarchical relation.

One particular discourse within law, the legal code, *circumscribes* the media through proscription (copyright, obscenity, etc.) in relation to particular practices. However, even such proscriptive strategies, always fluid, become highly provisional as techno-cultural issues constantly transcend the boundaries of modernist legal frameworks as refracted through the media – notably the disembodiment of the social through virtual technologies and the modalities of genetic engineering. The media may exist in legal discourse as an 'object' of regulation, but far more powerfully, the embeddedness of the media within the legal and vice versa leaves any Cartesian notion of the law in disarray (Boyne 1990). The popular legal imagination acquires more and more prominence as the practices and ethics of law become mediatized, become more visible in, and more vulnerable to, public contestation. In a mediatized culture, the authority of the law is relentlessly questioned. Final statements such as 'it is illegal' are more often portrayed as questionable across a whole range of legal genres, and the contestable-legal is repeatedly emphasized across the complex array of media forms.

That 'crime' is an entity separable from the media is an untenable proposition. The development of the popular press from its inception confirmed 'crime' as a moveable feast in everyday life. Crime–media discourses reveal the multifaceted nature of the constitution of crime as metaphor and myth, a vocabulary through which are articulated the experiential and psychological impacts of increasing ontological insecurity and crises of trust and risk in modernity (Giddens 1991; Beck 1992). It has also proved to be a central locus in consolidating broader normative constellations of knowledge/power in modernity: gender, race, imperialism, age, and class, and more broadly still, the human–nonhuman hierarchizations on which all of modern culture depends. The bestial darkness of the pre-Hobbesian psyche and the necessity for its containment is ultimately the stuff of all mediated crime.

Both crime and the law, then, have a long pedigree as media products: aesthetic, dramatic, and spectacular. Both 'fictive' and 'non-fictive' media representations have deployed the crimino-legal complex as 'entertainment' and 'spectacle'. Crime as material for display and expressivity has been utilized to the full: the visceral, the passionate, and the voyeuristic fulfilments of desire are endlessly recycled as news, drama, documentary, Hollywood blockbuster, literary and filmic noir, reality TV, horror flicks and tabloid shockers continue the rounds, increasingly feeding each other through a carnival of cross-dressing in each other's generic conventions and technologies. Similarly the mediation of law exploits the dramatic qualities of censure and chastisement, the public and the private, constriction and liberty, truth and falsehood, loyalty and treachery, justice and injustice.

'Real crime' and 'real law' *have no existence* prior to, or transcendent of, their inherence in the public – and therefore mediatized – domain. Broadly speaking the ways in which crime and law are articulated operate along three modalities. The modality of the pre-modern attends to the primordial: drives, urges, and states of nature form the basis of a morality play in various reworkings of sin and retribution; the modality of reflexive modernity employs interpretive strategies to peel back the surfaces of crime and law to 'reveal' their dynamics and tell origin stories; the content-less postmodern modality explores superficiality and intertextuality to display crime and the law as a bricolage of narcissistic, vacuous spectacle and aesthetic. The media does not so much re-present crime and law as *define* them through these modalities: the epochal products of nature–culture, which exist in, and not outside of, the mediations of everyday life.

Debates over the place of technology within media culture have become more prominent as the sophistication of media technologies accelerate. Featuring increasingly in the theorizing of the social-in-general, technologies of mediation have come to be seen as pivotal in attempts to comprehend (in the broadest sense) power and communication in modernity. From Marxism to feminism, Weberian sociology to postmodern refutation, technological form has remained something of a thorn in the side of social theory. Technological developments have gone hand in hand with the question of history; it is there, in the 'post' of social change: postindustrial, postmodern. Integrally bound up with power, change, and power *to* change, technology has been theorized as dynamic, catalytic, determinant in turn and turn-about. Technological determinism has been dismissed as a contradiction in terms; constructivism has it as a social product only contingent upon the 'real', social, dynamics of change; feminism has had it as an instrument of domination and control, notably through the technologies of reproduction. The intimate connection of the technical with the social, as in theories of labour, has proved perplexing. *Technology* has not caused the compression of time and space, but it is impossible to conceive of the latter without the former; *technology* has not caused the implosion of knowledges, nor the disembodiment of the social, yet these are inherently technological changes. Attempts to resolve the problem tend to stumble; Giddens could not manage it, nor could McLuhan. We have not really got further than the inherent confusion of the notion that the 'medium is the message'. The endless attempts to appropriate the 'meaning' of the latter reveal it as part of the problem and not the solution.

For the crime, law, media, culture articulation the technology problematic is as crucial as in any other area of theorization. Only the cartographic standpoint and the non-modern position, for me, hold the potential to be of help here. If we revert to the old usage, 'applied science', the term reveals its own theoretical possibilities. A theory-in-action, technology refers not to an object, a thing, but to the articulation of nature and culture in particular conjunctions of the human and the non-human. Neither can be *removed* from technology and leave it with any meaning. Technology is descriptive of the process and outcome of a particular knowledge form, of reflexive action and practical competences in articulation with the non-human. Technology is not an object, therefore, but a quasi-object, having human and non-human properties and consequences. Technology is central to the mediatized formations of crime and law in many ways. It defines the form *and* the content of these formations in equal part. The globalization that brings crime and the law instantaneously into the living room, smashing the public/private opposition, the glocality that comprehends universal and traditional forms of crime and law, the virtual that erodes the bases of embodied crime and law, the prosthetic that deconstructs the subject and object of crime and the law, the power of magnification and miniaturization that brings about the collapsing of intimacy and voyeurism and renders problematic the gaze of crime and the law, and the interactivity that disputes the ownership of crime and the law, are all technologically infused consequences of media form-content.

Taken together, these perspectives on crime, law, media and culture produce 'crime and law in media culture' – a rejection of the 'great divide' (cf. Latour 1993). I am treating crime and the law as a 'co-production of sciences and societies', articulating nature and culture through the media. This entails no necessity of seeing nature or the human subject as mere 'constructions'; the hybridization of crime and law is a mapping process that leaves both 'an external truth and a subject of law' intact (Latour 1993: 134).

Entailments, ethics and crime, law, media, futures

No theoretical position carries entailments in practice. Not even theories that may be most repugnant to individuals or collectivities do this. Neither genocide nor democracy arises of necessity out of theories. A retrospective process is more common, whereby theories are produced in practical contexts to account retrospectively for actions, to legitimate or supply reflexive coherences in memory and history, or to provide tools for the furtherance of objectives. Theoretical work is instrumental, but practical utilization of theory is ethical. I have always been perplexed by statements of the kind: 'it's just a theory', or 'what use is theory?' A theory is a reflective constellation of ideas about how things work or might work or have worked, and what things are, might be, or have been; which means (a) that it is constantly supplantable, (b) it is of necessity a fragment not a whole, and (c) it has possibilities but not imperatives. What theory leaves in its wake is the responsibility of decision making. Whatever is said of Baudrillard, his analysis cannot be deemed 'poisonous' because it abstains from claiming implications. This is not the same as saying that theory can be objective, for reasons I have explained.

Ethics however, carry entailments. Theory ends where ethics begin, and vice versa. It is not the question of knowledge, but what to do with knowledge, which is at issue here. The mediatization of crime and the law broadens the scope of this burden by metastasizing the domains of crime and law throughout everyday life. The rendering of crime and law as entertainment and spectacle do not undermine, for example, the possibility of rules of conduct. Truth is not the province of the media. The 'dangerousness' of the media should cease to be an issue in the sense that there are not 'good' and 'bad' media, the former true to reality and the latter distortive of it. All media distorts, all mediation distorts. They refract, are prismatic, as is all communicated meaning. 'Bias' in the media is not a question of truth and falsity; 'bias' suggests only the refraction of something in a way that implicitly or explicitly attempts to impose an entailment of action. By this token, a number of contingent points arise:

- *No text is privileged.* No domain of knowledge is *de facto* superior as a way of understanding the world. Therefore an academic episteme, for example, which insists on the primacy of its own narratives in understanding crime amounts only to an assertion of some conceit. This enables academia to assess 'the media' as if it were an entity quite different from, say, criminological discourse. Such a criminology would see its conventions as offering a theory of the media without recognizing itself as part of the media network. 'Media' narratives, whether as novels and films, television drama, or the news, are seen as genres of representation to be addressed in terms of their relation to, derivation from, or effect on, crime. If the academic text is *not* privileged, then fictive and other crime texts provide other equally legitimate ways of reading crime. Mediated crime is not then treated as an object of criminological knowledge but as part of a broader mapping of crime and law. This does not prevent criminology from addressing the ways in which nature and culture are mobilized by 'the media' in their readings of crime, but does entail reflexivity on the part of criminology in assessing the ways in which *it* does so. There is a relation of equivalence between 'criminological' analyses and other readings of crime. It is *what crime texts do* that is important, not what method they use. Concepts such as 'entertainment', 'spectacle', and 'ideology' need to be reassessed as coterminous with the criminological. Equally the contention that 'no text is privileged' denies the high/low culture dichotomy which has long been used to justify allegations of perniciousness against the popular media.
- *The media are not the poisoners of the social.* The scapegoating of the popular media as a vehicle for the corruption of culture merely obfuscates ethical contestation. This fails to acknowledge the media as inhering in social practices which may or may not be deemed desirable depending upon one's preferred outcomes. Censorship is logical on one ground only: the explicit desire to suppress the public expression of cultural practice. The impossibility of attaining such a goal arises from the impossibility of suppressing culture-in-general. Partial attempts to achieve such a goal usually result in subversion, since they are dependent upon unrealistic expectations of control over technologies of

communication, of which satellite broadcasting and the Internet are cases in point.

- *The media are the fora for the contestation of crime and law.* The boundaries of the criminal and the bases of law are rendered inevitably provisional by media culture. 'The art of law', the 'law of art', and the 'death of law' (Redhead 1995) are expressions of the mediatization of crime and law and the possibilities (or impossibilities, as in 'post-law') of crime, law, media futures. Contingent upon mediatization in the twenty-first century, there is not law and 'pop law'; there is only 'pop law'.

- *The real is not dead.* The hyperreal and the simulacrum do not dissolve the experiental dimensions of hurt. Hurt may be caused by murder, burglary, assault, imprisonment, torture, verbal abuse, and a myriad of other practices. Mediated crime and law bear a metaphoric resonance with this hurt, and as language (image) is practice, can also inflict it (as with pornography) and ameliorate it (as with 'morality plays'). Logically, 'censorship' (a hypothetical harm-reduction strategy in its most liberal interpretation) is replaced by specific remedies (a hurt must have been inflicted). The hyperreal and the simulacrum constitute not the separation of media representation from reality but their distancing from direct experience.

- *Fact and fiction elide.* Truth claims are made across a range of crime genres; from criminology, to news, documentary, drama, fiction, film and 'art'. These truth claims are not identical, but in a context where the forms of the media increasingly borrow from each other formats, genre conventions, technologies and techniques (videocam, fast forward, flashback, dramatic reconstruction, sampling, looping, sound bite, digital reimaging etc.), it becomes increasingly difficult to characterize what would distinguish crime 'fact' from crime 'fiction'. Reality TV is the apotheosis of this, where the apparent distance between the viewer and reality is closed by editing and production techniques and technologies, an illusion of faithful description is created, while at the same time the genre can also act to distance the viewer from its subject matter by its hyperreal presentation.

Mediatization is a state of being which places the ethical decisions of societies, constituted in what is established as crime and what is established as law, in a constant state of provisionality and doubt. The media–crime problematic has historically been framed in a way which 'separates out' the media as *a* quasi-object with institutional, normative, and material properties which can therefore *impact upon* crime and the law. In this scenario the media are a *product of* formations of inequalities of power and of cultural and material capital; they serve to *reinforce and perpetuate* these formations through their institutional natures. In this sense, we should be debating not the death of law, but the death of the media as a quasi-object. In de-objectifying the media, we acknowledge that crime and law, and the media, form an indivisible network, a hybrid formation. Crime and law futures are media futures.

■ NOTES

Chapter 2

1 Frederick West was arrested on 25 February 1994 for the murder of his daughter, Heather. The remains of other young women were subsequently found beneath his house in Gloucester, UK and he would have faced 12 charges of murder had he not committed suicide in his cell while awaiting trial. In the absence of a protagonist to bring to justice, attention turned to his wife Rosemary West, who had also been charged with all except two of the murders. Masters (1996) contends that prior to West's suicide 'it seemed as if the charges against Rosemary West would be dropped' (Masters 1996: x). However, with the media and the public cheated of a culprit, he suggests, Rosemary West's being brought to trial became inevitable despite disturbingly questionable evidence, and 'the presumption of innocence was largely ignored even in court, and utterly derided by the popular press, which scented a new source of gold' (Masters 1996: 337). In other words, with the victims and the primary suspect dead, the absence of knowledge was used to construct a richly textured discourse of guilt and retribution around the simple assumption of complicity: that 'she must have known'.

2 On 3 March 1991 Rodney King, a black man, was the driver of a car

in Los Angeles, California, which did not stop when signalled by a police car. A police chase ensued. When police stopped the car they delivered 56 baton blows and six kicks to King in a period of 2 minutes, causing 11 skull fractures, brain damage, and kidney damage. A videotape shot by a bystander of the event was broadcast worldwide by TV stations on 4 March. On 15 March 1991 four police officers were arraigned on charges of assault with a deadly weapon and use of excessive force. On 29 April 1992, over a year later, a jury acquitted the defendants. The response was six days of rioting in Los Angeles in which 54 people were killed, an estimated 2383 injured, and 13,212 arrested (http://www.crimsonbird.com/history/rodneyking.htm, accessed 8 August 2002.)

3 *Big Brother* started in the UK on Channel 4 in 2000, based on a Dutch idea. The first final, on 16 September 2000 was seen by 10 million viewers (http://news.bbc.co.uk/1/hi/entertainment/, accessed 8 August 2002). In terms of the telephone voting, BT reported that the programme attracted the highest ever figures, smashing the record for telephone polling of 2.6 million callers held by ITV's *The Monarchy Debate* (http://media.guardian.co.uk/overnights/story.htm, accessed 8 August 2002). During the second series in 2001, on the night of 30 May, *Big Brother* attracted 4.4 million viewers, compared with BBC1's 4.3m for the *10 O'Clock News* during, ironically, the UK Election campaign (http://media.guardian.co.uk/overnights/story.htm, accessed 8 August 2001). *Pop Idols* began on ITV1 in the UK in October 2001 and 'made entertainment history by letting the public in on the business of actually choosing the candidates for stardom in the first place' (http://news.bbc.co.uk/1/hi/entertainment/tv_and_radio/, accessed 8 August 2002).

They marked a distinctively 'postmodern' turn in their interactivity, self-referentiality and intertextuality (the progress and finals of both programmes ousting even news items such as the Election Campaign from prestige news slots), in their apparent 'reality base' while simultaneously celebrating fantasy, in their rendering of the 'ordinary' person into the 'celebrity', and in their explicit elevation of the 'banal' into the seriously 'cultural' and 'newsworthy'. Their very depthlessness, as it were, dominated not just the tabloid but the 'serious' news, and gripped the UK in a taste for parodic democratic participation.

4 8-year-old Sarah Payne disappeared from near her grandparent's house in West Sussex on 1 July 2000. After 17 months and a trial

lasting 3 weeks Roy Whiting, a 42-year-old local man on the sex offenders' register, was found guilty of the murder (http://www. forensic.gov.uk/forensic/news/casefiles/sara_payne.htm, accessed 9 August 2002).

Chapter 3

5 A traditional lawyer whose definition and concept of application of the law derives narrowly from within its formal codes; that is, the polar opposite of the popular articulation of the notion of law.

Chapter 4

6 *Facelifts from Hell* (ITV1) was shown in the UK on 14 February 2002 and drew an audience of 8.5 million viewers. *Fat Club* (an ITV1 series) began in February 2002 and achieved an average of 6.1 million viewers with a 26 per cent audience share (http://www2.carlton./ com/mediasales/listings/factual.jhtml?nav=tvlist, accessed 10 August 2002).

Chapter 5

7 *Mondo 2000* is described by Sobchack (2000) as a 'hot' new magazine that emerged during 1989 and 1990. Not easily characterized, it 'proclaimed its own position as "surfing" the "New Edge" of a . . . social formation called "cyberculture" ' (Sobchack 2000: 138).

■ REFERENCES

Adam, A. (2000) Cyberstalking: Gender and computer ethics, in E. Green and
A. Adam (eds) *Virtual Gender: Technology, Consumption and Identity.*
London: Routledge.

Adorno, T.W. and Horkheimer, M. (1972) *Dialectic of Enlightenment.* New
York: Herder and Herder.

Adorno, T.W. and Horkheimer, M. (1973) *Dialectic of Enlightenment.* London:
Allen Lane.

Adorno, T. and Horkheimer, W. (1993) The culture industry: enlightenment as
mass deception, in S. During (ed.) *The Cultural Studies Reader.*
London: Routledge.

Allan, S. (1999) *News Culture.* Buckingham: Open University Press.

Appardui, A. (1990) Disjuncture and difference in the global cultural economy,
Public Culture, 2(2): 1–24.

Bankowski, Z. and Mungham, G. (1981) Lawpeople and laypeople, *International Journal of the Sociology of Law*, 9: 85–100.

Barak, G. (ed.) (1996) *Representing O.J.: Murder, Criminal Justice and Mass
Culture.* Guilderland, NY: Harrow and Heston.

Barker, C. (1997) *Global Television: An Introduction.* Oxford: Blackwell.

Barker, C. (1999) *Television, Globalization, and Cultural Identities.* Buckingham: Open University Press.

Barker, M. and Petley, J. (eds) (1997) *Ill Effects: The Media/Violence Debate.*
London: Routledge.

Barnes, B. (1977) *Interests and the Growth of Knowledge*. London: Routledge and Kegan Paul.

Barthes, R. (1972) *Mythologies*. London: Jonathan Cape.

Baudrillard, J. (1983) *Simulations*. New York: Semiotext(e).

Baudrillard, J. (1995) *The Gulf War Did Not Take Place*. Sydney: Power Publications.

BBC (1998) *News*, Home. 31 March. http://www.bbc.co.uk/home (accessed 2 February 2002).

Beck, U. (1992) *Risk Society: Towards a New Modernity*. London: Sage/TCS.

Becker, H. (1963) *Outsiders: Studies in the Sociology of Deviance*. New York: Free Press.

Bell, D. (2000) Cybercultures reader: A user's guide, in D. Bell and B.M. Kennedy (eds) *The Cybercultures Reader*. London: Routledge.

Bell, D. and Kennedy, B.M. (eds) (2000) *The Cybercultures Reader*. London: Routledge.

Bennett, T. (1986) Introduction: 'The turn to Gramsci', in T. Bennett, C. Mercer, and J. Woollacott (eds) *Popular Culture and Social Relations*. Milton Keynes: Open University Press.

Berger, J. (1972) *Ways of Seeing*. Harmondsworth: Penguin.

Bibbings, L. (2000) Boys will be boys: Masculinity and offences against the person, in D. Nicolson and L. Bibbings (eds) *Feminist Perspectives on Criminal Law*. London: Cavendish.

Bordieu, P. (1984) *Distinction*. London: Routledge.

Bourke, J. (1996) *Dismembering the Male: Men's Bodies, Britain and the Great War*. London: Reaktion Books.

Boyne, R. (1990) *Foucault and Derrida: The Other Side of Reason*. London: Unwin Hyman.

Brite, P.Z. (1996) *Exquisite Corpse*. London: Phoenix.

Brown, S. (1991) *Magistrates at Work: Sentencing and Social Structure*. Buckingham: Open University Press.

Brown, S. (1994) *Time of Change? Adult Views of Youth and Crime in Middlesbrough*. Middlesbrough: Middlesbrough City Challenge Partnership.

Brown, S. (1998) *Understanding Youth and Crime*. Buckingham: Open University Press.

Burrows, R. (1997) Cyberpunk as social theory: William Gibson and the sociological imagination, in S. Westwood and J. Williams (eds) *Imagining Cities: Scripts, Signs, Memories*. London: Routledge.

Butler, R. (1999) *Jean Baudrillard: The Defence of the Real*. London: Sage.

Callinocos, A. (1989) *Against Postmodernism: A Marxist Critique*. Cambridge: Polity Press.

Callon, M. (1986) Some elements of a sociology of translation: Domestication of scallops and the fishermen of St Brieuc Bay, in J. Law (ed.) *Power, Action and Belief: Towards a New Sociology of Knowledge?* London: Routledge and Kegan Paul.

Caputi, J. (1988) *The Age of Sex Crime.* London: The Women's Press.

Carlen, P. (1974) *Magistrates' Justice.* London: Martin Robertson.

Castells, M. (1996) *The Rise of the Network Society.* Oxford: Basil Blackwell.

Chancer, L. (1996) O.J. Simpson and the trial of the century? Uncovering paradoxes in media coverage, in G. Barak (ed.) *Representing O.J.: Murder, Criminal Justice and Mass Culture.* Guilderland, NY: Harrow and Heston.

Chibnall, S. (1977) *Law and Order News.* London: Tavistock.

Clerc, S. (2000) Estrogen Brigands and 'Big Tits' Threads: Media fandom on-line and off, in D. Bell and B.M. Kennedy (ed) *The Cybercultures Reader.* London: Routledge.

Cohen, S. (1973) *Folk Devils and Moral Panics: The Creation of the Mods and Rockers.* St Alban's: Paladin.

Cohen, S. (1985) *Visions of Social Control.* Cambridge: Polity Press.

Cohen, S. and Young, J. (1973) *The Manufacture of News.* London: Constable.

Connell, R.W. (1987) *Gender and Power: Society, the Person and Sexual Politics.* Stanford, CA: Stanford University Press.

Connell, R.W. (1995) *Masculinities.* Cambridge: Polity.

Craig, D. (1997) Psychonalytic sociology and the Holocaust, in C. Sumner (ed.) *Violence, Culture and Censure.* London: Taylor & Francis.

Curran, J., Gurevitch, M. and Woollacott, J. (1977) *Mass Communication and Society.* London: Edward Arnold.

Denvir, J. (ed.) (1996) *Legal Reelism: Movies as Legal Texts.* Urbana, IL: University of Illinois Press.

Denzin, N. (1991) *Images of Postmodern Society: Social Theory and Contemporary Cinema.* London: Sage/TCS.

Derrida, J. (1978) *Writing and Difference.* London: Routledge.

Derrida, J. (1981) *Dissemination.* London: Athlone Press.

Diski, J. (1997) *Skating to Antarctica.* London: Granta Books.

Ditton, J. and Duffy, J. (1983) 'Bias' in newspaper reporting of crime news, *British Journal of Criminology,* 23: 159–65.

Douglas, M. (1966) *Purity and Danger: An Analysis of the Concepts of Pollution and Taboo.* London: Routledge and Kegan Paul.

Drucker, P. (1992) *Sisters and Strangers: An Introduction to Contemporary Feminist Fiction.* Oxford: Blackwell.

During, S. (ed.) (1993) *The Cultural Studies Reader.* London: Routledge.

Durkheim, E. (1969) *The Division of Labour in Society.* London: Collier Macmillan.

Dworkin, A. (1981) *Pornography.* London: The Women's Press.

Eco, U. (1976) *A Theory of Semiotics.* Bloomington and London: Indiana University Press.

Eldridge, J. (ed.) (1995) *Glasgow University Media Group, Vol. 1.* London: Routledge.

Ericson, R.V. (ed.) (1995) *Crime and the Media.* Aldershot: Dartmouth.

Ericson, R.V., Baranek, P.M. and Chan, J.B.L. (1987) *Visualizing Deviance: A Study of News Organizations.* Toronto: University of Toronto Press.

Ericson, R.V., Baranek, P.M. and Chan, J.B.L. (1991) *Representing Order: Crime and Justice in the News Media.* Toronto: University of Toronto Press.

Featherstone, M. (1995) *Undoing Culture: Globalism, Postmodernism and Identity.* London: Sage/TCS.

Featherstone, M. and Burrows, R. (eds) (1995) *Cyberspace, Cyberbodies, Cyberpunk: Cultures of Technological Embodiment.* London: Sage/TCS.

Featherstone, M., Hepworth, M. and Turner, B.S. (eds) (1991) *The Body: Social Process and Cultural Theory.* London: Sage/TCS.

Ferrell, J. (1996) Slash and frame, in G. Barak (ed.) *Representing O.J.: Murder, Criminal Justice and Mass Culture.* Guilderland, NY: Harrow and Heston.

Fiske, J. (1996) *Media Matters: Race and Gender in U.S. Politics.* Minneapolis: University of Minnesota Press.

Foucault, M. (1977) *Discipline and Punish.* Harmondsworth: Penguin.

Foucault, M. (1981) *The History of Sexuality.* Harmondsworth: Penguin.

Fowles, J. (1999) *The Case for Television Violence.* London: Sage.

Friedman, J. (1990) Globalization and localization, in M. Featherstone (ed.) *Global Culture: Nationalism, Globalization and Modernity.* London: Sage.

Gair, C. (1997) Policing the margins: Barbara Wilson's *Gaudi Afternoon* and *Troubles in Transylvania*, in P. Messent (ed.) *Criminal Proceedings: The Contemporary American Crime Novel.* London: Pluto Press.

Garland, D. (1990) Frameworks of inquiry in the sociology of punishment, *British Journal of Sociology,* 14(1): 1–15.

Garland, D. (1994) Of crimes and criminals: The development of criminology in Britain, in M. Maguire, R. Morgan, and R. Reiner (eds) *The Oxford Handbook of Criminology.* Oxford: Clarendon Press.

Genosko, G. (1999) *McLuhan and Baudrillard: The Masters of Implosion.* London: Routledge.

Gibson, W. (1984) *Neuromancer.* London: Victor Gollancz Ltd.

Gibson, W. (1995) *Neuromancer.* London: Voyager.

Giddens, A. (1985) *Nation State and Violence.* Cambridge: Polity.

Giddens, A. (1989) *Sociology.* Cambridge: Polity.

Giddens, A. (1990) *The Consequences of Modernity.* Stanford, CA: Stanford University Press.

Giddens, A. (1991) *Modernity and Self-Identity: Self and Society in the Late Modern Age*. Cambridge: Polity.

Giddens, A. (1992) *The Transformation of Intimacy: Sexuality, Love and Eroticism in Modern Societies*. Cambridge: Polity.

Giddens, A. (1999) Lecture 1 – Globalization, *The BBC Reith Lectures 1999: Runaway World*. BBC Online Network.

Glasgow University Media Group (1976) *Bad News*. London: Routledge.

Glasgow University Media Group (1980) *More Bad News*. London: Routledge and Kegan Paul.

Glasgow University Media Group (1982) *Really Bad News*. London: Routledge and Kegan Paul.

Goodman, S. (1997) Nihilism and the philosophy of violence, in C. Sumner (ed.) *Violence, Culture, and Censure*. London: Taylor & Francis.

Grabosky, P.N. and Smith, R.G. (1998) *Crime in the Digital Age*. New Brunswick, NJ: Transaction Publishers.

Graham, S. (1997) Imagining the real-time city: Telecommunications, urban paradigms and the future of cities, in S. Westwood and J. Williams (eds) *Imagining Cities: Scripts, Signs, Memories*. London: Routledge.

Gramsci, A. (1971) *Selections from Prison Notebooks*, ed. and trans. Q. Hoare and G. Nowell-Smith. London: Wishart.

Greek, C. (1996) O.J. and the Internet: The first cybertrial, in G. Barak (ed.) *Representing O.J.: Murder, Criminal Justice and Mass Culture*. Guilderland, NY: Harrow and Heston.

Green, E. and Adam, A. (eds) (2000) *Virtual Gender: Technology, Consumption and Identity*. London: Routledge.

Greenfield, S. and Osborn, G. (1995) Where cultures collide: The characterization of law and lawyers in film, *International Journal of the Sociology of Law*, 23: 107–30.

Greenfield, S. and Osborn, G. (1996) Pulped fiction? Cinematic parables of (in)justice, *University of San Francisco Law Review*, 30: 1181–98.

Grisham, J. (1999) *The Testament*. London: Arrow.

Hagell, T. and Newburn, E. (1994) *Persistent Young Offenders*. London: Policy Studies Institute.

Hall, S. and Jefferson, T. (1976) *Resistance through Rituals: Youth Subcultures in Post-War Britain*. London: Hutchinson.

Hall, S., Critcher, C., Jefferson, T., Clarke, J. and Roberts, B. (1978) *Policing the Crisis: Mugging, the State, and Law and Order*. London: Macmillan.

Hannerz, U. (1990) Cosmopolitans and locals in world culture, in M. Featherstone (ed.) *Global Culture: Nationalism, Globalization and Modernity*. London: Sage.

Haraway, D. (1985) A manifesto for cyborgs: Science, technology and socialist feminism in the 1980's, *Socialist Review*, 15: 65–107.

Harbord, V. (1997) 'Natural Born Killers': violence, film and anxiety, in C. Summer (ed.) *Violence, Culture and Censure*. London: Taylor & Francis.

Harley, R. (1987) Hiding in the light: Extended club mix with Dick Hebdige, *Art and Text*, 26: 70.

Haut, W. (1999) *Neon Noir: Contemporary American Crime Fiction*. London: Serpent's Tail.

Heim, M. (1998) *Virtual Realism*. Oxford: Oxford University Press.

Held, D. (1980) *Introduction to Critical Theory: Horkheimer to Habermas*. Cambridge: Polity Press.

Howitt, D. (1998) *Crime, the Media and the Law*. Chichester: John Wiley and Sons.

Hunt, D.M. (1999) *O.J. Simpson Facts and Fictions: News Rituals in the Construction of Reality*. Cambridge: Cambridge University Press.

Inglis, F. (1993) *Cultural Studies*. Oxford: Blackwell.

Ito, M. (1997) Virtually embodied: the reality of fantasy in a multi-user dungeon, in D. Porter (ed.) *Internet Culture*. London: Routledge.

Iyer, P. (2001) *The Global Soul: Jet-Lag, Shopping Malls and the Search for Home*. London: Bloomsbury.

Jay, M. (1973) *The Dialectical Imagination: A History of the Frankfurt School and the History of Social Research 1923–1950*. London: Heinemann.

Jefferson, T. (1997) Masculinities and crimes, in M. Maguire, R. Morgan, and R. Reiner (eds) *The Oxford Handbook of Criminology*, 2nd edn. Oxford: Clarendon Press.

Karnow, C.E.A. (1994) Recombinant culture: Crime in the digital network, Defcon II, Las Vegas, NV, July. www.cpsr.org/cpsr/computer_crime/net.crime.karnow.txt (accessed 7 February 2002).

Kerekes, D. and Slater, D. (1995) *Killing for Culture: An Illustrated History of Death Film from Mondo to Snuff*. London: Creation Books.

Kidd-Hewitt, D. and Osborne, R. (eds) (1995) *Crime and the Media: The Post-Modern Spectacle*. London: Pluto Press.

Kitchin, R. (1998) *Cyberspace: The World in the Wires*. Chichester: John Wiley.

Lacey, N. (2000) General principles of criminal law? A feminist view, in D. Nicolson and L. Bibbings (eds) *Feminist Perspectives on Criminal Law*. London: Cavendish.

Lacey, N., Wells, C. and Meure, D. (1990) *Reconstructing Criminal Law*. London: Weidenfeld and Nicolson.

Lakoff, G. and Johnson, M. (1977) *Metaphors We Live By*. Chicago, IL: University of Chicago Press.

Lansing, A. ([1964]2000) *Endurance: The Greatest Adventure Story Ever Told*. London: Ted Smart.

Lash, S. and Urry, J. (1994) *Economies of Signs and Space*. London: Sage/TCS.

Latour, B. (1986) The powers of association, in J. Law (ed.) *Power, Action and Belief: Towards a New Sociology of Knowledge?* London: Routledge and Kegan Paul.

Latour, B. (1987) *Science in Action: How to Follow Scientists and Engineers through Society*. Cambridge, MA: Harvard University Press.

Latour, B. (1988) *The Pasteurization of France*. Cambridge, MA: Harvard University Press.

Latour, B. (1993) *We have Never Been Modern*. Cambridge, MA: Harvard University Press.

Law, J. (ed.) (1986) *Power, Action, and Belief: Towards a New Sociology of Knowledge?* London: Routledge and Kegan Paul.

Lemert, E.M. (1972) *Human Deviance, Social Problems and Social Control*, 2nd edn. Englewood Cliffs, NJ: Prentice-Hall.

Levi, M. (1997) Violent Crime, in M. Maguire, R. Morgan, and R. Reiner (eds) *The Oxford Handbook of Criminology*, 2nd edn. Oxford: Clarendon Press.

Levinson, P. (1999) *Digital McLuhan: A Guide to the Information Millennium*. London: Routledge and Kegan Paul.

Loader, B.D. (ed.) (1997) *The Governance of Cyberspace: Politics, Technology, and Global Restructuring*. London: Routledge.

Lupton, D. (2000) The embodied computer/user, in D. Bell and B.M. Kennedy (eds) *The Cybercultures Reader*. London: Routledge.

McBeath, G.B. and Webb, S.A. (1997) Cities, subjectivity and cyberspace, in S. Westwood and J. Williams (eds) *Imagining Cities: Scripts, Signs, Memory*. London: Routledge.

McColgan, A. (2000) *Women Under the Law: The False Promise of Human Rights*. London: Longman.

McDermid, V. (1996) *Booked For Murder*. London: Women's Press.

McDermid, V. (1997) *The Blood in the Wire*. London: HarperCollins.

McGuigan, J. (1999) *Modernity and Postmodern Culture*. Buckingham: Open University Press.

Mackay, H. and O'Sullivan, T. (eds) (1999) *The Media Reader: Continuity and Transformation*. London: Sage.

McLuhan, M. ([1964]1997) *Understanding Media: The Extensions of Man*. Cambridge, MA: MIT Press.

Maguire, M., Morgan, R. and Reiner, R. (eds) (1997) *The Oxford Handbook of Criminology*, 2nd edn. Oxford: Oxford University Press.

Marcuse, H. (1968) *One Dimensional Man: The Ideology of Industrial Society*. London: Sphere Books.

Masters, B. (1996) *'She Must Have Known': The Trial of Rosemary West*. London: Doubleday.

Matthews, R. and Young, J. (eds) (1992) *Issues in Realist Criminology*. London: Sage.

Messerschmidt, J. (1993) *Masculinities and Crime*. Lanham, MD: Rowman and Littlefield.

Millard, W.B. (1997) I Flamed Freud, in D. Porter (ed.) *Internet Culture*. London: Routledge.

Mills, C.W. (1959) *The Sociological Imagination*. Harmondsworth: Penguin.

Moreiros, A. (1993) The leap and the lapse: Hacking a private site in cyberspace, in V. Conley (ed.) *Rethinking Technologies*. Minneapolis, Minn: University of Minnesota Press.

Morley, D. and Robins, K. (1995) *Spaces of Identity: Global Media, Electronic Landscapes and Cultural Boundaries*. London: Routledge.

Muncie, J. and McLaughlin, E. (1996) *The Problem of Crime*. London: Sage.

Muncie, J. and McLaughlin, E. (eds) (1996) *The Problem of Crime*. London: Sage.

Muncie, J., McLaughlin, E. and Langan, M. (1996) *Criminological Perspectives: A Reader*. London: Sage.

Murdock, G. (1997) Reservoirs of dogma: An archaeology of popular anxieties, in M. Barker and J. Petley (eds) *Ill Effects: The Media/Violence Debate*. London: Routledge.

Newson, E. (1994) *Video Violence and the Protection of Children*, Report of the Home Affairs Committee. London: HMSO, 29 June.

Nichols, B. (1994) *Blurred Boundaries: Questions of Meaning in Contemporary Culture*. Bloomington, IN: Indiana University Press.

Nicolson, D. and Bibbings, L. (2000) *Feminist Perspectives on Criminal Law*. London: Cavendish Publishing.

Norris (1992) *Uncritical Theory: Postmodernism, Intellectuals and the Gulf War*. London: Lawrence and Wishart.

Palmer, P. (1997) The lesbian thriller: Transgressive investigations, in P. Messent (ed.) *Criminal Proceedings: The Contemporary American Crime Novel*. London: Pluto Press.

Patton, P. (1995) Introduction, in J. Baudrillard, *The Gulf War Did Not Take Place*. Sydney: Power Publications.

Pearl, D., Bouthilet, L. and Lazar, J. (eds) (1982) *Television and Behaviour*. Washington, DC: National Institute of Mental Health.

Pearson, G. (1983) *Hooligan: A History of Respectable Fears*. London: Macmillan.

Pearson, G. (1985) Lawlessness, modernity and social change: An historical appraisal, *Theory, Culture & Society*, 2(3): 15–36.

Poster, M. (1995) *The Second Media Age*. Cambridge: Polity.

Raab, C.D. (1997) Privacy, democracy, information, in B.D. Loader (ed.) *The Governance of Cyberspace: Politics, Technology and Global Restructuring*. London: Routledge.

Redhead, S. (1990) *The End of the Century Party: Youth and Pop Towards 2000*. Manchester: Manchester University Press.

Redhead, S. (1995) *Unpopular Cultures: The Birth of Law and Popular Culture*. Manchester: Manchester University Press.

Redhead, S. (1997a) *Subcultures to Clubcultures: An Introduction to Popular Cultural Studies.* Oxford: Blackwell.

Redhead, S. (1997b) *Post-Fandom and the Millennial Blues.* London: Routledge.

Redhead, S. (2000) *The Repetitive Beat Generation.* Edinburgh: Rebel Inc.

Reiner, R. (1997) Media made criminality: The representation of crime in the mass media, in M. Maguire, R. Morgan and R. Reiner (eds) *The Oxford Handbook of Criminology*, 2nd edn. Oxford: Clarendon Press.

Rheingold, H. (1993) *The Virtual Community: Homesteading on the Electronic Frontier.* Reading, MA: Addison-Wesley.

Robins, K. (1995) Cyberspace and the world we live in, in M. Featherstone and R. Burrows (eds) *Cyberspace, Cyberbodies, Cyberpunk.* London: Sage/TCS.

Robins, K. (2000) Cyberspace and the world we live in, in D. Bell and B.M. Kennedy (eds) *The Cybercultures Reader.* London: Routledge.

Ross, A. (2000) Hacking away at the counter-culture, in D. Bell and B.M. Kennedy (eds) *The Cybercultures Reader.* London: Routledge.

Roy, A. (1998) *The God of Small Things.* London: Flamingo.

Rubenstein, R.L. (1978) *The Cunning of History: The Holocaust and the American Future.* New York: Harper and Row.

Rushkoff, D. (1996) *Media Virus! Hidden Agendas in Popular Culture.* New York: Ballantine.

Santos, B. (1987) Law: A map of misreading. Towards a postmodern conception of law, *Journal of Law and Society*, 14(3).

Sardar, Z. (1998) *Postmodernism and the Other: The New Imperialism of Western Culture.* London: Pluto.

Scoppettone, S. (1993) *I'll Be Leaving You Always.* New York: Ballantine Books.

Scott, M. (1996) *Hen's Teeth.* London: Women's Press.

Scott, M. (1999) *Stronger than Death.* London: Headline.

Sherwin, R. (1996) Framed, in J. Denvir (ed.) *Legal Reelism: Movies as Legal Texts.* Urbana, IL: University of Illinois Press.

Shute, J. (1995) *Life-Size.* London: Minerva.

Shute, J. (1997) *Sex Crimes.* London: Secker and Warburg.

Sinha, I. (2000) *The Cybergypsies: Love, Life and Travels on the Electronic Frontier.* London: Scribner.

Smart, B. (1999) *Facing Modernity: Ambivalence, Reflexivity and Morality.* London: Sage/TCS.

Smart, C. (1984) *The Ties That Bind.* London: Routledge.

Smart, C. (1989) *Feminism and the Power of Law.* London: Routledge.

Smith, A.D. (1990) Towards a global culture?, in M. Featherstone (ed.) *Global Culture: Nationalism, Globalization and Modernity.* London: Sage.

Smith, D.J. (1994) *The Sleep of Reason: The James Bulger Case.* London: Century.

Sobchack, V. (2000) New age mutant ninja hackers, in D. Bell and B.M. Kennedy (eds) *The Cybercultures Reader*. London: Routledge.

Sparks, R. (1992) *Television and the Drama of Crime: Moral Tales and the Place of Crime in Public Life*. Buckingham: Open University Press.

Spelman, E.V. and Minow, M. (1992) Outlaw women: An essay on Thelma and Louise, *New England Law Review*, 26: 1281.

Spelman, E.V. and Minow, M. (1996) Outlaw women: Thelma and Louise, in J. Denvir (ed.) *Legal Reelism: Movies as Legal Texts*. Urbana, IL: University of Illinois Press.

Stanko, E.A. (1985) *Intimate Intrusions: Women's Experience of Male Violence*. London: Routledge.

Stevenson, N. (1995) *Understanding Media Cultures: Social Theory and Mass Communications*. London: Sage.

Stevenson, N. (1999) *The Transformation of the Media: Globalization, Morality and Ethics*. London: Longman.

Stivale, C.J. (1997) Spam: Heteroglossia and harassment in cyberspace, in D. Porter (ed.) *Internet Culture*. London: Routledge.

Stone, A.R. (1996) *The War of Desire and Technology at the Close of the Mechanical Age*. Cambridge, MA: MIT Press.

Stone, A.R. (2000) Will the real body please stand up? Boundary stories about virtual cultures, in D. Bell and B.M. Kennedy (eds) *The Cybercultures Reader*. London: Routledge.

Sumner, C. (1992) Introduction, in R. Sparks, *Television and the Drama of Crime: Moral Tales and the Place of Crime in Public Life*. Buckingham: Open University Press.

Sumner, C. (ed.) (1997) *Violence, Culture and Censure*. London: Taylor & Francis.

Tarantino, Q. (1996) *Pulp Fiction*. London: Faber and Faber.

Taylor, P.A. (1999) *Hackers: Crime in the Digital Sublime*. London: Routledge.

Thompson, J.B. (1990) *Ideology and Modern Culture*. Cambridge: Polity Press.

Thompson, J. (1995) *The Media and Modernity*. Cambridge: Polity Press.

Thompson, J. (1999) The media and modernity, in H. Mackay and T. O'Sullivan (eds) *The Media Reader: Continuity and Transformation*. London: Sage.

Townsend, C. (1998) *Vile Bodies: Photography and the Crisis of Looking*. Munich: Prestel.

Ussher, J. (1991) *Women's Madness: Misogyny or Mental Illness?* London: Harvester Wheatsheaf.

Vanacker, S. (1997) V.I. Warshawski, Kinsey Millhone and Kay Scarpetta: Creating a feminist detective hero, in P. Messent (ed.) *Criminal Proceedings: The Contemporary American Crime Novel*. London: Pluto.

Vine, I. (1997) The dangerous psycho-logic of media 'effects', in M. Barker and J. Petley (eds) *Ill Effects: The Media/Violence Debate*. London: Routledge.

Walklate, S. (1995) *Gender and Crime: An Introduction*. Hemel Hempstead: Harvester Wheatsheaf.

Wall, D. (ed.) (2001) *Internet Crime*. London: Routledge.

Watson, G. (1996) An archaeology of the soul, in R. Wollen (ed.) *Derek Jarman: A Portrait*. London: Thames and Hudson.

Webster, F. (1999) What information society? in H. Mackay and T. O'Sullivan (eds) *The Media Reader: Continuity and Transformation*. London: Sage/The Open University.

Weinstein, D. and Weinstein, D. (2000) Net game cameo, in D. Bell and B.M. Kennedy (eds) *The Cybercultures Reader*. London: Routledge.

Welsh, I. (1993) *Trainspotting*. London: Minerva.

Westwood, S. and Williams, J. (eds) (1997) *Imagining Cities: Scripts, Signs, Memory*. London: Routledge.

Willis, P. (1977) *Learning to Labour: How Working Class Kids Get Working Class Jobs*. Farnborough: Saxon House.

Wilson, B. (1984) *Murder in the Collective*. London: Virago Crime.

Wilson, B. (1991) *Gaudi Afternoon*. London: Virago Crime.

Wilson, C. ([1956]1990) *The Outsider*. London: Victor Gollancz Ltd.

Wings, M. (1986) *She Came Too Late*. London: Women's Press.

Wollen, R. (ed.) (1996) *Derek Jarman: A Portrait*. London: Thames and Hudson.

Wood, D. (1992) *The Power of Maps*. New York: Guilford Press.

Wykes, M. (2001) *News, Crime and Culture*. London: Pluto Press.

Young, J. (1986) The failure of criminology: the need for radical realism, in R. Matthews and J. Young (eds) *Confronting Crime*. London: Sage.

Young, J. (1995) Left realist criminology: radical in its analysis, realist in its policy, in M. Maguire, R. Morgan and R. Reiner (eds) *The Oxford Handbook of Criminology*. Oxford: Oxford University Press.

Young, A. (1996) *Imagining Crime: Textual Outlaws and Criminal Conversations*. London: Sage/TCS.

Zahavi, H. (1991) *Dirty Weekend*. London: Macmillan.

Zickmund, S. (2000) Approaching the radical Other: The discursive culture of cyberhate, in D. Bell and B.M. Kennedy (eds) *The Cybercultures Reader*. London: Routledge.

INDEX

MATERIAL CULTURE
IN THE SOCIAL WORLD

Tim Dant

This should become a core text for second year courses in sociology and cultural studies . . . it synthesizes a vast body of literature and a complex range of debates into a text which is at once accessible, engaging and stimulating . . . it will lead to students seeing and thinking about the material world in a totally new light and can be used as a way into key theoretical debates.

Keith Tester, Professor of Social Theory, University of Portsmouth

- In what ways do we interact with material things?
- How do material objects affect the way we relate to each other?
- What are the connections between material things and social processes like fashion, discourse, art and design?

Through wearing clothes, keeping furniture, responding to the ring of the telephone, noticing the signature on a painting, holding a paperweight and in many other ways, we interact with objects in our everyday lives. These are not merely functional relationships with things but are connected to the way we relate to other people and the culture of the particular society we live in – they are social relations. This engaging book draws on established theoretical work, including that of Simmel, Marx, McLuhan, Barthes and Baudrillard as well as a range of contemporary empirical work from many humanities disciplines. It uses ideas drawn from this work to explore a variety of things – from stone cairns to denim jeans, televisions to penis rings, houses to works of art – to understand something of how we live with them.

Contents

Introduction: the cairn and the mini-strip – Consuming or living with things? – Fetishism and the social value of objects – Building and dwelling – Wearing it out: written and material clothing – Playing with things: interacting with a windsurfer – Objects in time: modernity and biography – Turn it on: objects that mediate – Who's that? People as objects – Conclusion – Further reading – Bibliography – Index.

240pp   0 335 19821 X (Paperback)   0 335 19822 8 (Hardback)

MORAL PANICS AND THE MEDIA

Chas Critcher

- How are social problems defined and responded to in contemporary society?
- How useful is the concept of moral panic in understanding these processes?
- What does an examination of recent examples reveal about the role of the media in creating, endorsing and sustaining moral panics?

The term 'moral panic' is frequently applied to sudden eruptions of concern about social problems. This book critically evaluates the usefulness of moral panic models for understanding how politicians, the public and pressure groups come to recognise apparently new threats to the social order. The role of the media, especially the popular press, comes under scrutiny. Two models of moral panics are initially identified and explained, then applied to a range of case studies: AIDS, rave/ecstasy, video nasties, child abuse and paedophilia. Experience is compared across a range of countries, revealing many basic similarities but also significant variations between different national contexts. Common to all is an increasing focus on threats to children, evoking images of childhood innocence. The conclusion is that moral panic remains a useful tool for analysis but needs more systematic connection to wider theoretical concerns, especially those of the risk society and discourse analysis.

Contents

Series editor's foreword – Acknowledgements – Introduction: original thoughts – Part one: the models – Made in Britain: the processual model of moral panics – Notes from a big country: the attributional model of moral panics – Part two: case studies – Unhealthy preoccupations: AIDS – Out of their minds: ecstasy and raves – A rocky horror show: video nasties – Suffer the little children: child abuse in families – Monstrous ideas: paedophilia – Part three: implications – Universal pictures: international comparisons – No news is good news: the role of the media – Time for a make-over: the models revisited – Myth appropriation: the childhood theme – Underwriting risk: moral panics and social theory – Afterword – Glossary – References – Index.

c. 192pp   0 335 20908 4 (Paperback)   0 335 20909 2 (Hardback)